DROUGHTS & DREAMS

Stories of Self-Reliance During America's Darkest Times

With Forewords By

GLENN BECK &

MATT REDHAWK

Droughts & Dreams

Stories of Self-Reliance During America's Darkest Times

As compiled by Matt Redhawk

Foreword by Glenn Beck

Foreword and commentary by Matt Redhawk

Printed in the United States of America

First Printing, 2015

ISBN 978-0692505250

Authors' Special Thanks

This book couldn't have been written without the people who contributed their own, personal family stories and memories about this nearly forgotten era of American History. Our grateful thanks are especially for you. Also thank you to Daria Lacy and to Heidi Wallenborn for their efforts on this project.

Contents

Contents

1935. There wasn't much to be happy about for most during the Great Depression. Franklin D. Roosevelt Presidential Library & Museum

Foreword

Glenn Beck

I am a lover of history.

I haunt museums, memorials, ruins, and battlefields, imagining myself amidst the victories and defeats that have brought out the very best and worst in us. I collect and preserve artifacts and heirlooms that have been a part of extraordinary events in our amazing, fading past. And I read, every day (and often far too late into the night) not only books, but the personal letters, private journals, and original documents handwritten by the men and women who, whether in the service of good or evil, helped make our world what it is today.

But if you know me, you probably already know all of that. What you might not know is the *why* behind it all, and if history has taught me anything, it's that the *why* of things is usually the most important part.

So here's why I'm so consumed with history: because if we ignore the teachings of our past, we may not survive our future.

Yes, I know it can sound cliché, but there is nothing

we face now that smart people of the past have not also faced and usually figured out. Sure, the exact circumstances and players involved may change, but the underlying issues are the same.

I am a self-educated man, and I've found that history is the most patient and ruthless of teachers. When it comes to the fundamental questions — those simple spiritual crossroads that will either lead us toward heaven or straight into hell — this teacher knows the devastating cost of taking the wrong path. And so for every crucial lesson we face, history finds a way to test us again, and again, and again. Each time, we either learn and rise as a people, or we die with our ignorance, leaving it to the next generation to try and pass that same fateful exam.

With that in mind, let's switch to a lighter topic and talk about the Great Depression.

This is a book of stories about good people in hard times, told by individuals who lived through one of the most difficult periods in our national memory.

How tough was it? People wanted to work, to do whatever it took to support their families, but there were no jobs to be had. Companies wanted to build and produce, but capital dried up as the bankers shut off the tap, and customers had no money to pay for goods and services. Investments became worthless, trade plummeted, the great engine of the American economy stopped dead and had no fuel left in its tank to restart again. And for many, as the months of despair turned to years, there was simply no reason to believe that things would ever get better again.

The experts, God bless them, still debate about the *why* of the Great Depression, what caused it, and even which factors (other than the effects of World War II) finally helped bring it to an end. I have my own theories, of course, most involving the economic legacy left by our first and only president with a PhD: Woodrow Wilson. His progressive spirit is still hard at work in our government, and I'm among those who believe that, if we don't change course soon, we may be headed toward an even greater economic disaster today.

But as important as the cause of it may be, for now let's put aside the *why* of the Great Depression, and focus on the more practical lessons that the era can teach us.

As you read the stories in this wonderful book, it's my hope that together we can learn how some extraordinary, everyday Americans rolled up their sleeves and made it through a trial by fire with their spirits still intact. Their experiences can warn us, and guide us, and even show us what to do in case such terrible times should ever return.

I've studied every one of these pages, of course, but I see something new every time I read them. Here's a sample of the lessons these stories have confirmed for me so far.

1. As long as you're still breathing, you *never* have nothing.

When your last dollar is gone, when your business goes under, when there's no food in the cupboard and you come home to a sheriff's eviction notice tacked to your front door, when you're so far down that you can't get any lower, that's when a realization hits: there are some precious things that no one can ever take away from you.

Your faith. Your family. The love of your spouse, for better or worse. The strength of true friends. The trust in the eyes of your children that says they know you'll never fail them. There's great power in those things—enough to overcome any obstacle and start again from wherever you're standing. And once you've stared into that abyss and made it back alive, nothing will ever truly scare you again.

2. Be prepared.

Eighty years ago, if you gave the average American family four chickens and a goat, most of them would know exactly how to use those resources to provide eggs, milk, cheese and meat through a long, hard winter. Today, not so much. We're much better with selfies now than self-preservation. As a culture we've largely forgotten how to fend for ourselves, and, despite the way that mainstream media spins it, that's not real progress.

Start now, if you haven't already: learn to do-it-yourself, make essentials at home instead of buying them, sew clothes, quilt and knit, repair instead of replace, learn cooking and canning and preserving, fermenting and pickling. Re-discover the joys of creating what you need with skills and tools and your own two hands. And while you're at it, teach your kids how to love doing those same marvelous things.

3. Easy credit is a trap.

Debt is a prison we build for ourselves, and many powerful lenders are more than happy to send us all the bars, bricks, and chains we need to finish the job. A healthy dedication to savings, on the other hand, can be a ticket to life-long freedom and security. There are no flashy ads on TV promoting frugality and impulse control, though, while cool movie stars are hawking credit cards on every commercial break.

It seems the big banks learned more from the bailouts than from the financial crisis itself. A dose of reality is badly needed, and no one is going to give your family that bitter pill if you don't.

Stop spending money you don't have. If you're in debt, start today to work your way out of it. Remember: Wants aren't needs. *Simplify.* Instant gratification leads to long-term pain. And always pay your future self first at the end of each month, in the form of savings, because rainy days always come when you least expect them.

4. Be a good neighbor.

Find a community that feels like home, and then take an active part in making it a great place to live. Help one another, put your trust in those friendships, and learn not to expect any help from some faraway, wasteful bureaucracy. In good times, life will be richer and far more enjoyable. And if the next crisis arrives, you'll know who you can count on when push comes to shove.

That's just a start. I know you'll find plenty of other wisdom in these stories on your own.

One last thing: enjoy this book, and then share it with someone who might need a refresher course in the things that really matter. Remind that person that every event retold in these pages actually happened here, in this country, and not so long ago.

And help them understand that we're the authors of our own living history, right here and now. How tremendous it would be if future generations read a book about us, and marvel at how much we accomplished and all we restored, rather than how far we fell.

I'm hard at work at writing my chapter in that thrilling, still unfinished book. How about you?

Hunger Line, Sixth Ave and 42nd Street, NY City.

Franklin D. Roosevelt Presidential Library & Museum

Foreword

Matt Redhawk
Preparedness leader, founder and
CEO of My Patriot Supply
Sandpoint, Idaho

"Those who don't know history are doomed to repeat it."
~ Edmund Burke, 1700s Irish Statesman and philosophical founder of Anglo-American conservatism

I boarded an airplane in late summer 2014 with the intention of getting caught up on work before my meeting the next day with Glenn Beck.

My seat-mate was an older woman who had recently celebrated her 90th birthday. We got to talking and I found out that she was returning home after a celebration with family and friends. Because I am an avid student of history, I knew that she had spent her formative years during America's Great Depression. I asked if she would mind sharing her personal experience with me and memories she had from that time.

I knew my plans to get some work done just went out the window. I put away my laptop and for the next two hours sat enthralled as I learned from a first-person perspective what life was like during one of our nation's most devastating economic times.

The next morning as I sat across from Glenn in his office, I asked if he had any projects I could help with. In a moment of beautiful serendipity, without hesitation he said that he wanted to see a book of stories from people who lived through the Great Depression.

The Roaring Twenties was a time when most Americans were comfortable, and confident that the prosperous industrial boom time would last forever. Excess and lavish lifestyles were the norm. It wasn't long before supply far outweighed demand and the foundation of the castle built on sand started to crumble.

Sound familiar?

Beginning with Black Tuesday on October 29, 1929, 16 billion shares were dumped in a single day, wiping out thousands of investors. Billions of dollars disappeared in a matter of weeks from the tumbling stock market. In the days following, frightened investors and families who had trusted banks with their money panicked and made rushes demanding their hard-earned cash. Banks handed out what they could, liquidated the rest, and many had to shut their doors. By the mid-1930s, more than half the banks in America were boarded up.

We came pretty close to that in 2007.

In the 1930s, riots birthed out of desperation erupted across the country when families lost jobs, businesses and homes, and parents struggled to find a way to at least partly fill their children's empty bellies.

To survive, Americans turned to homesteading. Going back to the basics, those who were able grew their own food — from livestock to vegetables — and learned how to be creative masters in their kitchens. Food wasn't fancy, but it sustained.

In recent years, similar disasters have happened.

Americans have faced hurricanes Katrina and Sandy, market crashes, bank disasters, Midwest tornadoes, terrorist attacks, domestic rioting in the streets and other catastrophes. We found that governments and organizations are woefully ill-prepared. They cannot be relied upon to help the average citizen: they are slow to respond and sometimes outright fail to provide basic needs such as food, water and shelter.

In fact, the government-run FEMA shelter at the Superdome in New Orleans quickly became a dangerous — even deadly — place to be. The government insisted, and in some cases forced, people to stay there.

Being self-reliant means that you don't have to rely on the government or anyone else to survive.

I believe that true patriotism is not the expectation that others will care for your needs but that freedom comes from attaining a certain level of self-reliance. When people think of living off the grid and being self-sufficient, they often think of a Grizzly Adams-type mountain man survivalist. They assume that preparedness means living off the beaten path with a rugged lifestyle that wouldn't change much if civilization as we know it collapsed.

But that's not true. In many cases, they are people like you and me who live in cities and urban areas who want to be prepared for whatever comes down the road -- independent of assistance or oversight from unstable government agencies.

There is no ultimate guide about how to become self-sufficient. Instead of focusing on specific steps, it's important to change the way you look at and think about your actions. What is your level of dependency on the government and others?

Several accounts in this book tell of how family providers shunned government assistance as a matter of pride – and they somehow found the means to provide. It might not have been much, but what was put on the table was by their own hard work. In other stories, government support helped keep food on the table for as long as they needed relief. But agency support was never meant to be a cure-all forever.

After reading these stories, I hope that you seek self-reliant alternatives in each area. Consider the importance of becoming debt-free, growing your own food which will include poultry and other meats, housing with a yard or other area big enough for a sizable survival garden, and finding alternate ways of transportation.

As I listened to my fellow passenger on the airplane – a survivor of the most tragic economic disaster in America -- I was reminded again of the absolute need for self-reliance and self-sufficiency. Hers is a generation who understands what it means to be prepared and do what it takes to survive the hard times.

Will we learn from their lessons? Will the current generation sink or swim in the unsteady days ahead?

Educating ourselves about our shared history – distant past and recent -- through both written word and oral accounts handed down from our families is an important aspect toward understanding where we've been not only as a Nation, but as a people.

In remembering, we will learn from the highs and lows of the past and recognize signs of history repeating itself with those who didn't learn those lessons.

My hope is that the personal stories, tips and anecdotes provided by Great Depression survivors in this book will help families find their way toward lasting self-reliance and freedom.

Matt Redhawk

Farm foreclosure. public domain

The Great Depression of 1929-1939: What happened?

Matt Redhawk

During the crisis of World War I (1914-1918), American food production — specifically wheat — soared. The price of wheat for farmers was at an all time high and their pockets prospered. Some historians and farmers agree that they were greedy during their prosperity and they wanted more; so they plowed more land, planted more wheat and spread out across the nation onto the virgin prairie to set up homesteads.

Native grassland in the Midwest was turned under in a hurry without taking care to ensure the soil could recover. Natural buffalo grasses that held moisture from scant rainfall were plowed to make way for more wheat fields. Men doubled their incomes by selling all that they grew.

After the Great War demand lessened but the supply didn't. To make up for the loss of income, farmers doubled their plantings. As a result, wheat glutted the market and sat unused, spilling out of silos and blowing away in the ever-present prairie wind. Most of the 1920s saw farmers struggling with their own economic depression due to drought and falling food prices. At the lowest point, prices fell by nearly 60 percent.

During the summer of 1929, the American economy entered a recession as consumer spending dropped and unsold goods piled up, which slowed production. However, stock prices continued to rise and by autumn of that year reached levels that could not be defended against anticipated earnings.

On October 24, 1929, the Wall Street stock market's bubble burst when investors started dumping shares. That day, infamously known as "Black Thursday," a record 12.9 million shares were traded.

Five days later on October 29, another 16 million shares were traded after yet another wave of panic swept Wall Street investors. As a result, millions of shares were worthless. Those investors who bought stocks with borrowed money or who sold everything to purchase shares were completely wiped out.

Over the course of that week in October, the stock market lost an astounding $30 billion. It took 23 years for the stock market to hit the high it was at before the crash.

As confidence disappeared despite newly elected Republican President Herbert Hoover's assurance that the crisis would run its course, businesses and factories slowed production. In March 1930, Hoover declared that the country had "passed the worst" and argued that the economy would sort itself out.

However with production slowing, positions were no longer needed and jobs vanished. Those who were lucky enough to still have jobs found that their wages decreased significantly.

Families who had purchased items on credit fell deeper into debt with no way to pay their commitments. Foreclosures and repossessions on homes and farms, automobiles, farm equipment and other goods climbed. Shantytowns and tent cities popped up across the country, named "Hoovervilles."

But the end of 1929 was just the beginning. The country held steady at its low point until autumn 1930. By then, 4 million Americans were out of work and couldn't find jobs of any kind. By 1931 that number rose to 6 million.

During that same time in the Midwest, relentless drought and wind picked up loosened prairie soil from bad farming practices and created the Dust Bowl — ruined land that would not sustain crops for many years. Year after year in the 1930s brought blinding sand and dust storms that forced farmers off their land and sent them — with or without their families in tow — to other parts of the country looking for work.

Meanwhile, industrial production dropped by half. Bread lines, soup kitchens and rising numbers of homeless people became more common. Hobos "riding the rails" increased to the point that one hobo described a train car as looking like it had a flock of blackbirds perched on it.

In the fall of 1930 the first of four waves of banking panics began. Many people lost confidence in the creditworthiness of their banks and demanded their deposits in cash. This forced banks to call in loans to supplement insufficient on-hand cash reserves. More bank runs followed in the spring and fall of 1931 and the fall of 1932. By early 1933 thousands of banks had closed their doors. Hoover's administration tried to support failing banks with government loans; his idea was that the banks would loan to businesses again and employees could be hired back.

By 1933 the Great Depression reached its lowest point — about 13 to 15 million Americans were unemployed; nearly half the banks across the nation had failed, and the Dust Bowl of the Midwest floundered under persistent drought and dust storms.

In March 1933 Democrat Franklin Delano Roosevelt took office in his first of four terms as President of the United States. In 1933 the economy hit rock bottom and nearly 9,000 banks failed. Nearly $2.5 billion in bank deposits were lost. Unemployment soared to nearly 13 million — or about one person in four of the labor force.

Over time, Roosevelt instituted relief and reform measures such as the Works Project Administration, Civilian Conservation Corps and Social Security to help lessen the worst effects of the Great Depression. But the economy did not fully turn around until after 1939 when World War II kicked American industry into high gear.

In 1938 the Fair Labor Standards Act introduced the nation's first minimum wage of 25 cents an hour. Until then, weekly earnings in manufacturing dropped from $27 in 1929 to $18 in 1932. In other words a five-day/eight-hour work-week wage dropped from 67 cents per hour to 45 cents per hour. But much more common were jobs that paid 10 cents per hour or $1 per day — or in food.

Common food prices in the 1930s

Dozen eggs, 18 cents
Peanut butter, 23 cents
Bran flakes, 10 cents
Jumbo sliced loaf of bread, 5 cents
Toilet tissue, 9 cents for two rolls
Camay soap, 6 cents bar
Cod liver oil, 44 cents pint
Toothpaste, 27 cents
Lux laundry soap, 22 cents
Applesauce, 20 cents for three cans
Bacon, 38 cents per lb
Ham, 27 cents can
Ketchup, 9 cents
Potatoes, 18 cents for 10 pounds
Sugar, 49 cents for 10 pounds or $1.25 per 25 lb sack
Pork and Beans, 5 cents can
Oranges, 14 for 25 cents
Heinz beans, 13 cents for 25 oz can
Spring chickens, 20 cents per pound
Wieners, 8 cents per pound
Pure lard, 15 cents per pound
Cabbage, 3 cents per lb
Sharp Wisconsin cheese, 23 cents per lb
Corn Flakes, 8 oz for 8 cents
Campbell's tomato soup, 20 cents/three cans

Following are stories of people who were adults or children from the 1920s and 1930s who stared into the worst economic abyss the United States has ever faced. These are the generation referred to by many as "the greatest."

Dorothy (seated in grass) - approx. 1931

Dorothy (seated in grass) and Bob (in "stroller") - approx. 1932

Doris (left), Dorothy (back), Herb (front) and Bob (right) - approx. 1943

"Our poor mom"

Dorothy (Irey) Wycoff Richardson

Born November 1930 in Grant County, Oklahoma

Late in 1930, I was born in a farmhouse west of Caldwell, Kansas in the same bedroom that my dad, Lee Othel Irey, was born in 31 years earlier. His parents, my grandparents, participated in the Cherokee Strip Land Run in 1893 and settled one mile inside of Oklahoma, because that is where their wagon broke down.

I am the eldest of four children — two brothers, Bob and Herb born 1932 and 1938, and one sister, Doris, born 1934. We had neither electricity nor telephone. Our house was a wooden frame with four rooms: three bedrooms with the fourth being a kitchen-bathroom-living room.

I remember the dirty '30s. It got so dark the chickens went to roost. Dust sifted through our windows and doors. The only way to clean was with a broom, which made more dust. We stuffed rags in all the cracks of our windows, but it didn't seem to help. Every morn-

School photo - Dorothy (Second row far left), Doris (front row far left), Bob (second row far right) and Herb (front row far right) - approx. 1939

ing the windowsills were full. Dust drifted into the ditches and covered the fences in places. We also had blizzards; but we escaped the tornados.

My dad was a wheat farmer and when we were big enough we helped, from putting up hay in the barn to scooping wheat into the granary. We also took our turn on the tractor and binder. Then we put the bundles into shocks and learned to drive in the field.

There were also chores such as milking, feeding chickens and gathering eggs. We had turkeys, guineas, geese and calves. I can still see Mom, Lorena Mae, picking feathers from geese. She made our pillows and featherbeds with the feathers that she collected.

Our mom was always working. She cooked on a three-burner gasoline stove and made all our bread and food. She had three children before she ever got a washing machine. On wash day we pumped water, carried it in and put it in a boiler to heat, then put it into the washing machine. Also, the rinse tubs had to be filled then carried out. Before she got the washing machine she did all the laundry on a washboard. I remember that sometimes we went swimming in our underwear in the red mud ponds. The red Oklahoma clay always stained them. Our poor mom. She was my favorite person.

My dad's mother, Grandma Mary, lived with us. She was quite a character. I never saw her take a bath, brush her teeth or change her clothes. We have no pictures of her, as she wouldn't let us take one. She was about 5-feet tall, about 140 pounds, and had grey hair that she wore combed back into a bun. After the threshing crew finished in the field, she would empty her ticking bed and refill it with fresh straw. The pillow spanned the bed and was filled with straw also. All four of us took turns sleeping with her. One night was enough, as the straw was scratchy.

Grandma stayed fairly active on the farm. When she milked our cows, she knelt down on one knee, held the bucket with her left hand and milked faster than the rest of us who used two hands. As potatoes grew, she took a butcher knife and dug around the plant until she would find enough fresh potatoes for the family. She was busy every day, fixing fences, doing chores, raising turkeys, making shelters for them and hatching the eggs. One time she came running and yelling because the bumblebees were after her. I guess she came in contact with a nest while she was building shelters.

Grandma was also somewhat of a superstitious person.

In the dry seasons she hunted a snake, killed it and hung it on the fence so the rain would come. Surprise! It usually worked until she took it off and then the rain stopped.

She despised the prairie dog; they undermined our pasture and she was afraid that the farm animals would step in the holes and break their legs. To get rid of the prairie dogs, she rolled rags and tied them in a small ball then dipped them in liquid that she called Hokey Pokey. My oldest brother went with her as she dropped each rag ball into a hole then covered the hole with dirt. Eventually she ridded the pasture of the critters.

She sewed her long dresses and aprons by hand out of grey chambray material. She only went to town twice a year — when she went to the doctor and to the bank. She pulled her own teeth and was fairly healthy until her stroke. When she went to town, she dressed in a full-length black dress and a velvet hat.

We kids dressed up one Halloween as witches by wearing her clothes and riding a broom. Boy did that make her mad. Every time she got mad, she "moved out" into the granary. But that wasn't the only time she got upset. I remember a time when my mom got curtains. She "moved out" whenever Mom got something new. During those times she would eat raw vegetables and not have anything to do with any of us.

In later years, she saved every used envelope and scrap of paper and old clothes to make quilts "just in case." She worked hard until the day she had a stroke while milking a cow. She lived about six hours and died at age 77 in her own bed at home.

Looking back, I have often wondered how we ever grew up safe and sound.

We played in the barn, climbed trees or made our toys from things on the farm. We swam nude in the horse tank. Company drove in one day and we had to stay in until they left. We had stripped in the chicken house a hundred feet away.

We decided to run away one day and moved into the barn. We took cereal from the house, milked a cow for milk and made our beds in the hay. There was an old buggy in the barn and we "smoked" the stuffing in the seat. We also pushed the buggy to the top of a hill — one guided it up with a rope and one pushed while the other two wrapped themselves inside the spokes for a ride down the hill.

One time, I remember I was in the first grade, I was swinging high and jumped out like most of the boys did — and tore a three-corner hole in the back of my dress. The teacher sent me to a house a bit north of the school and the lady there stitched up my dress.

All four of us took turns with childhood diseases — we even had the seven-year-itch. Mom would stand us up on a chair and rub us with something that smelled terrible. It didn't last that long, but it was awful.

On Saturday nights we took turns bathing in a square wash tub behind the potbellied stove — from youngest to oldest. Mom would add a teakettle of hot water now and then. I was number four in line.

We attended Sunnyside School, two miles from home. It had one room and grades one through eight with one teacher. We walked to school every day and carried our books and lunch. When it was muddy our feet got so heavy. When it was cold, Mom made us wear long, brown stockings and long underwear with our brothers' coveralls over the top. When we got to school, we took off the over-

Doris (left), Dorothy (back), Bob (right) with their pet turkey approx. 1937

alls, rolled up the underwear and rolled down the socks. We were girls with dresses!

Our school only lasted eight months of the year and the only day off was Christmas. At the time that we came down with the Chicken Pox we were the only students in school, so school was dismissed and our teacher took a vacation. That's the only year we received perfect attendance. One year I attended the east school with four boys — I was the only girl. When I graduated 8th grade I had to pass the state exam before high school.

We had a pet turkey named Gobbler. The turkey played with us when we played outside. We'd lie down on the ground and the bird would walk on us and all around us — really playing.

We wanted a horse to ride. All we had were two work horses, Daisy and Nell, so we coaxed, petted and fed them until one day my brother Bob tried to get onto Daisy, the black one; Nell was grey. He bridled her in the barn, got on — and out the door she went! She finally settled down and he and my sister rode double thereafter. My little brother and I rode Nell after awhile. Because they were workhorses and were very big, our legs practically stuck straight out from the sides.

Our trips to town were usually on Saturday. Our folks took cream and eggs to sell and this bought our groceries for the week. We kids received a dime each to spend, but we never saw a movie until we were in high school.

One time Dad loaded the cream into a pickup to go to town. He went around a corner too fast and it upset, spilling both cans. How do you clean 20 gallons of cream from a pickup and no hose?

We would have ice sometimes if mom put the card in the window for delivery. She turned it to how many pounds she wanted with a choice of 10-25-50 or 100. Mom had the delivery person put the ice into a wash tub then covered it with newspapers and quilts. This would keep on the porch for a week. That was our only refrigerator.

As children, our daily thing was to get to the outhouse, talk and wish from the Sears Roebuck catalog. We had a double-holer. Also, we got to listen to the radio if the wind had blown enough to charge the battery. We liked to listen to *Inner Sanctum Mysteries* and *The Lone Ranger*. It was the only way the folks had to hear the news. The end of the Depression years was war-time, so we always had to hear the news. We also had a wind-up record player with cylinder records.

I lived on the farm until I was 16-years-old, when my parents moved to the south of Wellington.

My parents are gone now, but as I look back I don't know how they managed all of us. My two brothers are gone now also. My sister Doris and I remember all the good and bad times. We live 100 miles apart but visit on the phone and in person once in awhile. She raised six children and I raised two and we have both lost our husbands — I have lost two. But we have our church families and our faith and are doing fine.

Contributed by niece Donna Abbott, Oklahoma

Curing the seven-year-itch and other ailments

In her personal account, Dorothy Richardson remembers, *"All four of us took turns with childhood diseases – we even had the seven-year-itch [scabies]. Mom would stand us up on a chair and rub us with something that smelled terrible. It didn't last that long, but it was awful."*

During the Depression era, the disease or ailment had to be serious before anyone went to a doctor or sent for one to make a house call. A visit could cost $4 — which could buy a wagonload of groceries for a small family.

In 1934 a ruptured appendix, which required hospitalization, could result in a bill of nearly $54. A tonsillectomy for a child with a full day of hospitalization could total $6. Doctor bills could easily set a family back for years.

Following is a list of "cure-alls" used to fend off illness:

Saleratus: Similar to baking soda, this medical potion was used for upset stomachs and general internal aches and pains. A glass of the bubbling water more often than not cured the ailment. The potion was concocted with 1 tablespoon into a large glass of water. Add a tablespoon of vinegar, then another teaspoon of soda. Briskly stir, and then drink before the fizz has gone down. Children drank it more willingly with a teaspoon of precious sugar added to the mixture.

White liniment: Rubbed onto skin and used to reduce swelling; 1 part cider vinegar, 1 part turpentine and 1 tablespoon salt.

Sore muscles: Wintergreen oil.

Loosen phlegm in chest: Goose or skunk grease with a bit of kerosene added then rubbed on the chest.

Remedy for eczema: Mixed well and rubbed onto affected areas; 3 tablespoons lard, 1 tablespoon sulphur and 2 drops iodine.

For chronic cough and to rid oneself of parasites: Chew one clove raw garlic on a cracker between meals and before bedtime — three times per day until relief comes.

Sore throat: Salt water gargle and a chicken feather dipped in alum to swab the throat. A bit kinder remedy was 2 tablespoons of honey with a pinch of black pepper mixed in a shot of whiskey or hot tea.

Mouth sores: Alum, with a bit of pucker, cured mouth sores.

Insect stings: Wet cigarette tobacco on bee and wasp stings draws the poison out quickly.

Sunburns: Vinegar bath.

Upset stomach: Mint, peppermint or chamomile mixed into tea. Ginger also helped cure motion sickness.

Scrapes and cuts: Raw honey onto the injury for its antibacterial properties.

Migraines and flu/cold fevers: Feverfew tea.

Boils and splinters: Baking soda and oatmeal mixed with a bit of clay will draw it out.

Poison ivy/oak/sumac: Witch hazel and oatmeal poultice.

Sore teeth and gums: Clove oil.

Seven-year-itch, or scabies: Sulphur mixed with lard applied to affected areas over the course of several days.

Cough syrup: Slice whole onions onto a platter or bowl. Cover with sugar and let stand overnight. Drain juice into glass jar.

Ernie and Peter Gunther on cotton planter. Photo courtesy of Wes Gunther.

Picking cotton. Photo courtesy of Wes Gunther

We lost the farm

Reba (Stuart) Chamberlain

Born 1925 near Jonesboro, Arkansas

I was born on a farm in Arkansas in 1925 between Paragould and Jonesboro out in the country near the county line. There were six of us children. I had two older sisters and an older brother, and a younger sister and brother. We are Scotch and Irish and a little bit of Native American. My father's mother was ¼ Indian, so he was ⅛, and I guess that makes me 1/16th.

My parent's names are Arthur Stuart and Dora Chambers. My mother's first husband passed away six weeks before she was due to give birth to my oldest sister. Even though she is my half-sister I never thought of her that way.

Before the Depression started my dad had 40-60 acres of farmland. He grew cotton, corn and soybeans. We had two mules instead of horses, one jersey cow for our home use, and chickens, geese and turkeys. We had lots of eggs unless they weren't laying much. Mother said the men had to work, so they would have eggs for breakfast, but the rest of us had oatmeal.

Mama had all kinds of vegetables in her garden.

Sweet potatoes, squash, beans, cabbage, tomatoes and okra are some that I remember. We also had fruit trees. Mama canned and stored it all in the smokehouse with butchered meat so we had food over the winter. She also made saurkraut — we cut the cabbages by hand with a crop cutter.

When the Depression came on we lost the farm — oh, in about 1931. There was no money in the bank either. There had been a three-year drought and we could not keep the farm. So Dad worked with the WPA (Works Progress Administration) on county roads for awhile.

We moved six or seven miles away. My uncle had an abandoned schoolhouse in timber on his property, so we moved into that. It was a large home — we had three beds. Mama still raised chickens and had a little garden, but there wasn't much space. Later, we moved again about another six or seven miles away.

That is where we worked picking and chopping cotton, and gathered peaches and apples for other people — mostly peaches. One of my jobs was thinning the cotton so that it would grow closer. I got $1 a day for that. It was my first job. I was six- or seven-years-old. After my baby brother was born Mama put him on a cotton sack in the field and dragged him along behind. We all did that. It was how we made ends meet.

We helped our neighbors too, and they helped us. When they killed hogs or other meat we helped and were able to take some of it home. We always had beans and potatoes. There was always food on the table; we never went hungry. Dad hunted, so we had squirrels and rabbits to eat too.

Mama made some of our clothing and all the bedding. She made feather beds and the ticking, and that would sit on top of the springs — we didn't have box springs. She also made pillows. But twice a year we made the seven-mile trip into town to get new clothes and once a year we got new shoes. Dad always got us high-top shoes so that our feet would stay warm. He cut our hair too, and did a pretty good job of it. Sometimes he cut the neighbors' hair because he was just a compassionate fellow.

We didn't have transportation. When it was time to go to town we'd all walk out to the highway and stand there. Everyone knew everyone and there were always relatives around. They'd pick us up and take us in if they had room. If they didn't, they'd slow down and roll by, saying, "Milk!" or "Butter!" or "Eggs!" to let us know why they couldn't pick us up — they were making deliveries and had no room.

Even though everyone was poor there wasn't any crime that I can remember. We never locked our doors. Stealing wasn't an issue with our chickens — they all ran wild in the yard and in the trees.

When my older three brothers and sisters went to school they had to walk three miles. But by the time I started,there was a bus that picked me up. I was able to go to school, but when school was not in session I worked in the fields alongside everyone else in my family.

I graduated from high school when I was 17. My parents let me go to St Louis, Missouri to look for a job because it was closer than Little Rock. In those days if you wanted a good paying job you had to go to a large city. A cousin let me stay with her. I found a good job that I liked at a dry cleaners for $9 a week with a half day off on Saturdays.

I wasn't there very long when I met an older gentleman who was in town from California visiting his mother. We became acquainted and we married a short time later. I moved to California with my new husband, James Chamberlain, and I was very happy. I worked in the shipyards in San Pedro for a bit.

We never had any children so I don't know how that would have been. But I know that the Depression time affected me in other ways as I grew older. Because of my skill in dry cleaning I prided myself on being able to make our clothes look nice myself. I enjoyed it. I did my own hair and fingernails and toenails — I never had them "done." I cook and eat very healthful, and I know how to shop for bargains.

How to describe my childhood? It was a good one. I have fond memories. It was a part of life and I didn't know we were poor. Our relatives had homes and uncles had cars to drive and we didn't. But that was it. When we moved from the farm I got the idea that we didn't have a home anymore, but I was very young and didn't understand everything.

I'm very pleased with my life. I'll be 90 next year. I have done well. Yes, I would say that I have done well.

Reba Chamberlain, California

Rabbits, hares and squirrels — oh my

Although Reba Chamberlain started life on a farm where animals were raised, her large family was a challenge for her parents to feed, especially after the family lost the farm in Arkansas in 1931.

But they made do. As Reba said, "*Dad hunted, so we had squirrels and rabbits to eat too*."

Following is a Depression era recipe for cooking them. Measurements for some items are not listed because most cooks knew offhand exactly how much to use for the amount of meat they had.

"Choose rabbits with soft ears and paws — stiffness is a sign of age. Also, be sure they are fresh and free from any unpleasant odor. Neither hares nor rabbits should be drawn [gutted] before hanging, as they may become musty. In winter, select a dry place for hanging and they may remain for some time."

Roast Squirrels

Squirrels
Salad oil
Lemon juice or tarragon vinegar
1 cup bread crumbs
Cream
1 cup button mushrooms, diced
Pepper and salt
Oil
Onion juice
Brown stock (broth)
1 cup boiling water
1 teaspoon Worcestershire sauce
Paprika

Clean the squirrels thoroughly, wash in several water baths and slather with salad oil mixed with lemon juice or tarragon vinegar. Let stand for an hour on a platter. Soak with a cup of bread crumbs in just enough cream to moisten them, add a cup of diced mushrooms, pepper, salt and onion juice.

Stuff each squirrel with this mixture, sew and truss as you would a fowl. Rub with oil, place in a dripping dish and partly cover with brown stock diluted with a cup of boiling water.

When the squirrels are well roasted, make a gravy out of the liquor in the pan by adding a teaspoon of Worcestershire sauce, paprika, salt and lemon juice to taste.

Rabbits can be cooked the same way.

“I think I have one of these”

Jackson Conner

Grandfather born 1908 in Floyd County, Virginia

My grandfather Sherman Jacob Conner was born in 1908 in a rural farming area of Floyd County, Virginia, not near any particular township.

He had only obtained a third grade education which seemed to be fairly common for rural areas at the time. After the onset of the Great Depression he and his parents along with his 11 siblings relocated to Roanoke, Virginia to look for work.

While still living at home, my grandfather did have two intermittent jobs during the Depression. The first was at a local furniture plant named Johnson Carper Furniture Co., and the second was for a local plumbing outfit named E.R. Carr Plumbing.

Interestingly as fate would have it, he started his own plumbing company in 1939 — S.J. Conner Plumbing. It was later renamed S.J. Conner & Sons Plumbing after the birth of his second son.

Having no money to actually start a business, it was his common practice to go out and find work and get a verbal agreement for such and such expected amount then go to a local plumbing supply house and convince them that he was good for the money in a day or two when said job would be completed. And that's the way he operated for several years.

In the early 1970s at the ripe age of 11, I began working in the family business as a plumber's helper and was for the most part assigned to help my grandfather. My main job was to dig plumbing parts and tools from the car's trunk — he would not drive a truck like most plumbers at the time — and take them to him while he worked.

It was during the next few years that I learned by way of many conversations with him about the difficult era of the Great Depression. I noticed some apparent characteristics of a man who lived through such difficult times: my grandfather would almost never take a vacation and viewed doing so as an unnecessary waste of money; he spoke often of how people in general "nowadays" spent way too much money; he was an avid saver and would always pay cash for larger ticket items such as automobiles and appliances.

His first house that he owned as a married man did not originally have running water or toilets and was paid for in cash. As the family grew, he added on for size and basic necessities by paying cash only.

Borrowing money was not considered. The only option was to wait until one could afford to pay for whatever was wanted or needed.

Grandfather would occasionally have to call a customer for details about when they wanted him to come over for repairs. Because he had no phone he would drive across town to use a land line, although putting in that unnecessary quarter in a nearby pay phone would have been much easier.

One of the stranger traits at that time that didn't make much sense to me was the way that he would look at spare parts — even used parts — evaluate them and stash them somewhere in the parts room of his shop or attic for a possible "some day" use. Invariably many times he might need to go to a plumbing supply house and buy the same said piece for repairs. That's when he would say, "I think I have one of these in a particular place," and drive to the shop where he would reach into some corner or crevice in storage and pull put the needed part for reuse or resale. This parts hoarding was something of a habit that neither of the two sons or any other plumber seems to have done or even considered then.

After a considerable passage of time working with my grandfather even into my 20s, I eventually realized that a lot of his seemingly conservative behavior patterns were in fact caused by living through an era that was quite foreign to the time in which I lived. It was obvious — to me at least — that the Great Depression left a lasting impression on my grandfather.

Jackson Conner, Virginia

Raisin grapes drying on paper trays.
Photo courtesy of Wes Gunther.

Paid in movie popcorn

Taressa Crawford
Grandmother born 1921 in Glennville, Georgia

My grandmother's name is Willie Mae Lindler Durrance. She lived in Glennville, Georgia and was born on August 19, 1921. She had an older sister and brother, Bessy and Frank Hall. Their daddy died when they were very young in a farming accident.

Grandmother's mother, Fostina Gertrude Pierce, remarried to William Lindler, who was much older. He was a blacksmith until someone stole his tools and equipment, then he became a cobbler. Grandmother's father was 62 when she was born. She also had a younger sister, Annie Laura. Grandmother was named Willie after her father. He passed away when she was 12. Her mother remarried again to John Morgan, who outlived her.

The family lived in a house in Glennville. They didn't have grass in their yards back then, so they would sweep the yard with a broom to keep it neat. Their

April 1940. Farm Security Administration

clothes were made from flour sacks and hand-me-downs. They walked to school. For Christmas sometimes they got an orange, which was a treat. Grandmother doesn't remember getting any Christmas gifts.

They used to get their food mostly from gleaning, or going over someone's garden after the crop had been harvested. In other words they gathered the leftovers and the rejected fruits and vegetables.

To make ends meet her mother used to get paid 10 cents to clean up the local movie theater after the movies were over for the day. Once the Depression started, instead of getting her dime or sometimes a quarter, the theater owners started paying her in leftover popcorn.

My grandmother and her sisters and brother were allowed to see the movie for free on Saturdays and their mother could bring home all of the leftover popcorn when she finished cleaning the theater.

They would eat that popcorn all week. My grandmother told me that her favorite dish was popcorn with milk on it. I said, "So you liked cereal." She said, "No," they never bought any cereal. But she loved popcorn with milk.

I asked her what her other favorite things to eat were and she said that she loved fried chicken. But she usually ate the neck or back piece even as an adult. I asked her why, when those had the least meat of any of the pieces. She said she just got used to eating those pieces when she was young, and when she was grown and had children of her own she kept eating them so that her children and husband could have the meatier portions.

Grandmother started working at a grocery store to help with paying bills when her children began attending school. She went on to work as a cashier for Winn-Dixie, which is where she worked until she retired.

Grandmother learned to sew at a young age and made most of her clothes and her children's clothes. She also made many quilts. I figure she's made at least 30 handmade quilts and has given most of them away to family.

Grandmother is still alert and active at 93-years-old.

Taressa Crawford, Georgia

Popcorn rescued many

For Fostina Gertrude Pierce, movie theater popcorn likely saved her family from starving during the Depression years. She was paid in popcorn weekly to feed her three children. Popcorn with milk and sometimes a little sugar was a staple breakfast food. Popcorn soup made with a bit of broth, diced onion, diced potatoes and evaporated milk was filling.

Popcorn also saved the movie theater business during the late 1920s through the Depression and into World War II.

Before 1927 silent movies were attended only by people who could read and had spare change for such frivolity. Adding sound in 1927 opened the industry up to a wider clientele. By 1930 attendance in movie theaters across the nation reached nearly 90 million per week.

But selling snacks inside theaters was frowned upon; movie house owners did not want expensive carpets ruined. As a result, ticket sales dropped because the entertainment venue wasn't family-friendly and the Depression was in full swing. Why spend money on a talking picture and not enjoy it? By the mid-1930s the movie business started to go under.

Popcorn was already popular with street vendors at the onset of the Depression. Opportunistic fellows pushed carts with steam or gas-powered poppers on them and followed the crowds. They were a common sight at fairs, parks and expositions.

If theater owners couldn't see the financial lure of popcorn and turned their noses up at installing popcorn equipment, enterprising street vendors didn't miss a beat: they brought their popping machines and sold popcorn outside the theaters before moviegoers entered.

The Great Depression presented an excellent opportunity for both movie theater owners and popcorn sellers. Looking for a cheap diversion from their troubles, audiences flocked to the movies. Popcorn was a luxury that most people could afford at 5 to 10 cents a bag. Popcorn kernels were a cheap investment — a $10 bag could last for several years.

For many theaters the transition to selling snacks helped save them from the crippling affects of the Depression. Those who began serving popcorn and other refreshments survived.

1930s Movie Theater Popcorn

For each person:

- 1/4 cup popcorn kernels
- 3-4 Tablespoons lard
- 1 Tablespoon butter, melted
- ¼ tsp salt

Photo courtesy of Jean Akens

We were one of the more fortunate families

Jean (Fike) Akens

Born 1929 in Fresno County, California

My story may be a little different. We were one of the more fortunate families during the Depression.

I was born in 1929 to Floyd Fike and Nell (Bateman) Fike in Fresno County, California. We lived on a large dairy farm near Layton. It was about 40 acres then before Dad started expanding. He also grew grain to feed his cattle. Mother was a schoolteacher.

We had a winter and a summer garden. You could have a winter garden in central California because the weather was so mild. We had a few acres of fruit trees — I remember apricots. There was also a big walnut tree in the back yard.

My grandparents were immigrants from Germany and settled in the Kansas area. When Dad was 13 he went with his dad and dogs and brought dairy cows to Fresno on flatbeds on the railroad. He bought his own place a short time later.

When the banks closed it didn't really affect his income. My father was already quite well-off financially. He wasn't really affected. He bought land when he was 13-years-old and expanded. I grew up on that same land. I do remember that he said there were people standing in line on the road to help on the farm. He paid them each 25 cents a day to work.

My mother died when I was five-years-old. There had been a little brother before me who died in infancy and then another brother. I'm not sure what she died of, it might have been cancer, but I never heard the word cancer. She was 39-years-old when my dad took her to the hospital. She knew then that she'd never return home. Before they operated on her she sat up in bed and wrote out her Last Will and Testament.

Grandma came to live with us after that to help take care of things around the house. She only lived about 12 miles away. She moved out about a year later when Dad married a Portuguese woman named Lillie Rose. She had daughters from an earlier marriage. Dad and Lillie had another child together.

Dad was extremely well off. I was brought up by a black mammy. Her name was Mrs. Hunt. She took care of the cooking and cleaning, too. Her husband, Mr. Hunt, took care of my brother and helped out on the farm. No one else in the neighborhood had anyone like that.

We always had food on the table and store-bought clothes. We didn't suffer. My stepmother liked that we were pretty well-off. She had fur coats and she liked her shoes. Dad was frugal in the fact that he wasn't generous with money outside of the family. He didn't give to charities that I know of. He wasn't flamboyant, but we lived comfortably. He had a big ol' Studebaker and we had a summer home in the mountains and a boat. He liked to fish and hunt, go dancing and dine out and socialize. He expanded his dairies to four and increased his land.

Jean Fike on left, with siblings..

But I didn't feel different than anyone at school, really. We walked or rode our bicycles or a horse to grammar school like everyone else. I didn't know what "poor" was until someone told me they ate lots of beans and potatoes and I didn't know why. They said it was because they were poor. In school there was no class line — at least not as far as I was concerned.

There was a class line as far as color though in our neighborhood. One day a neighbor came to the door and my step-mother answered it. The neighbor said she just wanted to see if she was a white woman. Oh, my step-mother could out-cuss any man. She cussed that neighbor all the way down to the end of our long driveway!

Although my father was the only rich person in the Valley, money didn't seem important to us kids or our friends. Our home was a little nicer, but it wasn't a real big house. There were other dairies around but they were smaller.

Most of my clothes were hand-me-downs. My step-sister was 11 months older than me and she had older sisters so 75 percent of my clothes were hand-me-downs from them. But they were still nice clothes. I remember to this day two brand-new outfits my father bought me: one was for Easter and the other for Christmas.

My closest girlfriend was Portuguese. I'd spend the night at her house or she would stay at mine. We were friends all though grade school and high school. Our time in grammar school was fun. We played in the yard, rode horses, played in the barnyard and in the loft — we did a lot of things together. I had dolls and things like that but not expensive toys. When we were in high school I was a cheerleader and loved my freedom. I had a lot of happy times hanging out with my friends. They compensated for a lot because there wasn't a lot of attention at home.

I think how I grew up in the Depression era affected me mostly in how I showed affection to others for a long time. My father was a good, kind man, but he and my stepmother weren't affectionate toward me. I can see the consequences of that in how I was with my own children. But I'm older and I lavish love on my children now. It's never too late. We've come around to a better way of life with showing love and giving love. That's what matters.

Jean Akens, California

Children didn't ask questions in those days

Katherine (Sigera) Dillon

Born 1926 in Earlimart, California

My father, Mehar Singh Sigera, came to the San Fernando Valley in California in 1917 from India. When he first arrived he was a farm worker. He wasn't able to own land because of California's Alien Land Law so he leased farms — mostly in grapes.

Dad married my mother, Ybana Guadelupe Lopez, who was a seventh-generation Mexican-Californian. I was born in 1926 in Earlimart, Tulare County, California. I had a brother two years older. My mother died in 1931 when I was four-years-old.

After my mother died I went to live with her Aunt and Uncle Senton and Mary Burdick and their son in Alberhill, near Lake Elsinore, California. My great-uncle worked at the Los Angeles Pressed Brick Company, which was founded in 1918. It closed in 1932 or 1933 because of the Great Depression.

I remember that Alberhill was a little company town, a little blip on the road. There was a one-room school, a little store and a grove of trailers where the workers lived. I think the whole town belonged to the company. We had a house across the highway. I don't remember electricity in Alberhill; we had coal oil lamps.

Meanwhile my father earned money from his leased farms in order to buy his own grape farm in San Fernando. He and a few other Indian men in the area put their money together. Dad was the only one with an education so he got to be the "big boss." He helped them buy farms of their own.

Dad was able to buy land from the bank during the Depression in 1933 — his way around the Alien Land Law was to put it in me and my brother's names because we were Americans. He bought a block of 160 acres; he raised grapes and raisins and made wine. Not all of the land went into production — only about 40 to 60 acres. Farm workers lived in some of the buildings and the rest of the open land gradually went into more grapes and citrus and peach orchards.

When the brick company closed down we moved to San Fernando and stayed one year — this was after Dad bought his land. My uncle did odd jobs. We always had something to eat and I know we went on welfare for one year until my great-uncle got another job. Children didn't ask questions in those days — you got in trouble if you did.

My great-aunt took care of their son and me; she didn't work outside the home. There was washing on Monday, ironing on Tuesday — that sort of thing. She had two washtubs of warm water that were heated up over a fire outside. Then she'd wash everything by hand. As kids we didn't really think about it. It was hard work for adults.

She sewed our clothing, raised chickens, tended her garden — maybe that's why we never went hungry; we always had chicken to eat and fresh vegetables. I remember picking a radish out of the ground, washing the dirt off of it and eating it. She also raised carrots, tomatoes and other things and canned different vegetables. Sometimes my great-uncle and his brother would go fishing, so we sometimes had fish to eat. I just ate what was put in front of me.

I had two dresses: one to wear when the other one was dirty. I also had one pair of shoes, but we ran around barefoot a lot of the time too. I liked to play games such as cops 'n robbers, jacks and stuff like that. Most of my friends and I each had one doll and we'd visit each other's homes to play. It was easier to do that when we lived in town — otherwise the nearest neighbor was a mile or more away if you lived out in the boonies.

My dad and brother stayed in touch when I lived away from them. There were letters occasionally and they usually visited once or twice a year, mostly in the summer when there wasn't as much to do at the vineyard; picking didn't begin until August. We didn't have a telephone until 1939 in the city.

At age 14 I moved back in with my dad and brother in San Fernando. When my brother and I were teenagers we'd wander into the open fields and shoot jackrabbits. I graduated from Caruthers High School in 1943.

I think those years affected me to some degree. My husband and I started our family after WWII — my husband was in the Army. We married in 1947 and had four children. Dad helped us get a farm in Caruthers, California where we raised grapes and peaches.

We raised our children differently than how we were raised. I was essentially raised in two different cultures. But my husband's parents died when he was four so he didn't have a "home." He was the fourth of eight children and there was a seven-year gap between the first and second groups of four. The older children raised the younger ones. To earn money they went "fruit bumming" from camp to camp. During the school year my husband stayed with his older sister. He's lucky he had older siblings.

Raising our own children after living through the Depression has given us a different perspective, certainly. We have been very affectionate with our children. I wouldn't say we were too frugal — we were generous with them.

It wasn't until later that I was cognizant of those things that made such a difference. It didn't occur to me until I was an adult that a lot of things that happened during my childhood were because of the Depression. I thought having cereal for dinner was wonderful. But now I can piece it all together. It was very difficult for the adults.

Katherine Dillon, California

"Make Do or Do Without"

Times were tough.

Money was scarce; if there was any, the household budget was tight. Many families made do with what they produced on their own — from meat grown on the hoof to vegetable gardens — or they did without, such as Katherine Sigera Dillon's family in California.

In the 1930s most people didn't travel to the grocery store on a whim when they needed a recipe ingredient, forgot to buy butter or ran out of bread. Rural families typically travelled weekly or monthly and even then it had to be necessary. Most often a trip to the grocery store was a chance to barter what they grew for what they couldn't. Eggs were handed over to the grocer in exchange for flour; butter churned on the porch bought brown sugar or a pair of shoes.

Reading a Depression era recipe with a modern-day mindset will change the recipe. When the instructions call for a can of something it is usually vegetables or fruit that were preserved in glass jars or bottles on top of hot woodstoves after the year's harvest then stored in a pantry or cellar.

Meat wasn't a staple at every meal and rarely used in recipes. Proteins were obtained through dairy if a family was lucky enough to have a cow or two along with eggs, lard and/or dried beans. Servings of meat were typically reserved for Sundays and special occasions. If a family was part of a community co-op for beef or pork, they saved their portion for the special weekly meal. Chicken dinners were most common. But they weren't neatly killed, plucked, cut-up and packaged off-site. A live chicken in the yard that morning ended up on the table in some form for the afternoon or evening meal. Those who lived near forested areas could supplement their diets with venison. Fish were handy too and often salted for later use.

Recipes refer to using lard more often than butter. Lard is rendered pig fat from last season's hog butchering where every part "except the squeal" was used. Also known as "pig butter," lard often replaced precious dairy butter. It provided protein and was spread thickly on a sandwich made from homemade bread. A raw, sliced onion added flavor. Onion and mustard sandwiches were not uncommon either; onions hold a lot of vitamins.

Cooks used ingenuity to feed larger families. To make food and recipes stretch, oatmeal and cornmeal were used as fillers. Soups were common — it didn't take much to add water, a bit of salt and a handful of beans to eke out extra bowlfuls.

Simple recipes with basic items define household cooking during the Depression era.

Chicken Soup

After the chicken is killed and plucked, boil the chicken and remove meat from bones. Heat broth until boiling, then reduce heat and sprinkle in a handful of cornmeal. Whisk until thickened then stir in chicken. Add salt and pepper to taste.

Chicken Soup with Vegetables

One clean, 3-4 lb. chicken. Place chicken in 2-gallon stockpot with an onion and 2 stalks celery. Bring to boil and simmer an hour. Lift out chicken, pull apart and remove bones. Return chicken pieces to pot and add veggies from garden including at least two carrots and potatoes. Fill pot with water again and bring to boil, then simmer till done. Season with salt and pepper.

Depression Yeast Cornbread

Dissolve 1 pkg yeast in 1/4-cup warm water

Scald 2 cups milk

Pour over 1/3 cup lard and 1/3 cup of sugar.

Cool and add 2 eggs well beaten and 1 tsp. salt and the yeast mixture.

Mix well and add 4 cups flour and 1/2 cup cornmeal.

Pour mixture into two loaf pans and let rise until double.

Bake in 350-degree oven for 45 minutes.

Dessert

Put stale bread in a coffee cup. Pour enough warm milk or coffee over it to make it moist. Sprinkle with a little sugar.

Potato Soup

In a saucepan, add a bit of lard or butter, flour and salt.

When it is melted, add milk and a handful of potatoes.

Vegetable Soup

Peel and dice about 6-8 potatoes.

Put potatoes in a large pot and add a diced onion or two and a chopped-up head of cabbage.

Pour water in to cover all vegetables, then bring to a boil.

Salt the water to taste but remember that you will not drain the water.

When these have all softened, add one can of tomato juice or some ketchup, 2 cans of corn, 2 cans of green beans

Simmer for at least 15 minutes and serve.

Hot dish

A pot of cooked rice

A lb. of bacon cut into pieces with rendered fat saved and set aside

A can of sauerkraut

Mix together rice, sauerkraut, bacon and bacon fat. Add black pepper.

Pea Casserole

1 can peas
1 small onion
2 cups bread crumbs
3 T lard
1 1/2 cups milk
2 eggs
Salt, pepper

Brown onion and bread crumbs in lard. Add milk, cook until thickened. Add peas and mix together; put in greased pan. Beat eggs and pour over casserole. Bake like meatloaf.

Meat Patties

1 lb. ground beef, pork, or bison
1 lb. mashed potato
1 medium onion, diced
1 egg
1 tsp. salt
1/4 cup bread crumbs (made by roasting in the oven)
Flour
Oil

Combine ground meat, mashed potatoes, diced onion, breadcrumbs, egg and salt. Mix together thoroughly.

Form into 6 patties about 1" thick.

Coat patties lightly with flour; fry in oil on medium to medium-low heat until the meat inside is just done.

Creamed Rice

Two cups of water to 1 cup rice.
Boil — after about 15 minutes as the rice finishes, add 1 – 1 ½ cups milk.

It has a somewhat soupy consistency.

For a treat, sprinkle with a bit of sugar or cinnamon.

Cabbage Soup

Put coarsely chopped cabbage in a pot and fill with water 2-inches over the cabbage until the cabbage is almost soft. In another saucepan melt a heaping tablespoon of lard or bacon fat and sprinkle with 3-4 T flour, stirring constantly until the mixture is a tan color. Mix this into the boiled cabbage. Stir until well-mixed — it will thicken the soup. Add ham or bacon if you have it. Otherwise, salt and pepper to taste.

Tomato/Cracker Soup

Hot water poured over broken-up saltine crackers with melted butter or lard. Add ketchup for "tomato" soup.

Corn Meal Mush

1 cup cold water
1 cup corn meal
1 tsp. salt
3 cups boiling water

Mix corn meal, cold water and salt. Slowly pour mixture into boiling water. Cover and cook 15 minutes on low heat. Stir as needed. Cool it until you can cut it with a knife then it fry in a pan and serve.

Fried Cabbage

Use scraps from ham or bacon grease as a base. Add sliced cabbage and cook down until soft and almost translucent. Serve over mashed potatoes or rice with cornbread.

Anything to bring in some income

Pat (Babb) Earnest

Father born 1915 in Baldwin, Georgia
Mother born 1919 in Middlesboro, Kentucky

Daddy, George Bernard Babb, was born January 27, 1915 in Baldwin, Georgia. He was an only child. His daddy passed away when he was two-years-old so he and his mother, Mary Alma Perry Babb, moved back to Macon to be near her family.

I remember my dad telling me about one place they lived when he was about five-years-old. It was out in the woods. When his mother was getting him ready for bed she opened the dresser drawer to get his pajamas and there was snake coiled up on top! YIKES!

When he was 12 they moved to Atlanta, Georgia. They lived in the Virginia Highlands area, always in rented rooms or a duplex or something. Daddy and his mother always lived with somebody else after his dad passed away. To my knowledge, my grandmother never owned a home; she couldn't afford it. Consequently, their "home" was always just two to three rooms in someone else's house.

His mother worked for a group of lawyers, taught piano, did sewing for people — anything to bring in some income. She never remarried.

Daddy had several jobs as a young man — worked in a grocery store, worked for a jeweler, had a paper route and was head usher at The Loew's Grand Theatre where *Gone With The Wind* premiered on Dec. 15, 1939.

Mother, Ina Marie (Standifer) Babb, was born on December 26, 1919 in Middlesboro, Kentucky to Joe and Cashie Standifer. She is the second oldest of 11 children. Mother's youngest sister is only nine months older than I am.

Mother grew up in Middlesboro and didn't leave there until she graduated from high school and went to Atlanta. Middlesboro, right on the Kentucky/Tennessee state lines, is known today as Appalachia. It was a coal-mining town; Granddaddy worked in the mines. They had a very, very hard life. They raised all their own meat and vegetables.

Mother's family lived in a "bare bones" clapboard house that my grandfather built. He only had a third grade education but he was blessed and gifted to know how to build. He could compute measurements and figure quantities and techniques — amazing.

They never had indoor plumbing in this house. I remember having to go to the "outhouse" to go to the bathroom and in the winter it was absolutely freezing in the house. I think the only thing that kept us from freezing to death was the fact that there were three to four people sleeping in each bed!

My mother's mother made their clothes out of feed sacks.

A Depression era Appalachian shack. Wikipedia Commons

I actually had some feed sack clothes myself that Mother made for me when I was around six or seven-years-old. They also only got one pair of shoes a year, at the end of summer when school was starting. They pretty much went barefoot during warm weather.

Mother told us many times how little they had growing up, but they never thought they were poor because they knew so many people who had so much less than they did. I do know they got some type of government assistance with food because Mother talked about "commodity" items such as cheese, flour, soda crackers, peanut butter and other staple items.

I also remember Grandmother insisted that ALL the children (three boys, eight girls) take typing in high school. For almost all of them that was their ticket out of Appalachia — even the boys. All 11 of the children were very good in school but only one — the youngest — ever got a college degree. Most of them graduated from high school and immediately went to work and/or got married.

Mother also had a paper route when she was very young. She graduated from high school a year early and went to work for a lawyer in his office and then became a court reporter for a few years.

Eventually Daddy went to work for Lever Brothers (now Unilever) in Atlanta. He spent 1943-1945 in the US Navy and retired from Lever Bros. in 1977.

When Mother moved to Atlanta she (coincidentally) went to work for Lever Brothers as my dad's secretary. They married in 1942. When Daddy came home from WWII, I was just a year old and Mother never returned to the workplace. She was a full-time mother. How fortunate we were! Wish I could've done that when my three daughters were young. I had to return to work when my first-born was only six-weeks-old.

My daddy's mother lived within six to eight miles of us in a rented apartment in someone else's home when we were growing up. As I mentioned earlier, she never remarried, so she was single and actually still working when we were very young.

I remember spending weekends with her occasionally and what a great cook she was. I remember that she had an iron bed and a "chifforobe" and a couple of old trunks that I just loved to plunder. There were old photographs, old jewelry, Daddy's baby clothes, etc. I have all these items in my home now. She made clothes for me on a Singer treadle sewing machine which I now have.

Mother's parents always lived in Middlesboro so we only saw them once a year or so. I was sort of afraid of those "big, rough" people. They weren't very outgoing and I was very shy.

Granddaddy built another house when I was about nine or 10, so that would've been around 1954. That's the first time they had indoor plumbing and a "larger" wood stove. This new house was on 22 acres, much of which was on the side of a mountain. But I loved going up there and exploring what to me was a wilderness. Didn't get to do that in the city where we lived.

Granddaddy's father passed away when Granddaddy was only 12; he had four sisters. He had to take his dad's job in the coal mine the very next day in order for the family to eat.

Grandmother's mother passed away when she was only four. She had a couple of sisters and four brothers I think. Her father took her and her sisters and put them in an orphanage until they were 12-years-old. Then he went back and got them and brought them home to cook and clean for the boys. Sounds almost like slave labor doesn't it? No wonder they all married as soon as they could.

There are five children in my family. I am the oldest and I have four younger brothers.

The way my parents lived during the Depression filtered into their lives later in many ways.

To say Mother was frugal would be an understatement. She made every piece of clothing I wore including slips, coats, zip-up leggings and dresses until I was in high school. At the time I thought that I was really deprived. But looking back I can really appreciate her expert sewing skills and self-reliance.

She made many things for my brothers also but boys' wardrobes don't lend as well to homemade as girls' do. Mother cut our hair and gave me and others "permanents." The learning curve was pretty painful for us sometimes.

Once or twice I looked like Little Orphan Annie and my brothers endured a week or so of "gapped up" hair. Back then boys wore their hair very short, even flat tops.

Her hairdresser skills improved though, and she would do shampoos and sets or perms for many ladies in the neighborhood and our church. That was a huge financial boon for us. I'm thinking she charged $2.50 for a shampoo and set.

Probably the main thing that they passed on to me and my brothers is that there is value in just about everything. Experiences, clothing, skills, relationships — all have at least some value and you must not waste it.

And we never threw away food. There was a time or two when that turned out not to be as beneficial as hoped.

Also a very strong sense of family. I only knew one schoolmate growing up whose parents were divorced. There was honor and strength in working together and to being a good example for your children. For them, family came first.

Mother passed away on Dec. 5, 2012, age 92 — almost 93. Daddy passed away on July 25, 2014, at age 99½.

Pat Earnest, Georgia

Needy Family food program begins

Over the course of American history there have always been poor families who had fallen on hard times and struggled to make ends meet. This was nothing new before the Great Depression.

However, until 1932 help with food and money was the responsibility of local communities and charity organizations such as churches and the Red Cross. The Federal government was not involved – why should it be?

From 1900 until the end of WWI in 1918 farmers – especially in wheat -- enjoyed relative prosperity. But the end of the Great War brought slackening demand for wheat and renewed competition from other countries. By 1920 farmers and their families slipped into a period of long-term stagnation coupled with drought.

During the start of the Great Depression farming products became effectively unmarketable. The Farm Administration bought surplus wheat that depressed markets could no longer absorb. As a result, millions of bushels of government-owned wheat accumulated in warehouses while photos of widespread hunger and malnutrition appeared in newspapers.

Americans were bothered by the contradiction of suffering amidst abundance and wanted some of this surplus to be distributed to the hungry.

But Republican President Herbert Hoover, his Administration and Congress opposed that idea, believing that to give away anything for free would undermine the country's work ethic. Hoover and others believed that the Red Cross and churches should care for the needy, not government programs.

Hoover also reportedly questioned the extent of hunger in America, which began a long debate over the definition and meaning of American malnutrition and hunger.

President Franklin Roosevelt took office in March 1933. Along with rehabilitating the farm economy, his Administration worked to create a program that would distribute surplus food to the hungry.

Commodity items were foods that the federal government had the legal authority to purchase and distribute in order to support farm prices.

It was a radical idea – the equivalent of a federal Robin Hood – the Government bought from those who had too much in order to give to those who had too little.

Pat Earnest, whose mother is one of 11 children raised in a poor family in Appalachia Kentucky, shared this memory: *"I do know they got some type of government assistance with food because mother talked about commodity items such as cheese, flour, soda crackers, peanut butter and other staple items."*

The first commodity distribution program was known as the Needy Family Program. Distributions were usually made once a month which made it difficult for a poor family to plan ahead; but something was better than nothing.

Eventually lost the business

Denise Murphy-Gerber
Grandfather born 1903 in
West Salem Township, Pennsylvania

My grandfather Chauncy McClimans used to speak about the Great Depression and the effects on his family.

Prior to the Great Depression my great-grandfather, Frank McClimans, was a successful businessman who owned McClimans' Hardware store in Greenville, Pennsylvania; it was a thriving town in western Pennsylvania when the Depression came on. They had a farm that they had sold when they moved into town and bought the hardware store. I'm guessing the house they lived in was paid off before the Depression hit because they didn't lose their home. They raised seven boys; one died of diphtheria when he was very young.

As people in the community had needs such as materials to fix a roof, repair a broken water pipe, etc. and no way to pay for the items, Frank began to offer

Franklin D. Roosevelt Presidential Library & Museum

credit. He said that as a Christian business owner he could not refuse a poor soul who desperately needed hardware items in order to take care of his family.

They eventually lost the business because folks had no way to pay for items — which meant that there was no money to restock the store and no money to make their own payments. When they lost the store someone else bought it and my great-grandfather was able to stay on as an employee. However, that employment was short-lived —Frank died in 1933 in a tragic hit-and-run car accident. At the time three of his sons were still living at home.

As the McClimans family struggled to make ends meet, my grandfather, who was a young man then, and his two other brothers needed to bring in some money to help the family survive. The only job that they were able to get was digging graves in the local cemetery. During the Great Depression my grandfather dug deep holes by hand with a shovel.

No one ever mentioned what my grandmother did to make ends meet. I assume that the three at-home boys were able to bring in enough money for food and incidentals.

Until the day my grandfather died he hated homemade bread. During the Depression the only hot meal that his mother could make the kids before they walked the mile to the one-room schoolhouse for daily classes was a slab of homemade bread that she had poured hot coffee over.

The "coffee bread" was indeed a reminder in later years about the lack of everything during the Great Depression including a decent breakfast. Homemade bread reminded him about the sacrifices the family made after the loss of their business and beloved husband/father.

One fun anecdote is that one of my grandfather's older brothers had to borrow a nickel off his wife to buy a toothbrush — they'd only been married a few days during the Depression. They were sort of on their honeymoon, although without any money to go anywhere I suppose it wasn't what people think of when they think of a honeymoon today. Years after the Depression they would tell that story over and over.

Dr. Denise C. Murphy Gerber, Pennsylvania

Bread for Life

Bread made at home was a diet staple of most Depression era families. Purchasing bakery bread was indeed a treat; one loaf of store-bought bread was often half of one day's wages in some of the poorer regions of the nation.

Denise Murphy-Gerber's grandfather and many others had home-baked bread for breakfast with warm coffee or milk poured over the top. Most families couldn't afford cereals. Sandwiches made with thickly cut slices rounded out lunch pails for adults and children alike.

Most often, flour was purchased in 50 lb. cotton sacks that were then used to make shirts, dresses and underwear. When companies learned that families were using the sacks to make clothing they started producing sacks with colourful prints.

Clara Bonfanti Cannucciari, of the Web series *Great Depression Cooking with Clara* and author of *Clara's Kitchen*, was born in 1915. She grew up in a suburb of Chicago during the Depression era and learned to cook from her mother.

Following is Clara's rough recipe for bread:

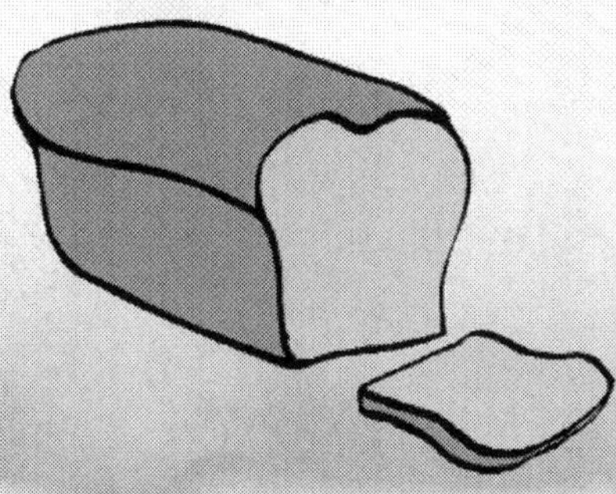

Basic White Bread

5 lbs of flour
2 oz. of cake yeast
4 cups warm water
Lard

Dump most of the flour in a very large bowl. Make a well in the flour and put the yeast in. Pour a bit of warm water into the well. Crumble the yeast cake into the well and mix the yeast and water with your fingers to dissolve. Mix in more flour with your hands, adding water as needed. You will eventually end up with a great big bowl of dough. Knead it until all is mixed well, then dump the dough on the counter.

Wash out the bowl and then grease it with lard. Put the dough back in and turn to coat with the grease.

Let the dough rise in a warm place for about an hour. Cover loosely with a clean towel while it rises to keep the dough from drying out. After it's risen, punch it down and divide it up for 8 loaves.

Place the loaves in greased bread tins and cover with a clean towel again and let rise for about 30 minutes.

Remove cloth and place them in the center rack of a 350-degree oven; bake 45-60 minutes until lightly browned.

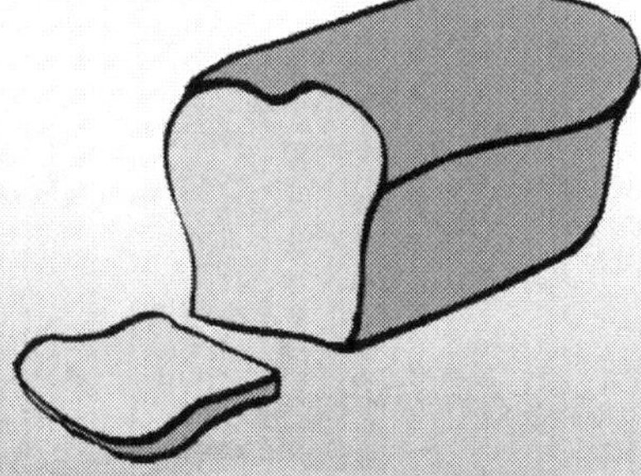

Wes Gunther hauling milk cans to the road for pickup.
Photo courtesy Wes Gunther.

Bartered raspberries

Taylor Goodwin

Great-grandmother born 1918 in Fillmore, Utah

My great-grandmother Leila Mae Taylor was born October 13, 1918 in Fillmore, Utah. It was a rural area — not a farm and not a city. She always went by her middle name, Mae.

She was about 11-years-old during the time of the Great Depression. She told me in one of many phone calls that I enjoyed with her in later years that there wasn't much to go around in their large family.

Great-grandmother's family had several raspberry plants in their backyard. They all took part in caring for them which included dividing them to increase the bounty for ensuing years. Eating raspberries as they

were picked when ripe was part of the fun.

At one time my great-grandmother needed dental work that the family could not afford. With a jar of raspberries in her hand she was sent off and made her way on foot to the local dentist. The dentist may have expected this arrangement already when my great-grandmother came or perhaps they talked a bit while she was there, but the bargain was done — raspberries in exchange for work and the family was able to have dental work done in exchange for what they could offer; the dentist was to have food for what he could offer.

Great-grandmother never lost her sense of humor,

House in Utah

despite growing up during such difficult times and she kept an able mind until her death. Though her memory was less sharp in her last few years, she could follow and offer word play and had more wit than many other people I know; she was always kind with her wit — it was without barbs and never was at another's expense. I don't know that I ever heard her say a negative opinion of another person.

I always enjoyed talking with her more than she knew.

Taylor Goodwin, Colorado

"Drive-in"

John Gunther and Helena Johnson Gunther, 1935.

Slept in an enclosed lean-to

Wes Gunther

Born 1927 in Kerman, California

By the time I was born in 1927 in Kerman, California, my parents already had 11 living children. Their firstborn, a son, died as an infant in 1911 when they lived in Oklahoma.

My dad, John P. Gunther, and Mom, Helena Johnson, started their lives together farming in Oklahoma. But due to family and other church members moving out they decided to move to California and make a living there.

After five years of unsuccessful farming in Kerman because the soil was so sandy, my dad sold his farm at a loss for $1,000 and put money down on a 40-acre farm south of Dinuba. Half of it was alkaline soil. It was terrible and only grew weeds no matter how hard Dad tried to improve the soil. Dad used parts of it as pasture for a small cattle herd. The other half was good soil and he grew alfalfa there. Gradually he introduced cotton to that part of the San Joaquin Valley and then grew all cotton.

Dad had put $2,500 down on the $6,500 price. He took out a loan for the rest intending to pay it off in five years. That was in 1930. Just a few months before the move the New York stock market crashed, sending the nation and our world into an economic depression such as it had never known. Over the course of the next 10 years Dad refinanced the land a few times and rented, or sharecropped, surrounding farmland to grow more crops and make more money to pay the bills and feed the family. He finally paid his farm off in 1939.

The first time I saw the farmhouse that was to be home for the next 25 years it was surrounded by dry weeds taller than me and had not seen a stripe of paint. I was less than three-years-old at the time but the scene burned itself in my memory. It was a fairly good size and had electricity,

Jack Gunther and Dad Gunther with truckloads of hay. In front is a 1929 Chevrolet, and behind is a Model T.

running water and an indoor bathroom with a toilet. There were only two bedrooms. Mom and Dad took one, and three of the seven girls took another with the other four sleeping on mats in the living room. The boys — five of us — slept in an enclosed lean-to on the back porch.

The dairy provided milk and cheese for our family but we sold as much as we could. Milk sold in the stores for 53 cents per gallon. Our milk went to a dairy processing plant in Tulare. We kept the milk cool in 10-gallon cans, and they sent out a truck to pick them up twice a day.

Mom always planted a huge garden. She could raise almost any kind of vegetable, flower or fruit tree. The vegetable garden was her biggest priority. She knew her family depended on the lettuce, cabbage, turnips, radishes, cucumbers, beans, carrots, beets, corn and tomatoes. She planted row after row knowing that many would be canned and used to feed her family during the long winter months. She would can up to 300 jars of fruit and vegetables. We also had an acre of fruit trees: peach, apricot, pear, cherry, plum and apple.

A few years later Dad built a huge chicken house to keep 1,000 chickens. He went to a sawmill in the mountains where he could get lumber for a reasonable price. It was my brother's and my job to collect the eggs everyday. Dozens and dozens had to be gone over one by one and weighed and cleaned. It was a one or two-hour job after school. We took the eggs to town on Saturdays. We could buy groceries in exchange for eggs — we usually got flour, sugar and potatoes. We didn't eat much rice.

Part of the blessing of having such a large family was that we could all work and earn money for the family. For two weeks at the end of summer we picked raisin grapes.

From the age of seven I helped. My first job was water boy and keeping the crew supplied with paper trays. It was hard, sweaty work. The next season I became a picker and my younger brother Ray took over.

That was hard work. My parents were up at 4 am to start their regular chores but I slept until 5 am. My goal as a regular crew member that first year (I was eight) was to pick 150 trays. We were paid by the tray so it was important that we pick as many trays as possible. During the early 1930s in the depths of the Depression we were paid 1½ cents a tray. That meant that my brother Peter who picked 400 trays a day was making $6 a day compared to the average day laborer who was glad to make $1 a day. Including me, seven of us children were able to work and contribute. I was proud that I did indeed make my goal.

Picking grapes paid for our shoes and school clothing for the coming year. Mom also stocked up on material to make t-shirts and underwear and the girls' dresses. We each had three pairs of shoes: school, church and work. They lasted until we grew out of them and passed them down or they wore out. But we went barefoot all summer long unless we were working in the fields.

The grade school we attended was three miles away. We walked in earlier years. When my older brothers got bicycles, they used those. Walking was always a big chore. I had a friend who lived on the back end of our 40 acres but he was in a different school district — those children had buses pick them up. I was so jealous. We all went on to high school — my wife and I were the first graduating class of Immanuel High School in Reedley.

We made our own fun. We never could participate in after-school sports because we had to get home and help with the chores. We had fun during the grade school years and we played during recess and sports in season and as a family: Red Rover, dodge ball, ante-over where we had to throw a ball over the roof of a garage. We had a lot of cousins and family that didn't live far away — we visited each other's houses. It was always fun to make big, 1 ½ gallon freezers of homemade ice cream.

We didn't have very many toys — they were all homemade. My brother had a knack of making toys from farm implements. We spent hours under a walnut tree playing "farm." We also had a coaster wagon but that's about it. We used it for chores along with a two-wheeled cart that we used to take milk from the barn to the roadside when the weather was cool enough.

In 1933 and 1934 our family experienced trials and sadness that we would never forget. At age 46 my mother gave birth to her 14th child, William Roger. He had serious

Mom and Dad Gunther weighing cotton.

health problems and developed pneumonia soon after his birth. There was no effective treatment in those days. He lived nearly three months. Shortly after that my 18-year-old sister, Martha, became ill. She was diagnosed with Crohn's Disease with complications of rheumatic fever and pneumonia. She died four months later.

The year and a half during which time Roger was born and died and Martha was so ill was a two-fold burden which took a toll on Dad and Mom's well-being.

As I have reflected on those early years it has occurred to me that although we were poor I never thought of our family as being poor — everyone around us was poor. No, I didn't have any fine store-bought toys to play with. I had to wear hand-me-down shoes and underwear. I seldom enjoyed a piece of penny candy. A slice of bread bought from the bakery was a special treat. The only time we left the house was to go to church on Sundays. We didn't have money for gas to go to church for Wednesday night prayer meeting during those early years. But we always had plenty of food on the table at least three times a day. I was well-dressed with clean clothes.

If it hadn't been for my father's work ethic we wouldn't have made it through as well as we did. My father was a great man, a great Dad. I couldn't have asked for better than him. God marvelously provided for this big family in spite of the poverty that surrounded us. The cattle on a thousand hills are His, and He allowed us to take care of some of them.

Wes Gunther, California
Includes some excerpts from "The Waters Run Deep"
used by permission

Games children played

Even during the Depression era, childhood was a time when girls and boys engaged in games and play. Besides having fun and getting exercise they learned leadership and cooperation, rules and social roles.

Several participants in this book said they were unaware that they were in the middle of the worst economic disaster in America's history simply because it's all they'd ever known. After chores and school they played even as their stomachs rumbled.

Popular games included: Red Rover, jump rope, King of the Mountain, Kick the Can, Hide-and-Seek, stick ball, marbles and hopscotch. Jacks, board games, cards and similar activities were played as well.

"We made our own fun. We never could participate in after-school sports because we had to get home and help with the chores. We had fun during the grade school years and we played during recess and sports in season and as a family [of 13 children]: Red Rover, Dodge Ball, and Ante-Over where we had to throw the ball over the roof of the garage." ~ Wes Gunther, California

Childhood in the city wasn't much different when it came to games – only the location. Mary Sweeney's mother, Shirley Wolff, grew up in Chicago during the 1930s in a poor area of town: *"She mostly spent her days playing outside. On a typical summer day she was outdoors as long as there was daylight. The neighborhood kids played Kick-the-Can and Red Rover. She'd come home hot, tired and dirty about 5:00 pm in order to be on time for dinner."*

During the Great Depression, the Reading Terminal Market was able to provide a vast variety of hard-to-get foodstuffs to Philadelphia shoppers, often stimulating sales with special events such as this fair.

Carol M. Highsmith Archive, Library of Congress,
Prints and Photographs Division

Food was scarce

Romy (Martinson) Hoffman

Great-grandparents lived in Hiawatha, Kansas

On a 200-acre farm in Hiawatha, Kansas, Melvin Honor and his wife, Bess, hand-built a modest home. My great-grandpa Melvin never trusted banks so he buried his money in coffee cans around his property. Melvin and Bess had Beatrice, my grandmother, on December 5, 1914; she had a sister, Dolores Honor.

Bess sewed all her girls' clothing. She dressed simply while she made dresses with fancy lace collars for her girls. She sewed on a Singer treadle sewing machine and this is how Beatrice learned to sew. Bess made feather mattresses for their beds out of feathers from the chickens on the farm. She made so many things: beautiful quilts and pillows and still found time to can all their food from extensive gardening. To prevent severe sunburn during her hard days out working on the garden and helping her husband, Bess wore bonnets.

When the Depression hit food was scarce despite all the canned goods they set up each year. Fields that had wheat were failing. The farm grew wheat for their income crop and had a limited number of cattle, pigs and chickens for their private use.

They managed to keep their farm by truly penny-pinching throughout the Depression and beyond. Bess ran a soup kitchen out her back door when she could to help her nearby small-town neighbors in need.

Times got very tough for them. There were times they ate food that would normally be thrown away. At one point they ate ham that had maggots in it — my grandma Beatrice's worst recollection. Despite hard times this farm remained in the family for over a hundred years.

After the Depression Beatrice was sent off to college, which was uncommon in those days. Grandma graduated from the University of Kansas before she met and married Arthur Martinson. He became a police officer in Los Angeles and Grandma worked at a bank for awhile. They had two children, Forrest (our father) and Sandra (our aunt). After their children were raised they bought a farm in San Louis Obispo, California.

But their dream was to go back to the way they had both been raised — so they did. Their land in California became quite valuable so they decided to buy a larger property in the Pacific Northwest. They moved a final time to Scio, Oregon, where they bought a 360-acre spread with their daughter, Sandra Gould. She was newly widowed and had two young children of her own: Kandi and Darien.

My grandparent's farm in Oregon was a working farm with goats, sheep, cattle, pigs and chickens. Grandma's gardens ranged about a half-acre and they planted their fields in corn, wheat and alfalfa. When I hit my teens, Grandma was still milking a cow, making butter and canning in mass quantities from the bounty of their fruit trees and farm. I learned a great deal about self-reliance from them.

The lessons learned during the Depression followed my grandparents until the end of their days. Grandma Beatrice had a food room in her basement that could feed several families. No one ever left their home hungry. She never let us waste a morsel on our plate when we dined at her country table. Grandpa Arthur used a slice of bread to wipe his plate clean — all food was eaten; none went to waste.

Grandma Beatrice was very kind and wonderful to know, however she was quite strict about food and no waste. We were expected to clear our plates and eat every morsel including the fat. Now, I have a natural aversion to fat that was clear when I was just a girl of five-years-old. The only time I saw my grandmother yield on her rule of eating the fat is when she saw me get sick after being forced to eat it on some pork chops. I was no longer required to eat it.

Bananas past eating were eaten anyway. She would remove mold from foods on occasion and still consume them. When we asked her why she did this, she told us that she learned during the Depression what it was like for people to be hungry. Out of respect for those people she would not waste food, she said. Leftover oatmeal was made into delicious cookies with her black Old English walnuts and chocolate chips — we would dip them in leftover coffee. Cornmeal mush became fried cornmeal patties the next day — drizzled with honey from her back property.

Grandma Beatrice's sewing talents produced clothing. When others bought socks, she was of the mind that they could always be saved. She would sit in the evenings darning socks while they watched the evening news. Old shirts and clothing became blankets. When one person was done with something it was passed on. She even made sock monkeys for the younger grandkids. Her idea of a gift was an item that you could use or consume.

When Great-grandma Bess passed on, Great-grandpa Melvin decided to move from Kansas and live in Oregon with his daughter Beatrice. His farm home in Kansas still had all the furnishings that my grandma had grown up with. Her parents had the same bed during their entire marriage; the mattress was made with feathers, replaced as needed. While most of the furniture was sold off, that last feather mattress was saved in order for Grandma Beatrice to make pillows for everyone.

The mentality created during the Depression ran deep in their family commitments too, and this never changed.

My grandma and grandpa opened their doors to four of their younger grandchildren, including me, during a tragedy that would have placed us apart in different homes. If not for them, we would have grown up without each other.

They believed most strongly that family sticks together and in helping their neighbors. After my siblings and I moved back into the city we stayed on their farm during summer breaks. When my cousin became a single mom, our grandparents stepped in and, along with my cousin's mother, provided all she needed for her five children.

The affects of the Depression have filtered down through our family to create different traits in all of us. I am the most frugal and resourceful of the four; one sister is now building a log house with her husband in order to live off-grid.

Grandma Beatrice lived to be 84, passing away in her farmhouse on Rogers Mountain near Scio, Oregon, on Dec. 25th, 1998.

Romy Hoffman, Oregon

"...she learned during the Depression what it was like for people to be hungry...she wouldn't waste food. Left-over oatmeal was made into delicious cookies with her black Old English walnuts and chocolate chips — we would dip them in leftover coffee."

~ Romy Hoffman, Oregon

Leftover Oatmeal Cookies

2 c. sifted flour
1 tsp. baking powder
1/4 tsp. baking soda
1 tsp. salt
1 tsp. cinnamon
1/4 tsp. nutmeg
3/4 c. sugar
2/3 c. lard or shortening
2 eggs
1 1/2 c. cooked oatmeal
¾ c. black Old English walnut pieces
½ c. chocolate chips

Sift dry ingredients together. Add lard or shortening and eggs and beat by hand until creamy (about 2 minutes). Stir in oatmeal, chocolate chips and walnuts. Drop from teaspoon onto greased baking sheets.

Bake in a preheated 375°F oven for 12-15 minutes.

Yield: 4 dozen

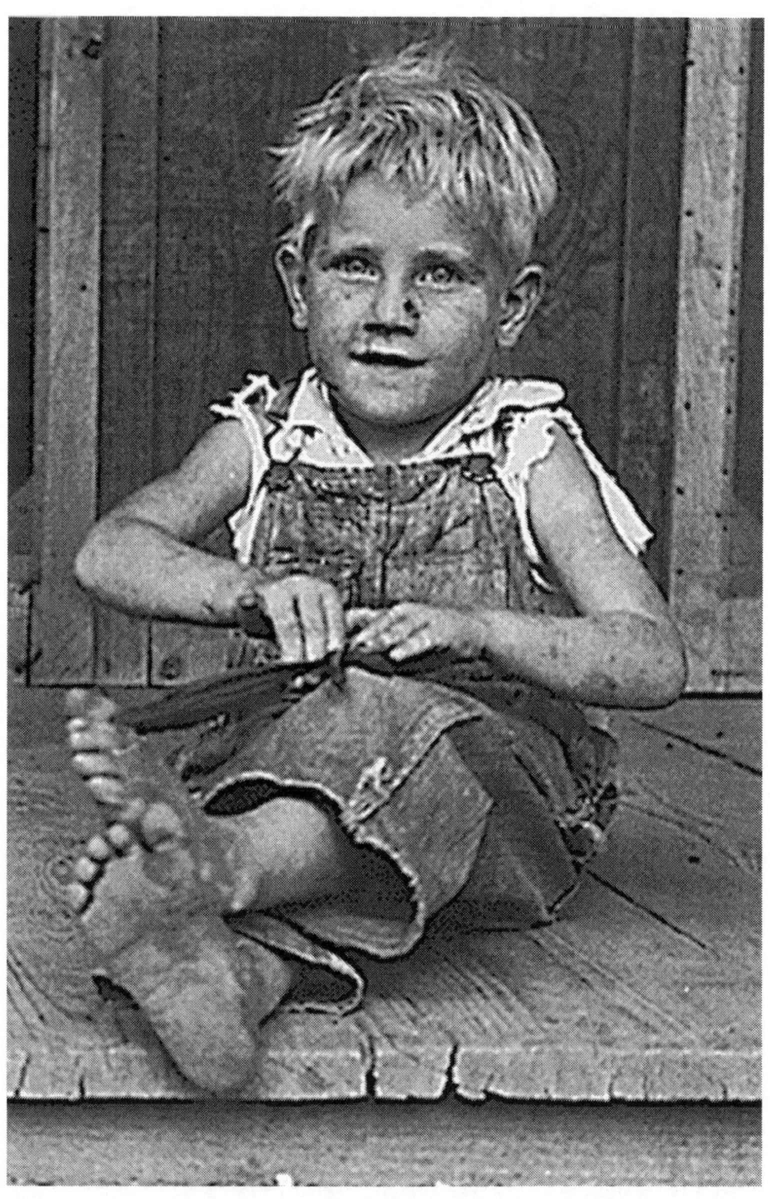

Children worked alongside parents in the effort to survive the Depression.
Creative Commons

Times were desperate

Maedell (Kramer) Dillon

Grandmother born 1892 in Greenvine, Texas
Father born 1916 in Burton, Texas

My grandmother Erna Heins was born Dec. 11, 1892 on a farm near Greenvine, Texas to Louis and Henrietta (Klump) Heins. She was the oldest of seven brothers and sisters. Erna's baptism and confirmation came in the years following her education at the school in the Klump community.

Erna married Charlie Kramer, my grandfather, on Nov. 4, 1915. They settled on a 115-acre farm in a house that Charlie built near the town of Burton, Texas. Erna bore two children: my father, Reinhardt, born Aug. 2, 1916 and Henry on June 5, 1918.

They raised cattle, pigs, chickens, cotton, corn, maize and sugar cane, had horses and grew vegetables in the garden to eat. My grandmother did all the canning on a wood stove in order to have food for the winter until the next garden came in. She also baked homemade bread, pies and cakes in the woodstove. She washed clothes on a washboard by hand. They made their own sausage and bacon in the winter in a smokehouse. They also had plenty of pecan trees, many of which are still standing today even after a tornado destroyed most of the trees and nearly wiped out the farm. If it could be grown, they probably grew it; if it could be made, they probably made it.

Their only source of heating was the wood-burning stove. They also had to gather wood for the winter not only for heating, but for cooking. The Kramer's house did not have electricity or running water during these years. The family's water came from a spring. Oil and gas lamps were used to light up the house at night. Electricity didn't reach the area until about 1940.

I remember my dad talking about drilling the first well. They used the horse to drill and neighbors would come to help. I don't know how many days or weeks it took — they were fixin' to give up but decided to try one more day. By dark there was still no water. The next morning they went to pull all the pipe out but water was running all over the ground. They realized that they had hit artesian water. It was capped and a hand pump was put on to draw it out. Now the water came from a well but still had to be carried to the house in buckets.

In the fall of 1928 tragedy struck the family. My grandpa Charlie suffered a stroke that paralyzed his left side. He was bedridden and unable to walk for more than a year. He was never able to work the farm again. But if my grandfather was able and his disability did not stop him, he would figure out a way to do whatever job needed to be done. If he was unable to do any job, he would be the one to teach someone how to do it — you would learn by what he knew.

Reinhardt was 12 and Henry was 10 at that time of their father's illness in 1928, so they were too young to perform some of the hard duties that farming requires.

Erna hired a work-hand after Charlie's stroke but mounting doctor bills made keeping the extra hand impossible. It took all of the family's savings to pay for the doctor's visits. Erna and her two sons were forced to make a living at farming — a difficult task for the strongest of men much less a mother and her two children.

Then as if things weren't bad enough, the Great Depression struck the very next year. The family struggled to survive. Times were desperate. They lived off the land and worked the land by hand. They grew a garden, cotton, corn and feed, and raised chickens, pigs and cattle. Erna provided the family's only source of income by selling eggs for two to three cents per dozen. Often, however, there was no one with two or three cents to buy anything. They would also have to pen up the chickens at night to keep people from stealing them and also to keep the varmints from catching them.

I remember my mom talking about Grandpa having their money in the bank and investing their money. He was given a paper for what stock he had in that company — and he had plenty of stock investments. Then the Great Depression hit and my grandparents lost all the money in the bank and all of the money they had invested, leaving them with only worthless paper. From that day on my grandparents never trusted banks or invested their money. At that time they only had what money was in their pockets when the Depression hit. From then on what money Grandpa made he kept on the place, later buying a money safe.

Grandpa Charlie was left paralyzed on his left side. He walked with a limp and used a cane. I still have his old cane. But he couldn't use his left hand because his fingers were curled inward. He was able to do some work, he was just slower. But my grandmother was the one that did most all the work.

If she needed help he could help with his right hand — he would pry open his left hand by using his right hand. Once he had his fingers around the item, (he was very strong) he could hold whatever it was in place, using his right to tighten or whatever needed to be done.

Charlie learned to use the cane to his benefit — he could still get around. He ran the beef club, kept the books, etc. He also used a horse to grind the corn people would bring to make cornmeal. People had no money so he would grind the corn on "half" — this would give his family cornmeal so they could keep their own corn for feeding the farm animals.

He and Grandma also raised sugar cane. He made ribbon cane syrup for his use and he made some for others.

Erosion of the soil caused problems that led to creating the Dust Bowl.
public domain

He also could do some blacksmith work — making or fixing what needed to be done on the farm. Neighbors would bring their items that he would either fix or make into something. He usually would trade in food for whatever they needed.

Charlie could drive their horse-drawn wagon by using the cane to pull himself up. They had no automobile, only a horse and wagon was their transportation. In later years, they bought an old truck and tractor. He was able to drive both.

Later Grandpa developed a hernia that would put him to bed until he could get it back in place. He did rest during the day, as did my grandmother. Their days were long and started well before daylight, ending by dark.

Erna was the saving grace of the Kramer family during these years. She worked both in the fields and in the house. She plowed by horse, picked up pecans, picked cotton, gathered the crops and did whatever else had to be done to keep the farm going. Her ability to pick cotton was second to none. She often spoke of the time when she picked 300 pounds of cotton in one day — a remarkable achievement to say the least.

My grandmother could saddle and still ride a horse in her 80s to bring back 40-50 lb. sacks of pecans she had picked up. She would lift those heavy sacks up, hang them on the saddle horn — one sack on each side — then walk the horse back to the house.

During those hard times money was extremely scarce. The ability to grow your own food was a must to survive. Families often joined together in their fight to make it through. One example was the beef club. Through the first several years of the Depression cattle had no market. To overcome this, families joined together every Saturday to butcher fresh meat. The Kramers were one of twenty-four families who banded together in their joint effort for survival.

Henry's daughter, Barbara, said she remembers the government men would come to buy the cows or calves when they needed to sell them, then shoot them in the pen 'cause no one could afford to buy the cattle.

My grandfather went to the third grade, my grandmother went to the first grade. They could read, write in long hand and do math. They were not able to go farther in their education, as they were needed on the farm. Their sons Reinhardt and Henry both got a sixth grade education over a period of many years. They were needed more on the farm.

The farm was open range at that time. Many years later it was fenced. As a boy, my dad, Reinhardt, would get up before daylight. He would have to find the horses in the dark, bring them back to the barn, saddle the horse and then go look for the cows on horseback. He brought the cows back to the barn so my grandmother could milk them before going to work in the fields.

My dad talked about when he was small he would watch the railroad men — men in ball and chain laying the railroad track along the front of their property. One day a big steam engine came down the track. Everyone stopped what they were doing to look at the train and wave; the engineer and all aboard waved back. My dad was so impressed, he said that when he gets big that is what he wanted to do, was drive one of those — which later he did.

Reinhardt got a job in 1936 laying railroad track which paid very little but was more money than was made on the

Horses were used for most of the work on farms in the 1930s. Photo courtesy of Maedell Dillon

farm. Later he married my mother and she would move around with him to different towns while he helped lay railroad tracks. She sewed clothes made from feed sacks for a few cents. He did work his way up in later years to become an engineer, driving a steam locomotive.

Uncle Henry stayed on the farm living with his parents and helped to run the farm. Later, he married my mom's sister but stayed on the farm after building his own house on the place. My aunt also took in sewing to make money. Henry did watch and clock repair in a nearby town and later he did both watch and clock repair and auto mechanics, becoming the master auto mechanic in a repair shop in Burton. He was self-taught in watch, clock and auto repair.

Dad and Henry would help pay for much of my grandparents' bills, leaving him and my mother very little money. Dad and my mother moved back to the homestead in the 1970s after his retirement from Southern Pacific Railroad.

As far as the elders talking about the past and hard lives, not much was said around children. We were not allowed to be with the adults. We were sent outside to play while the men gathered usually under a tree where they told their stories. The women were in the house telling theirs. When company would come or dinner was served, most would bring a dish of food, putting it all on the table with what my grandmother would fix. The men would eat first then dirty dishes were collected and washed before setting out clean plates for the women to eat off of. The children would then be called to eat what was left. That was the tradition for many years. Slowly the men and women would all sit and eat at the same time with children eating last. Finally years later we all ate at the same time.

If you would ask questions about years ago, they would talk about life being very hard — otherwise nothing much was said. I think they wanted to forget the past.

Erna and Charlie remained together on their farm until July 17, 1967, when Charlie passed away. Erna stayed in the house that Charlie built for her until April 1985 when she moved into a rest home — some 70 years after the family first settled. She died on May 31,1995.

Maedell Dillon, Texas

A pretty good life at the orphanage

Doris (Heathman) House

Born 1935 in Madison, Missouri

I was born in 1935, in Madison, Missouri and am one of six children. My parents, John Virgil Heathman and Lillie May (Newan), were farmers.

Farmers worked together then. They would go to one farm at a time planting and harvesting to help each other. At our farm, mother would bake everything in the cook-stove. One time she baked pies and left the door open. One of the boys backed up into it and burned himself. A neighbor was in the house and waved his hands over the burn — sort of like he was praying — and it healed without a scar.

Father grew sugar cane and made molasses. He had an old Model A or Model T and would load buckets of syrup and molasses to take somewhere to sell for extra money.

I liked going to Grandmother's place. We all went to town every Saturday whether we needed to or not.

Sometimes they'd pick up chicken sacks to use for clothes. Some of those feed sacks had nice prints. One time, one of my aunts lifted up my dress in public to see my chicken sack underpants. It's good to look back and see the funny parts in everything.

My dad died of a ruptured appendix in 1940 when I was five-years-old. The oldest child was 11, the youngest was 11-months-old.

Mother sold the farm and ended up in St. Louis to work in an aircraft defense plant. I remember her two older brothers came to the house with a wagon full of rice and pinto beans they'd picked up from the commissary or some place like that.

Child's flour sack dress.
Photos courtesy
textileranger.com

One day my youngest sister Judy went to a birthday party for the girl next door. Judy wore a special dress. The little girl dropped a candle in my sister's lap and the dress caught fire. She spent one

year in the hospital. Mother gave Judy skin grafts from her own legs.

During that time and because her legs were healing, Mom couldn't care for all of us while she was working so she put us in an orphanage. We would come home for one weekend a month — usually we'd do chores. Sometimes we came home for the summer. That was always nice.

But we had a pretty good life at the orphanage — churches helped support it. We always had donated clothes to wear and the Brown Shoe Company would use us children to test their shoes — so we always had shoes. Kids can be pretty hard on shoes.

There was no welfare back then. There were no radios or TVs to know what was going on. My mother was a private person and wouldn't tell us kids a lot of things unless we asked something. That was the way adults were back then.

Doris House, Texas

The wonder of sorghum

Used mainly as poultry and cattle feed, sorghum was also used to make molasses and illegal hooch during the Depression years in America.

For centuries, sorghum has been an important staple food for millions of poor rural people around the world. The tall, sugarcane-like plant with its clusters of tiny seeds is a good source of energy, protein, vitamins and minerals. It also grows in harsh environments where other crops do not grow well.

"Father grew sugarcane and made molasses. He had an old Model A or Model T and would load buckets of syrup and molasses to take somewhere to sell for extra money."

~ Doris Heathman House, Texas

Following are instructions for making molasses grown from sorghum:

RECIPE: When 40 to 60 gallons of juice have been squeezed out of the sorghum presses, strain the liquid — first through burlap, then twice more through a finely woven cotton sack — and pour it into a large pan.

Build a fire in a large outdoor pit. Place the pot over the fire and boil the juice. Burn the fire slowly and evenly or the molasses will burn. The sorghum juice needs to boil for about six hours.

As the juice boils, scum will rise to the surface and must be skimmed off. [A molasses skimmer looks like a stiff fly-swatter, easily made from win-

Sorghum. Wikipedia

dow screen.] As the batch boils down add fresh liquid occasionally to cook the impurities out.

Boil and skim until the juice is reduced to about an eighth of its original volume. At this point the product has a molasses-sweet smell, has a yellowish color, is thick and thready when pulled up with a spoon and "frog eyes" appear. Frog eyes are bubbles in the thick molasses.

As the syrup becomes thicker and darker, slow the fire and reduce boiling. Take up some of the hot juice in a dipper and pour it slowly back into the pan. When it forms strings or drips off the spoon in sheets, it is at the right point.

Quickly put out the fire, remove the drain plug and strain the contents one last time as the syrup runs into big pots.

After the syrup has cooled for about an hour, funnel into final storage containers such as pint or quart glass jars. It should be a rich red or brown, translucent and not too thick. Any foam on top will melt back into the contents within a few days.

If the molasses was overcooked, grains of sugar will form and settle to the bottom of the containers. If that happens, gently heat the molasses and add a little water to get the crystals back into the solution. Store it in a cool, dark place.

Fifty gallons of sorghum juice makes seven gallons of molasses.

Molasses Candy

1 c. molasses

3 c. sugar

1/2 c. water

1 tsp. cream of tartar

Mix sugar and Cream of Tartar together. Add molasses and water. Stir until sugar is dissolved. Boil without stirring until it hardens in cold water. Turn onto buttered pan. When cool, work and cut into sticks.

"Sorghum was grown to make our own molasses...on special occasions, there was dessert: usually teacakes, plain cakes and Dad's favourite molasses cookies."

~ Ginger Gill Brown, Louisiana

Molasses Cookies

2 c. dark brown sugar
1/2 lb. lard
1 tsp. salt
2 eggs, beaten
1 c. sour cream
1 tsp. soda mixed with a little water
1 c. molasses
1/2 tsp. ginger
7 c. flour (approximately)

Cream together the dark brown sugar and lard. Use only enough flour to make a soft dough. If you add too much flour, the cookies will be tough and bitter. After mixing all the ingredients together using a wooden spoon, place in refrigerator or on the back porch to rest overnight.

The next day, roll about half an inch thick and cut with a jar ring or large, sharp-edged tumbler. For topping, beat an egg, brush over the top of each cookie and sprinkle with white sugar.

Put the cookies on greased baking sheets and bake in a 350°F preheated oven about 12 to 15 minutes, watching carefully because they brown fast. These cookies are best made large.

Oklahoma was hit hard by the drought and Depression. Shown are a poor mother and her children, Oklahoma, 1936.

Dorothea Lange, US Farm Security Administration

"Now I'm not complainin'"

Edward House

Born 1930 in Oklahoma City, Oklahoma

I was born in Oklahoma City in 1930.

At the time of the Great Depression, I was two-years-old, and my dad, Jack House, was working as a traveling carpenter. He and my mom, Emma, had moved up from Houston, Texas.

While we lived there and I was about two-years-old, my dad was put in prison. He did a lot of things and was in and out of prison a lot. My mother and I moved back to Houston and lived in the back of Grandpa's house. It had one room, a kitchen and a bath.

In 1934 I had a hipbone disease and had casts on both of my legs. What I remember most about that time was that my mom, who was about four-foot-four-inches and weighed about 90 pounds, carried me every week from the house down to catch a streetcar to take us to the free medical clinic to see the doctors. Those casts weighed about 30 pounds.

When my dad got out of prison we moved to a shack in Sugarland — it was a WPA (Works Projects Administration) sponsored shack.

Because I was so young, I thought living like that was normal. I didn't have any friends. When I was five or six-years-old I had to learn to crawl when I got out of my cast. I remember playing with small pebbles on the floor. There were gaps in the floor and I tried to hit chickens on the head that were under the house. I never had anybody to play with. I wandered around the woods all the time after I could walk.

One time we visited some people who lived in a house on a hill. Their walls were lined with newspapers. I wanted that kind of house. I thought that it would be the only time I could be happy was if I lived in a house like that one.

Students at a crippled children's school are painting giant footprints at dangerous intersections as warnings to pedestrians.

Library of Congress, 1934

Some men in the community raised hogs. There was a Mexican, a white man and a black man who all raised one hog. We were the only family in the community that had a smokehouse. So we would get some of the meat whenever anyone wanted meat smoked. People all shared their food.

Sugarland had two big silos. One was full of white potatoes. The other one had sweet potatoes. At certain times people could climb in and get what they needed. Well, my mother was a little thing and was too small to push in to get the white potatoes, so all we got was sweet potatoes. Now I'm not complainin'; those helped us stay alive. They were real good for vitamins and we didn't have hardly any vegetables. We used to go down to Oyster Creek where there was wild spinach and kale. But to this day I won't touch sweet potatoes though everyone tries to trick me into it.

I had a nephew once complain that his shoes wore out. I told him that when ours wore out during the Depression, why, we'd scoop out the potato and wear the peelings as shoes. Boy, you should have seen the look on his face. It wasn't true, but it's good to joke about it.

Our community had a cow. When it was our turn to have the cow, Mom milked it and then sold the milk for 5 cents a gallon to the community. I remember the Mexicans would get some from her and then we'd see them walking down the road saying, "Nickel la leche!"

One house we stayed in was on the bank of Oyster Creek. One year there was a flood. I was looking out the window and saw a cow floating by. It looked at me and I looked at it. It looked helpless and said, "Moo!" Boy, that shook me up for the rest of the day.

At the age of eight or nine we moved to the suburbs. Dad stole lumber to build a house. Mom didn't know. He got people to build it. It was a nice house. We stayed there a couple of years and then Mom left him, taking me with her. Daddy went all over the country. He was a carpenter. He wouldn't take his family but he took his girlfriends.

We got stuck in San Angelo. Mom's older brother brought us back to Houston. Dad got picked up doing "paper-hanging," which is writing hot checks, and got sent back to prison. He had jobs in prison — they liked him. Back in those days, he'd get the itchy foot being in prison, and he'd up and leave. They'd track him down and catch up to him and put him back in.

So Mom and I started over again moving from house to house and finally stayed in a boarding house. It was a pretty tough life until I was 12 or 13. It's nobody's fault; it's just the way it was.

When the War [WWII] started, Mom went to work at a parachute factory in Houston. In 1943 she made a design for ropes on parachutes that made them safer and saved a lot of lives. She won a national award for that. She didn't have much education, but she sure was proud of that.

I think growing up in the Depression made me pretty tight-fisted with everything. Back then, people stayed married to survive, whether it was any good or not. I'm really proud of our children, Bob and Cindy, they are doing really good.

All us ones who lived through the Depression found things to make the bad things not so bad. In the memories it's best to find the good — the funny.

Edward Mandell House, Texas

The versatile sweet potato

"My mother's family survived by moving to her grand-parent's farm. They raised a lot of potatoes and sweet potatoes. Each morning they cooked lots of sweet potatoes in the oven and put them in a pan on the back of the stove. When someone got hungry they would just go get a sweet potato and eat it to 'tide them over' 'til suppertime when they had their next meal. They also poured hot tea with milk over bread that they toasted in the oven. My parents both say they never went hungry, but they didn't always like what they had to eat. They just ate it..."

~ poster K.A. Grama, from *Taste of Home*

Sweet potato roots Wikipedia

Raw sweet potatoes are rich in complex carbohydrates, dietary fiber and beta-carotene. Other nutrients include vitamins B5, B6, C and manganese. The nutritional value of sweet potatoes ranks fairly high in comparison with other foods.

But to five-year-old Edward House, none of that really registered.

"...so all we got was sweet potatoes. Now I'm not complainin'; those helped us stay alive. They were real good for vitamins and we didn't have hardly any vegetables...but to this day I won't touch sweet potatoes..."

~ Edward House, Texas

However Ginger Gill Brown, who grew up in Arkansas, has fond memories of the useful potato: *"If the sweet potato crop was good, Dad made sweet potato biscuits...boy that was a treat."*

Sweet potato field. by katorisi - Own work. Wikimedia Commons

Sweet Potato Biscuits

Ingredients

3 cups flour, sifted
¾ cup buttermilk
¾ cup sweet potato baked and peeled
¼ cup lard
2 Tablespoons sugar
¼ teaspoon cinnamon

Instructions

Lightly grease a biscuit pan with lard. Heat oven to 500F.

In a large mixing bowl, sift the flour.

In a separate bowl, add sugar and cinnamon. Sift together with your fingers. Create a well in the middle and add lard, sweet potato and buttermilk. Squish wet ingredients between the fingers until fairly smooth.

Stir the wet ingredients into the flour using a small, circular motion, drawing together while stirring. When a dough ball forms, flip the dough and knead it a few times, working in more flour as needed until a soft, smooth dough ball forms. Use a light touch; don't press the dough too hard.

Pinch off a small amount and roll it between your hands to form a ball. Roll it in flour to coat evenly. Pat the dough lightly to shape the biscuit, but don't press it together hard. Place biscuit on prepared pan. Repeat.

Bake at 500F for about 8-10 minutes or until tops are lightly browned. Remove from oven, brush with butter, cover with a clean cloth and let rest.

Coverall were the clothing of choice for many children during the Depression era. Arthur Rothstein/Library of Congress

Us girls mostly wore coveralls

Clara (Wanner) Lacy

Born 1926 in Belfield, North Dakota

I was born Clara Wanner in 1926, in a little town called Belfield, North Dakota. I was the fourth of six girls born to my first-generation American parents: Adam Wanner and Angeline Obritschkewitsch.

I earned my first nickel by being able to spell my mother's last name. She got tired of filling out forms for school and such. Every time I spelled her name for her I got a nickel.

Both of my parents' families are Germans who left Russia in 1891 and passed through Ellis Island. They lived in the Ukraine and farmed when the Russians expanded their borders and asked Germans to come and help them teach the peasants farming and to keep the Turks away from the borders. In exchange, their boys wouldn't have to go into the Russian military, they had exemption from taxes and had religious freedom — they were Roman Catholics, not Orthodox.

When Catherine the Great died all that changed over time. So they left.

To come to America there had to be relatives already there who would help them pay their way. There was an uncle I think, in North Dakota. They lived in a dugout in the side of a hill for awhile. It had a thatched roof. One time the cows stampeded; one fell through the roof and onto the baby on a bed. It crippled him badly, but my uncle learned how to get around and eventually became the postmaster of Dickinson, which was one of the larger towns. My mother was the youngest child of six and the first one born in America.

My parents and sisters and I lived in Schefield, which has gone down like the dust now. I think there's still a cemetery there where St. Pius Roman Catholic Church used to be. But when we lived there, there were two grocery stores, a blacksmith shop, some water wells and a few windmills, some homes and my daddy's shop called the People's Garage.

Daddy worked on farm equipment, cars and trucks and he also had a gasoline pump. That was when people pumped gas by the gallon, not the dollar. There was a little pop-up thing on the top that would show how many gallons were pumped. He kept pretty busy.

We lived in a two-bedroom house in town. It was a long walk to use the toilet out back. We were "rich" because we had a three-holer — two for adults and one closer to the ground for the children. It was my job to take the "thunder mug" from the house in the mornings and dump it in the outhouse. In the winter the contents were frozen — it got that cold in the house.

The Catholic church had a basement for shelter from

cyclones. The church was also a boarding school for all the farmers' kids. The top floor was where the students would board for $5 per month. Farms were too far away. Even to visit relatives we had to spend the night.

One time we heard the Gypsies were coming to town. When that happened we all had to stay inside the house because they would take anything that wasn't nailed down. One day my youngest sister Louise who was three-years-old and barely able to walk got out and we didn't know. We were all screaming and crying when we couldn't find her. Dad and Mom saw the Gypsy wagon and ran outside — she was in there. Evidently they were "collecting" their own children and took her by mistake because with her olive-toned skin and the fact that she wasn't wearing panties they thought she belonged to them. My daddy took her out of that wagon.

We didn't wear underwear until much later, and then we wore bloomers and stockings to school. It was just better that way.

I remember when Daddy put in our first light bulb. He would put each of us girls on a chair one at a time and have us pull the cord to turn it on and off. It was the thrill of the year.

He ran a waterline from the garage to the house too for running water for Mama instead of her having to use the well. In the wintertime he brought snowballs in and melted them for water and laundry. We'd hang the clothes out on the fences to freeze-dry.

In the summertime windmills were used to get water out of the ground and put up into the water tower. It sprang a leak one year after too much water and we made a swimming hole. Mother made us bathing suits and we wore stockings — I think they were called lisle stockings.

Mother had her own business in town working from home. She ran a creamery. Farmers delivered the milk in big cans and she would separate the milk and cream and make butter for them. It wasn't easy. I remember her slinging those cans around when she was pregnant. When she was older she blamed all her aches and pains from that time. She also sold eggs for the farmers. So she had to be at home all the time.

Mama kept all the dairy cold in a section of the ice house that was insulated, probably with hay. In the wintertime huge ice chunks were harvested and stored under hay. We children were not allowed in the ice house. But we followed the ice wagon down the street. The man would knock chips off for us — by us I mean all the kids in town — and we followed and picked them all up. Man, that tasted good.

Mom made all our clothing from flour and feed sacks. She used a Singer treadle machine. Us girls mostly wore

The Wanner family moved from North Dakota to Oregon in 1935. Pictured from left to right, Grandma Wanner, Clara, Marie, Mamma, Cathie, and Hildegard. Little sister Carrie is in front.

coveralls.

Mother had the best garden. We ate a lot of chicken, and rabbit that Dad hunted and shot. We called them the four-legged chickens. There was a bounty out for jackrabbits because they were so bad for the farmers. Dad got a bonus for shooting every jackrabbit and would have to show the foot as proof. It wasn't much, but it added up.

It was a big family time when it was time to bring in the pork. Our large family gatherings meant that we would make sausages and all kinds of things and the adults drank beer and partied and us kids ran around and found fun things to do. We had a large extended family and we looked out for each other.

When I was in first grade I brought my best friend Annie home from school once. We had a lot of fun that afternoon and my mother was real nice and polite. But as soon as Annie went home, Mama sat me down and sternly said, "Don't ever bring that girl here again. You are a nice German girl and nice German girls don't associate with Russians." I still played with her at school but I imagine she got the same lecture at her house.

There was a very strict line in our community. The Russians were Orthodox and the Germans were Roman Catholic. We didn't have anything to do with each other.

Our priest, Father Bede Dahmus, was German. I was five-years-old and he said to me one day, "Do you know that you have red hair and freckles? Do you want to get rid of your freckles?" He told me to go to my dad's garage and get crank case oil and mix it in with metal shavings that I would find on the floor. Then to rub the mixture into my face and keep it all on for as long as I could stand it. So I did. My skin started to come off. I tell you, I never heard my mother talk to any other priest like she did to that priest. He said he thought that I'd know it was a joke. She told him that I was just a little girl and that little kids look up to him like he's God and didn't he know what a big responsibility that was? I'm just glad my skin grew back even though the freckles did too.

We always had each other. We were perfectly content. We were never hungry. Mama always had something on the table: German sauerkraut, food from the root cellar, lots of chickens and we had a cow every year to breed for meat. We always had milk, eggs and potatoes. There were grape farms around us and we collected grapes to make juice and wine. We helped Mama save things.

The worst thing about clothing us was that I was hard on shoes. I never walked, I skipped and my shoes wore out very fast. When the bottoms wore out we used kits that had scrapers, glue and a half-sole. My biggest joy was when I got bigger than my older sister and no longer had to wear hand-me-downs. It was a blessing.

We went out west to Portland, Oregon in a covered truck in 1935 — I was nine or 10 at the time. Dad made a cover to go over the top in the back. In the way-back was a day bed that folded down and made a cot. Mama and all us kids rode back there. I rode backward all the way from North Dakota to Portland. I told my kids later that I never knew where I was going but I could tell them where I'd been.

Daddy had to leave the garage in North Dakota because all the farmers owed him money and couldn't pay because of the Depression. We couldn't afford to live there any-more. The cops came in and collected the money for him but since he had no way to go back and get it he never did get his money. When we left Daddy had just enough money to pay for gas.

We traveled mostly on gravel roads then and stopped by the roadsides to camp. One time in Montana just past Billings we camped by a river. My sisters and I were playing by the woods and heard Mama honking the horn. A Game Warden was there and Mama was trying to warn Daddy who was fishing. Now, he didn't have a license for fishing and he couldn't get his rod and reel put away fast enough. They were going to take him to jail, but he asked, "What are you going to do with my family?" They confiscated his fishing gear instead. Montana had suffered a lot during the Depression. Whatever they confiscated they could sell. It was a source of income for the Game Wardens. So there was no fish for dinner that night.

When we got to Portland, we stayed at a campground near Jantzen Beach. There were a lot of people there looking for work. It was like *The Grapes of Wrath*. We girls had no dresses; we always wore coveralls that Mama made. We stayed there for quite awhile. Daddy found places to stay but they were usually in bad parts of town, so we always moved. We finally ended up in a one-bedroom house.

Daddy ended up getting a job fixing trucks. And by 1939 and the start of WWII the diesel big rigs started showing up. Dad did really well as a diesel mechanic. He also had a part-time job on a road crew going to fix broken-down big rigs.

Our biggest problem was coming in from rural North Dakota to Portland. We looked like we'd just fallen off of a turnip truck. We wore stockings and bloomers to school and nobody else did. But my sisters and I rolled our stockings down to look like anklets and hiked the bloomers up to fluff out our dresses. We had a family member who already lived in Portland who was hep to fashion and she helped Mom.

My main goal was to lose my German North Dakota accent - "dese," "dem," "dose." I worked my butt off to make the "v" sound instead of "w," to say "village," instead of "willage." I didn't want to sound German.

When Pearl Harbor was bombed and the government started rounding up the Japanese, Mama sat us down and said, "Don't tell anyone that you're German. You are American." She was scared that they were going to gather the Germans and put us all in camps like they did to the Japanese.

But everybody was poor in those days. Everybody helped each other. I think it affected how I raised my children: make do or do without — waste not, want not. We really carried that through. If something was almost wore out we'd find another use for it. I used to save a lot of things but I got over it. I didn't want to feel "trashy" by saving up too many things. Things got better - we were more prosperous.

The biggest thing I passed on to my children was the importance of education. They all went to college. One thing I learned through the Depression was that education is major, major, major. Those who had it got better jobs and more money.

Clara Lacy, Washington

Refrigeration during the 1930s

Novel refrigerators actually sold quite well in the early part of the 1930s at the onset of the Great Depression era. In fact, sales increased by the middle of the decade.

However, dirt-poor farmers from the Dust Bowl in the heartland of America could hardly afford to even think about a newfangled refrigerator, let alone figure where they were going to get seed money for the next crop.

Families generally didn't overeat so there wasn't anything to keep cold after it was prepared. Most of what they ate was food preserved in jars from last year's harvest. Trips to the store were mostly weekly for nonperishable items such as flour and sugar, often in exchange for perishable butter and cream that had been produced at home.

"Our trips to town were usually on Saturday. Our folks took cream and eggs to sell and this bought our groceries for the week." ~ Dorothy Richardson, Oklahoma

Homesteaders stood by and relied upon their already tried-and-true ways of keeping things cold: *"In the wintertime, these leftovers were kept in a wooden crate nailed to the kitchen window sill [outside] because we didn't have an icebox."* ~ Nina Gilfert, Florida

Winter was the time to harvest natural ice for use through the summer. Men broke large chunks from creeks, rivers and lakes and hauled them into barns where they were packed in sawdust or hay to prevent melting.

Some homes had iceboxes either inside or kept on the back porch. In cities and some rural towns people could rely on the regular household delivery of large blocks of ice for their households and community ice-houses.

"We children weren't allowed in the ice house. But we followed the ice wagon down the street. The man would knock chips off for us — by us I mean all the kids in town — and we followed and picked them all up. Man, that tasted good." ~ Clara Wanner Lacy, Washington

With the onset of household refrigeration via iceboxes, the woman of the house could store dairy items and other things that needed to be kept cold. City dwelling housewives didn't have to go to market every day for vegetables or fresh meat; consumers could buy for more than one day of meals at once and keep extra food cold.

Although convenient, iceboxes had drawbacks. For example, the door couldn't be opened often because the ice could melt too fast. Iceboxes were also difficult to clean, especially if ice had been cut from outdoor bodies of water. As ice melted, sediment was left behind. And because the icebox was usually made of wood, food smells permeated it.

Iceman, Wikipedia, made available by Common Good.

But life was not nice

Ruth (Cohen) Mims

Born 1928 in Adel, Georgia

My name is Ruth Mims. I was born on December 15, 1928 in Adel, Cook County, Georgia. I was the last of seven girls, and the 14th of 17 children born to my father, Eddie Cohen, and Mother, Beauty Huff.

My daddy was a white Jew from Israel. His mother was Greek and his daddy was a Jew from Israel. Back then in the Middle East it would be like a black woman marrying a white man — they were ostracized. They got on a ship and came across in the 1890s and landed in South Carolina. They had eight children; my daddy was the oldest.

My mom was a full-blooded African girl of 14-years-old when my daddy saw her. My grandmother didn't like black girls but my daddy didn't pay her no mind. They obviously loved each other — look how many children they had!

My mom died when I was almost four-years-old in

October 1932. I don't remember much about life before then except that we all lived in a very small house. The day we went to the graveyard we all piled into an old wagon. I remember seeing a box being let down into a hole in the ground but I didn't understand until later that my mother was in it.

There was a fancy lady there, my grandmother. And do you know what she wore? She wore a bright white dress and a blood red sweater. She drove up in a very expensive, beautiful wagon drawn by beautiful horses. I noticed because ours was so old and run-down. I was sitting on the edge of our wagon and she walked over and reached her hands out to me. I took them and she picked me up and took me into her fancy wagon.

We rode and rode and rode for the longest time. Finally we came to the biggest house I'd ever seen. Inside, it was beautiful and big and very clean. She took me to a bedroom that had a white, chenille bedspread on it with a peace bird in the middle. I sat and plucked at that bird for the longest time before she came back for me.

The next time I saw her, she was standing at the door with my grandfather. He stood there looking at me. Then he walked over and held his hands out to me and I went to him.

They took me into the kitchen and we all ate together. There was just the three of us. I'd never done anything like that before — sit at a table in a kitchen and eat a meal much less have only three people eating.

But life was not nice.

I found out later that they agreed to take the youngest daughter in to help my daddy out. We lived in Adel on a plantation. My grandfather was a farmer. He raised cotton, corn, peanuts, tobacco, hogs and milk cows. Grandma kept the house looking beautiful and sewed clothes for me. They could afford to buy me new ones but I wasn't "white enough."

My brothers and sisters and Daddy would come to visit on the Fourth of July, Thanksgiving and Christmas, but I didn't see them very much outside of that. I wasn't allowed to make friends either, because my grandparents didn't want me to be around other black people. The white kids didn't want to play with me because I wasn't white enough. So I didn't go to school, I didn't get an education, and I didn't have any friends. I really knew nothing about the world outside the big house.

Slum housing often sat underneath finer homes.

Franklin D. Roosevelt Presidential Library and Museum

I spent most of my time playing with my cats and dogs. When my cats had kittens I'd name them all, mostly after my brothers and sisters.

When I was 14 I got away and found a pay phone to call my sister. I told her she'd better come and get me or I was going to kill Grandma. Now, I wouldn't have, but I was that mad and tired of it all. She walked nine miles to where I was and we walked nine miles back. She took me clothes shopping for the first time in my life. That was in 1942.

I was 17 when I met John Benjamin Mims. He was 11 years older than me and just out of WWII. He told me he was going to marry me so he could finish raising me. He knew all about what happened. He was so kind and gentle. He decided to not have children until I was 21-years-old. Then we had eight — seven boys and one girl.

We moved to New York City and I got a job at a mental institution handling patients. I didn't need an education for that. It paid well and I live on the retirement from that even today.

John's been dead some 37 years now. I came to Texas to live 13 years ago. I decided to get an education and I did. I go to the library for classes on how to read and write. And I take piano lessons. I am 85 years old now and I live in a beautiful house in a beautiful place and take care of my 9-lb puppy. I am the only black lady in a white neighborhood but it doesn't matter. We all look out for each other.

It wasn't a very nice life during the Depression. But life is good now.

Ruth L. Mims, Texas

They lost the house

Ann Patterson

Mother born 1920 in Roanoke, Virginia

I have a portfolio collection of letters that my grandfather James Albert Armstrong sent to many prospective employers during the Great Depression while looking for a job. He was laid off from his position as Assistant and then Commissioner of Revenue in Roanoke, Virginia.

What struck me most about his letters was the gracious tone, both in the requests and in the replies he received even in the midst of the dire circumstances that everyone faced in the 1930s. I doubt we'd see the same today — most employers don't even answer letters of inquiry, much less graciously!

My grandfather was out of work for six months then found another job as an accountant and did bookkeeping work for the Strietmann Biscuit Company. But he was let go again when they merged with Kroger and downsized in the late 1930s or early 1940s.

My mother, Martha Ann, was born in 1920 in Roanoke. She also had a sister, Sarah. Mother is 94 now and she was just a teenager when this happened. She was attending Woodrow Wilson Junior High.

The family survived on assistance from my grandfather's older brother, Charles Armstrong, who lived in Cincinnati, Ohio, and who sent money to help out. He also did some

Unemployed men looked for work.

Franklin D. Roosevelt Presidential Library and Museum

sort of office work to survive.

Before Grandfather lost his job in Revenue, they lived in a very nice, three bedroom, red brick home in the Raleigh Court area of Roanoke on Mt. Vernon Road — a middle-class neighborhood. They lost the house while he spent those six months looking for another job.

Grandmother's sister and her husband, Aunt Lucy and Uncle Prentiss Campbell, lived next door so my mother and her family moved in. Mother and her sister Sarah grew up with their cousins Prentiss Jr. and Betty.

Mother said that they lived there for a couple of years until her father got the job with the Strietmann Biscuit Company. Then they rented another bungalow-type house on Northumberland Avenue in the same area. They moved again later and rented Aunt Mary Preston's house on Glenheim Road after her husband died. She moved to Kingsport, Tennessee to live with her children.

Grandfather would never buy a house again, only rent, as the experience was so devastating. In later years, he ran for and was elected to the Office of Commissioner of the Revenue in Roanoke again and was in that position until he retired.

I have always thought that people were able to get through the Great Depression because of their inner strength that was born of faith, work ethic, strength of family, and strength of character. I doubt very much that our society would weather the same conditions today — because of a lack of those very things.

Ann Patterson, Colorado

Dust storm in Amarillo, Texas, 1936.
Arthur Rothstein/Library of Congress

How kind and compassionate people seemed

Lauri Plum

Great-grandmother born in Benton, Kentucky and lived in Paducah, Kentucky

I find myself many times during my life using my great-grandmother's experience of living in the Depression era as an example to show others how kind and compassionate people seemed to be back then, even in a very difficult and uncertain time.

My great-grandparents Lloyd and Norah (Benson) Gregory had a little farm of a few acres down in Paducah, Kentucky. It was just a little family farm with a few pigs, chickens, a big garden with corn, grapes and a few pear trees. They raised food to feed their own family. Great-grandpa sold whatever they could spare.

They were already financially poor long before the Great Depression so times got a little bit tougher. But

Franklin D. Roosevelt Presidential Library & Museum

as always, they dug in and made it work.

My great-grandma found work down at the local laundry and sewing shop. I remember her telling me that she made 5 cents a week and it was barely enough to buy a loaf of bread. Because of that she made her own bread and grew a garden in addition to having their meat animals.

During the Depression Great-grandma also took old chicken and horse feed sacks to make dresses for her daughters because they had no money for clothes. The material had prints and colors and she added bits of lace or buttons if she had them.

Great-grandma and her four adolescent daughters canned everything they could to put up for winter while Great-grandpa tended to the animals. My grandma, Wilma Gregory Babb, was about 10-years-old in 1929.

By the time the Great Depression hit, people were starting to suffer. Great-grandma told me that people who were down and out would come to their door, knock and put out one of their hands. They would ask for a handful of beans or just one potato so they could feed their families.

Of course my great-grandmother would give them what they asked for. People back then had compassion and love for others — something that is surely missing in today's world.

The funny thing is, that when all four girls grew up not one of them had anything to do with the country life. They all left farming when the railroad opened up and they left for Ohio for work — that's how we ended up here.

My grandma lived her entire life getting every convenience known to man. Money became very important to her, and they did well. Dishwashers, refrigerators, stoves, you name it. And my mother is just like her. We had the first color TV on the street. I remember kids looking in the window; it was a bit embarrassing. I'm the one going backward — I have a garden, I can fruits and vegetables and I have chickens!

How I would love to go back to a time when life was treasured and people looked to God above for help and guidance. I imagine that when the next Great Depression hits people will just come to the door, pull out a gun, shoot and take what they want.

My great-grandmother's story is of others having true love and compassion for everyone during a very difficult time.

Lauri Plum, Ohio

Margie, Bill and Clair Lohnes

Relentless dust storms that sent sifting sand

Herbert Petrie

Born 1915 in the Willamette Valley, Oregon

In 1929 the economic disaster that had been threatening the country came to a head: the stock market crashed, and many banks closed their doors. The big Depression was off and running, although our family didn't experience anything unusual or different because our existence had usually been depressed through the years.

My Dad, Bob Petrie, was the ninth of 11 children born in Scotland to James and Mary (Melvin) Petrie. At 19 he boarded a ship at Aberdeen in 1906 for Halifax, Nova Scotia with his trunk and a few coins in his pocket. He walked and "hopped" freight trains across Canada and headed for his brother Jim's place in Moose Jaw.

Through a series of unfortunate events, he landed in Minot, North Dakota for a "miserable" farmhand job at a homestead. He went back to Canada and worked the coal mines in Ontario while he earned a diploma from the Veterinary Science Association. He moved to Detroit and got a diploma from the Veterinary Dental College. With that background, he was hired as a government cattle inspector just above Blaine, Washington at the Canada border. He was successful, and became known as "Doc." He was carefree, energetic, had slightly wavy hair and a manly mustache.

Dad caught the eye of Minnie Burnley, and after a whirlwind romance they wed in Seattle in 1913. He sold his interest in a livery stable and headed to Pullman to increase his schooling at Washington State College. Before long he was promised an active veterinary career in the Willamette Valley of Oregon which was rife with stock, so they moved with my firstborn brother Bob in tow. I followed less than a year later in 1915.

The promised veterinary work didn't materialize, so my parents moved us to a wheat ranch west of Spokane. It was a prosperous venture. My mother proudly drove her own team of dappled gray mules hitched to a two-seater, rubber-tired buggy with a full-length cloth top. Another son followed in 1917. A "million miles away," the United States was at war. Wheat crops were good and prices high. The Petrie family enjoyed amazing prosperity, so they graduated to a much larger wheat ranch in Ruff, about 30 miles further west.

A bigger ranch needed more horses, machinery and farm hands with expanded meals and sleeping quarters. Dad accumulated the best of farm machinery along with a large herd of horses, using 19 at a time on the combine harvester over the rolling hillsides of wheat fields.

But the summer of 1919 saw relentless dust storms that sent sifting sand around rattling doors and windows, leaving drifts against buildings and machinery and playing havoc with wheat crops. The next summer fared no better, leaving wheat crops a disaster. After the War there was no market for what was left, so the government tied it up which left farmers without income for feed, machinery and farm payments and to pay hired hands.

It was a total disaster, both for farming and doctoring stock. We had to move. Machinery was left where it sat; our farm animals were given away except for a large gelding and the herd stallion to form a team to transport a wagonload of furniture to more promising land. One milk cow was tied to the back of the wagon to plod along behind. My dad had just turned 34 and my mom was 29.

Dad tried wheat farming again and hired himself out for veterinary services. He tried his hand at mining and we moved a lot following the work. We lived in a one-room schoolhouse, an unpainted two-story farmhouse, and a two-room log cabin all by the end of 1922. But we had a couple of hogs, a dozen laying chickens, several cows, a team of horses and a riding pony, and a "root house" with a double-thick door that was dug into the side of a hill that stored potatoes, dry onions, carrots, turnips and parsnips buried in straw. The barn was filled with alfalfa and the woodshed was full of dry pine.

But my dad decided it was time to move on to greener pastures. He sold his mining claim and our 40 acres for 20 acres of unseen stump land in Napavine in southwest Washington and a 40-acre farm with buildings, an orchard, and a year-round creek close to a place called Morton. After

10 years of marriage, five children and another on the way, Dad just stopped working the mines.

Farmers from the area came and left with our cows, pigs and chickens. We traded our 12-foot wagon bed and entire garden for a 16-foot wagon bed. We loaded the wagon with mattresses, bedding, tent, cooking utensils, a trunk full of personal valuables, clothing, foodstuffs, a five-gallon can of water, a canvas bag of drinking water, and hay and grain for horses. Dad and Mom sat on the wagon seat and us five kids were in the back.

For two full weeks we traveled by wagon and camped out in a family tent under the stars, eating food prepared over an open fire, watering and feeding our horses along winding roads and steep ascents and summits on the east side of the Cascade Mountain Range.

The 40-acre Morton farm ended up being on the side of a mountain covered in old-growth timber at the foot of a river with a broken-down orchard and the remnants of collapsed buildings overgrown with briar bushes and alder trees.

We moved on over two days, in wet weather to our new home -- a rental near the abandoned Haywire Mill in Napavine. It was a dilapidated, two-story, unpainted house with a woodshed and standard outhouse. It was too late in the year to put in a garden and what little money my parents had saved was spent on moving; no store would give us credit for purchases.

Dad couldn't find work, so he and we three boys spent all available time cutting and splitting wood, selling and delivering for 50 cents per rick. One such load was traded for a 30-cent, 50-lb bag of flour. Mom needed lots of flour and we needed a lot of bread, with little more than that to eat at times. Dad made frequent trips with a burlap gunny sack to the railroad unloading dock at the Napavine Feed Store to glean spilled alfalfa and grain to bolster the sparse diet of our animals and chickens. Circumstances weren't treating us too kindly, though we had milk, a few eggs and some grocery staples from wood sales — but with eight mouths to feed now, it wasn't unusual for us to go to bed hungry.

After a while, Dad joined on with a lumber company and we moved into "the old Caron place" nearby. It was a big two-story house, heaven-sent for our large family. There were six large walnut trees, a quince tree, several berry bushes and a nice garden spot. There were two large barns, pigpens, a well, a fruit orchard and pastureland for hay and grain.

Before long, Dad was without a job again. No income — no money. He traded some of our animals, sold his 30-30 rifle for a riding pony that he hoped to take on "hoped for" veterinary calls, and "witched" water wells and dug them at a dollar a foot. It wasn't enough to keep us going, and only one store would give us any credit. Without them, we really would have been in dire straits with nine mouths to feed by then.

Late that summer we were ordered by our landlord to move. We had been there two years with no money changing hands, and we had used two hay crops, quite a few trees for wood, and eaten amply from the fruit trees.

We had no place to go. Winter was on the way. Five of us were in school. Dad didn't have a car or a job. Dad came across someone he knew who told him about an abandoned 40-acre hilly stump ranch just two miles away. Fire had destroyed all but one building. He sold it to Dad for $750 with nothing down and 4 percent interest to be paid annually with the principal to be paid "as you can."

The place was a shambles on uneven ground strewn with rotting logs and stumps. Dad got someone to build a 14-foot by 34-foot chicken house for us to "temporarily" live in.

We moved in the day after Christmas. The wind blew through our shell of a house. With no partitions or ceiling, rain and snow blew through the cracks. Wet wood wouldn't burn and had to be pre-dried in the oven, which got our bedding and clothes wet from the steam. On freezing nights, frost gathered on the blankets from our breath, and every morning it was miserable to get into cold, damp clothes.

We kids were cold, bewildered and hungry most of the time, with no hope of improvement in sight. How we managed to survive that first winter remains a mystery.

So when the Depression began, Dad had a job working at a rock-crushing place, and we were eating quite well, bolstered with reserves from our summer garden. We already knew what living without was like.

Dad bought a 1926 Ford Touring car for his veterinary visits. It had bumpers and a self-starter so it didn't have to be cranked. I had been driving for a couple of years, and was delighted to get to drive at times when Dad went out evenings or weekends doctoring stock. One such place was the County poor farm in Newaukum Valley; here lived older people who had absolutely nothing left except the clothes on their backs when the Depression hit — some through misfortune, others from lack of planning for old age. The big farm with many big buildings was self-sustaining through the labors of these pitiful souls, although most of them just plodded around like zombies with nothing to look forward to and mostly misery for nostalgia.

We decided to make money by raising turkeys. But the few we had ran loose to forage for their existence. They nested in the brush. A few of the poults made it to maturity to provide us with turkey and dumplings. Before the year was out, no more turkeys — so that venture was abandoned.

With the coming winter of 1930-31, Grandma Burnley, my mother's mother, came to stay with us for a while. Being crowded for sleeping space, my brother Bob and I were relegated to spending our nights in the old Buick touring car that had a seat that folded down to make a full-length bed. It was under a roof, but no walls and some distance from the house. It was cold and damp, but we had no other alternative. Evenings were spent with all ten of us in our "one room" chicken house which comprised our living/dining/kitchen area. On nights when the wind howled and rain came down in torrents or the snow blew through the cracks, Dad would often make the statement, "What a dirty night out there." With a reassuring arm around Mom's shoulders, he'd add, "but it's the happiest days of our life."

In the spring of 1931, Grandma Burnley was put on the train with some boxes containing her few possessions and took her turn living with Aunt Blanche in Portland. Bob and I were happy to move back into the "house."

A round enameled pan was all that we had for a washbasin and it was a mad scramble for everyone to use it to wash hands and face and to be used as a receptacle for brushing teeth with salt or soda when bad weather prevented us from standing outside to do so. After the wash water was used, it was thrown out into the yard.

After I graduated from high school I headed to Wenatchee to pick apples — the only good paying job I could find. I needed a car, and planned to buy one with my earnings. I left with Bunch Chrisman and his dad, "Uncle Eldie," in his crudely built 1924 Overland pickup — with cooking utensils and dishes, extra clothes, bedding, and an empty coffee can for his dad's "weak kidneys."

We bunked and ate in Jess and Ada Graybill's packing shed then moved into their isolated single-car garage for living quarters: a wood cook stove, double bed for Bunch and me, a single cot for his dad, a small wooden table, three apple boxes for chairs, an old wooden rocker, and a broom and dust pan. It was "home" for the next month and a half.

Leftover peaches, pears and fallen apples were unlimited for gleaning. We all three had experience in cooking. We didn't eat fancy, but we had plenty. Van Camps canned pork and beans were a daily part of our diet, causing Eldie to constantly berate, complain and gag over the foul air.

We were paid a nickel for each 42-pound box — and 60 boxes was a good day's work. Early November completed one harvest, and we were paid in full. Bunch sold me his Overland pickup for $15. Now I had a car and money for completely neglected dental care. I could buy a few warm winter clothes, register the car, buy license plates and maybe have a couple dollars left for gas. After paying for living and traveling expenses and buying the car, I arrived home with $30 — all that in just two months.

We boys could do a man's job, but unemployed, experienced family men were flooding the labor market — willing to go anywhere and do anything at any wage. Having a car was no help without money for gas. We didn't have a chance to compete.

Herbert Petrie

Via family memoirs contributed by Lester Petrie, Oregon

Dental Care in the 1930s

"There were only two people in my dad's hometown of Honey Brook who had any money. Everyone else was thin. Everyone had crooked teeth."

Lynn Frank, Pennsylvania

During the mean 1930s, few families could afford to see dentists. As a result, they were left to themselves with few resources. Diets high in starch and sugar led to weak teeth, tooth decay and gum disease starting from childhood.

In her regular column about aging in the *Orange County Register*, the late Lucille de View wrote that reg-

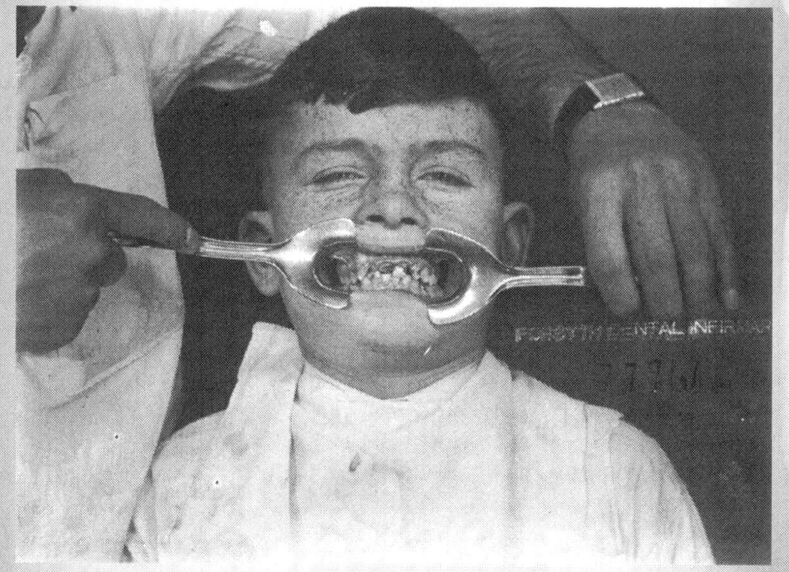

In the dental office. Green 'N' Growing Collection (The History of Home Demonstration and 4-H Youth Development in North Carolina), Special Collections, North Carolina State University Libraries, c. 1920. Copyright unknown. Original image housed by North Carolina Special Collections Research Center

ular dental care was not a priority during the Great Depression because few could afford it. *"We were lucky to have toothbrushes let alone store-bought toothpaste,"* she wrote and added that families used baking soda or salt instead.

Taylor Goodwin's great-grandmother Leila Mae Taylor bartered raspberries from her family's garden in Utah for her dental care: *"[She] needed dental work that the family could not afford. With a jar of raspberries in hand, she...made her way on foot to the dentist...the bargain was done – raspberries in exchange for dental work."*

Herbert Petrie and his eight brothers and sisters all shared one round, enameled pan as a wash basin, *"... and it was a mad scramble for everyone to use it and to wash hands and face and to be used as a receptacle for brushing teeth with salt or soda."* After spending a summer in eastern Washington picking apples, he used part of his earnings to get long-neglected dental care.

Appalachian Toothache Remedies:

Hold liquor in the mouth for several minutes, then swallow

Chew ragweed leaves

Put cinnamon oil on the tooth

Put clove oil on the tooth

Put persimmon juice on the tooth

Place a piece of cloth soaked in kerosene on the tooth

Hold a warm bag of ashes, salt or water on the cheek

If the cavity is deep in the tooth, stuff the hole with soda, spider webs, aspirin, burned alum, cow manure or salt

Always looking for ways to make money

Bill Lohnes

Born 1928 in McCracken, Texas

I was born William (Bill) Donald Lohnes in McCracken, Kansas in 1928. My grandpa's farm was located in Brownell between there and the Smokey Hill River. We lived in Ness City. From an early age my older sister, Margie, and I spent several summers on the farm with Grandma and Grandpa Fitzgerald.

My parents are Thornton Lohnes and Vera (Fitzgerald) Lohnes. My father was absent most of my life and my mother took care of the family and everything else. He had a number of odd jobs such as farming, welding and working for the WPA (Works Progress Administration.)

Mother was a homemaker and primary breadwinner. She took in all kinds of work to make money in-

Vera Lohnes and Grandma Jessie Fitzgerald, with Jane and June.

cluding sewing and ironing.

I didn't know we were poor. Almost everyone in town was in the same situation. Somehow my mother must have kept the worst of it to herself because I remember having a very happy childhood.

The grocery store owners and the funeral home were the only businesses that had any significant income. In fact, my uncle Brian Fitzgerald was often given quarter-sections of land in exchange for burying people's loved ones; often that's all they had with which to pay. Uncle Brian never asked for the land but people felt obligated to pay something. (Incidentally, the Fitzgeralds still own and operate a successful funeral home in Ness City.)

Because my father was mostly absent, my earliest memories are of living with Mother and my siblings — Margie, older brother Clair and younger brother Jerry — on my grandparent's farm before we moved to Ness City. Twin girls, Jane and June, came later. I have a few striking memories of this time; mainly seeing my first wild buffalo, and my grandfather trying to hold a trap door shut as a tornado struck the farm.

We had ice cream socials where all the farmers would get together and make all flavors of homemade ice cream. They would also get together to butcher hogs. This wasn't very pleasant to watch as they would stick the hogs and let them run around 'til they bled to death. I guess this was a better way of getting all the blood out as opposed to killing them and hanging them up to bleed. This always ended with a huge meal outdoors and Grandpa would start the meal by eating the pig's tail.

We had a smokehouse to cure and smoke the ham and bacon. Next to it was a pump house that had troughs made from the native limestone rock that circled all four walls. The windmill ran almost all the time and the cold water would circulate through the troughs in which butter and other commodities were kept.

My sister Margie and I were given the responsibility of finding the guinea eggs. This was a very hard task as they hide them real well. Guinea hens are excellent watchdogs as no one can come onto the place without them setting up a racket. If we found any eggs we were allowed to take them to the store in McCracken to exchange for candy. Grandmother traded eggs, meat, butter and other things for flour, sugar, salt and other necessities.

After we moved into a house in Ness City a few years later, I and my friend Donnie were always busy trying to find ways to make a little extra money.

Beardsley's Dry Goods Store in Ness City was the place to be in the early mornings during harvest time to be picked up for a job. I was there a lot of mornings (as young as I was), but never picked up for the job of shocking wheat. At this particular time of year wheat was cut, picked up and tied into bundles and then into shocks. Later the wheat was picked up and taken to a threshing machine where the grains were separated from the straw. These huge straw stacks were wonderful to play on. It was hard, back-breaking work and the guys picked to do the job were the larger ones.

One morning much to my surprise, I, along with six other boys was offered a job at $4 per day. Land was being cleared for a golf course. Our job was digging up cactus and poisoning Prairie Dogs with cotton balls dipped in some kind of liquid. At the end of the day I had cactus spines in my hand and on my clothes and shoes, as did all of the boys. When my dad found out what I was doing he made me quit. I don't believe that I ever earned a harder $4.

Ness City had a pool hall. We kids were forbidden to go into the pool hall and in truth, Mother didn't even like us to walk by the place. As usual, we were always looking for ways to make some money and brown beer bottles were worth a penny each. We searched through the alleys behind the places of people that we knew — or thought we knew — drank beer, and found half a dozen bottles. We took them in through the back door of the pool hall so as not to be seen and turned them in for the 6 cents. We noticed the proprietor stacked them with some others just outside the door. This was to good to be true. We waited an hour, then went back into the alley and helped ourselves to 12 bottles. We just carried them right on in to the proprietor and turned them in for 12 cents. This was a gold mine and being eager to exploit it we waited about half an hour, went back to the alley and picked up a whole case, then carried them in the rear door for the payoff. The proprietor grabbed us by the shirt collars and made us give back all the money — including the 6 cents that was really ours. At least he didn't tell my folks.

Every Wednesday there was a livestock and commodities sale at the sales pavilion east of town near the railroad tracks. We always hoped to get a job herding cows, pigs or other livestock into the arena to be auctioned off. Failing to do that we would walk around under the bleachers hoping that someone would drop some coins. The reason we wanted the money was for the hamburger stand. For 15 cents you could get a huge hamburger with all the trimmings and a Coke.

The other reason we wanted the job was for the apples and watermelons. Apple stealing was easy. Most trucks had an air vent in front of the bed that was covered with burlap. Since the vendor was at the rear of the truck taking care of business, it was simply a matter of making a hole in the burlap and helping ourselves.

Watermelons took more ingenuity and it helped to know the vendor and how tight-fisted he was. My cousin would bring his wagon, one of us would drop a penny then pick it up and announce loudly that he'd found a penny. The vendor would come over to stake his claim to it while the other bandit would load a melon into the wagon while his back was turned.

One of the many jobs that I had as a young boy was filling four large buckets of water from an outdoor pump for a widow woman. This job occurred in the wintertime. I was paid 5 cents each time, usually twice a week.

This was very hard pumping and the handle was always so cold. But the real downside of the story was the lemon pie. The widow always insisted that I come in, get warmed up and have a piece of lemon pie. It was gummy, sour and I hated it. To make matters worse I lied to her about liking it and she always gave me another piece. How do you tell an aging, good-hearted lady that she doesn't know how to make a lemon pie? I was lucky to get the 5 cents for the job though; Mother had told her I would do it for free.

One of the wealthier ladies in town hired me to mow her huge lawn. She had a rusty old mower that was hard to push even when it wasn't cutting grass. I wasn't very big and the going was tough. I think I only managed to cut a 12-inch swath with each push.

After working all day and with blisters on my hands, I went to the door to collect what I hoped would be a nice piece of change. She handed me a quarter and then gave me a dime to go to the bakery for a fresh loaf of bread. I bought her a day-old loaf for a nickel and pocketed the other nickel.

Donnie and I had a small business that was good for necessary funds. We searched for old copper, aluminum, zinc, lead or pewter to sell at the scrap metal yard. We spent many an hour at the county dump with a hammer and pry bar tearing metal from old cars or finding old kettles. During this time the price of scrap iron went up. This was in the late 1930s, so we branched out into scrap iron.

We found it in all sorts of places. Some of it was old farm equipment that was partially covered with dust drifts from the dust storms. We recruited other boys to help but they soon dropped out after we hinted that we may have come by some of it illegally and the sheriff might be looking for us.

We filled the pipes that we found with sand and pounded the ends shut for more weight. We paid a man 25 cents to haul our pile to the scrap metal yard with the understanding that we had to load and unload it. We stayed on the truck and when left alone, threw some of it over the fence and retrieved it at night. Our biggest haul was $26, or $13 each. This we proudly presented to our mothers. Five dollars would buy all the groceries you could haul in a wagon.

Earning money was always very difficult. One of the ways to make money was to shoot and sell rabbit furs. I had a .22 caliber bolt-action rifle that was older than the hills and because of a loose bolt would often spit burnt powder back in my face. The shells that I managed to get were Airways — I think they were called that because you could actually follow the arc of the shot. They were 20 cents a box.

We had a deep snow and the temperature was below zero. I headed out west of town, crossed over the frozen Walnut Creek and out into the pasture beyond. There in a depression I saw my first rabbit. Taking very careful aim so as to not waste any shots, I fired. I was sure that I hit him as I heard a loud "thud." I fired twice more with the same results. I went closer and soon discovered that the rabbit was frozen solid.

I was pulling a sled with me so I loaded the rabbit on it and started looking for more. This was great; I would make some money here. That hollow produced a wagonload of rabbits and I went back home to thaw them out and skin them.

From the start I knew that something was wrong. The skins kept tearing off in little pieces. The going price for rabbit was 10 cents — or 5 cents if the buyer had to skin them. I decided that I would sell them whole. After I got my money I went straight to the hardware store and bought several boxes of good Remington 22s.

By the time I got home the man that I had sold the rabbits to was there talking to Dad. He wanted his money back. I told him that I had already spent the money, and besides, how was I to know that you can't skin a rabbit that has been frozen? Dad agreed with me, and the man told me to never try to sell anything to him again. Those Remington shells lasted me for a long time.

The biggest way that growing up during the Depression affected me is that I vowed to myself to always be there for my wife and children. Despite having many happy childhood memories, my father's absence must have made a deep impression as I saw my mother work so hard to keep all of us housed, fed and clothed. She was an incredibly strong woman.

The Great Depression did not make me bitter; what I carried forward is my love of nature and wildlife, the value of hard, honest work and the responsibility of taking care of my family...always.

Bill Lohnes, Florida
Includes some excerpts from "Ness City Chronicles"
used with permission

Hog-killing time; "too many pigs"

For many families across the Midwest, raising their own food from gardens to livestock was paramount for survival during the Depression. Sometimes butchering for meat took place as a community.

Bill Lohnes, who was raised in Kansas, remembers: *"They would also get together to butcher hogs. This wasn't very pleasant to watch...this always ended with a huge meal outdoors and Grandpa would start the meal by eating the pig's tail. We had a smokehouse to cure and smoke the ham and bacon..."*

In Arkansas, James Gill counted on hog-killing time to keep his family of 13 children fed. His daughter Ginger said, *"After harvest, the weather turned cold and it was hog-killing time. Neighbors gathered and all the men hunted until they had six to eight hogs to share."*

Every part except the squeal and the entrails were used. Even the bladder was blown up and fashioned as a ball for children to play with. Fat was cooked out and stored as lard in jars. Hams, shoulders, pork loin and chops were cured over hickory chips in the smokehouse for about a month then hung in cloth sacks in the cold outdoors to keep flies out.

However, federal government officials panicked about dropping livestock prices in the early years of the Depression. New Deal officials believed that farmers still produced too much cotton and too many hogs. So they formed the Agricultural Adjustment Act (AAA) to reduce the supply.

As a result, in late spring 1933 the government carried out "emergency livestock reductions." According to writers and historians Claudia Reinhardt and Bill Ganzel, in Nebraska the government bought nearly 470,000 cattle and 438,000 pigs. Nationwide, six million hogs were purchased from desperate farmers. In the South, one million farmers were paid to plow under 10.4 million acres of cotton.

Following is an excerpt from Wessels Living History Farm in York, Nebraska:

"After the government purchased the livestock, they ordered them all to be killed. In Nebraska, thousands were shot and buried in deep pits. Farmers hated to sell

Fattening Herefords in a feedlot, Lincoln, Nebraska, 1941.
Farm Security Administration

their herds, but they had no choice. The federal buy-out saved many farmers from bankruptcy, and AAA payments became the chief source of income for many that year.

It was a bitter pill for farmers to swallow. They had worked hard to raise those crops and livestock, and they absolutely hated to see them killed and the meat go to waste. Critics charged that the AAA was pushing a 'policy of scarcity, 'killing little pigs simply to increase prices when many people were going hungry.''

Agriculture Secretary Henry A. Wallace said that because there was too little demand for pork products, farmers couldn't run an, 'old folks home for hogs and keep them around indefinitely as pets.' But even Wallace relented, recognizing the desperate need in the country. He pledged that the government would purchase agricultural products 'from those who have too much in order to give to those who have too little.' The AAA was amended to set up the Federal Surplus Relief Corporation (FSRC), which distributed agricultural products such as canned beef, apples, beans and pork products to relief organizations."

"...farmers couldn't afford to farm because the market prices were so low. President Roosevelt started a program to destroy food. While people starved, farmers were killing and burying cattle and pigs and pouring milk on the ground." ~ Lynn Frank, Pennsylvania

Child of rehabilitation clinic, Marie Plantation, Arkansas. Farm Security Administration. Franklin D. Roosevelt Presidential Library & Museum

Things went from bad to worse

Juanita Reid

Born 1933 in southwest Arkansas

My parents, Edward Thomas and Bernie Reid, lived in southwestern Arkansas near Gillham. They were already parents during the Great Depression.

My oldest sister was born October 1929 with five more siblings following at two-year intervals. I was a middle child, born in 1933. I also had a brother.

My dad worked in the timber industry and also worked in a mine — not a coal mine, it was another type of mineral mine. My mom had a big garden; she grew strawberries and sold them for a truck crop.

Things went from bad to worse for them after the stock market and banks failed in '29. All of the United States was affected by the Depression. Crime was rampant and there were no jobs.

The drought was followed by winds that blew away the topsoil then followed by rains that produced floods that washed away what little topsoil was left that might produce a garden. Bad farming practices left no stubble in the fields to hold soil and water. Insects such as boll weevils, grasshoppers and locusts were rampant and ate up what little did grow.

Most farm animals were sold or butchered because there was no money to buy food for the family much less to feed animals.

Arkansas normally has lots of wild nuts, fruits and berries. But the lack of water caused even the forests to abort almost all their bounty, making nuts and fruit scarce. What little plants survived and produced were appreciated.

My parents' survival skills kept us alive by foraging on wild plants and nuts, eating pokeweed and dandelions for greens and hunting wild game and fish for meat.

My mother was skilled at scavenging wild edibles and

Families walked away from homes and farms. public domain

made the most of them to feed her family. She learned those skills from her mother who was part American Indian.

Medicines were homemade from wild plants. Babies were born at home, delivered by a midwife or a member of the family.

My dad was a good hunter and killed deer to feed his family and close neighbors. The deer meat was cherished by all. Hunting laws were on the books and Game Wardens knew that folks were in need of meat. To my knowledge, my dad never got caught poaching.

Once the Game Warden came looking for my dad just shortly after he got home with a newly killed deer. My dad put that field-dressed deer in bed with my great-grandmother who was sick. The Game Warden could see into her room through an open door but never suspected there was evidence of a deer kill hidden under her covers.

My mother died in 1942, leaving Dad with six children to raise — my youngest sister was two-years-old. We lived on Irish and sweet potatoes and beans. After Mom died we pretty much fended for ourselves because Dad had to make a living.

I think growing up in the Depression affected me because I am frugal. I still can fruits and vegetables every day of my life and I make soap — I remember my mom and Grandma making soap from ashes. I make beauty products for my friends and family. I have chickens and live on a mini-farm with horses, dogs and cats.

I'm 81-years-old and I'm still gardening, canning and cooking.

Juanita Reid, Ohio

Truck gardening for extra dollars

If a family had enough acreage, truck farms also known as truck crops and truck gardens brought in extra income.

These were farms with extra land set aside to produce one or more vegetable and/or fruit crops for commercial sale, usually to local markets or at their own roadside stands.

People who lived on farms were able to make it through the Great Depression mostly because of their garden. They might not have had much money but they had vegetables, maybe some fruit trees, a flock of chickens, a dairy cow and sometimes pigs.

"My mom had a big garden; she grew strawberries and sold them for a truck crop." ~ Juanita Reid, Ohio

"Daddy had 'truck patches' of corn, peas and potatoes, so our table was set with the most basic of foods, but we never went to bed hungry," ~ Alfred Farris, Alabama

In the years before WWI truck farming was popular and depended entirely upon local or regional markets. Its popularity dropped off during the war but soon rebounded as the use of railroads expanded and refrigerated carriers for perishable foods were introduced. Because of this, truck farms spread to the cheaper lands of the West and South, shipping seasonal crops to distant markets where certain produce couldn't be grown because of climate.

According to Shawn Kidd with Salisbury University of Maryland, a typical truck crop of the Depression era would have included "quick harvest" fruits and vegetables such as strawberries and raspberries, sweet corn, snap peas, tomatoes, watermelons and cantaloupe, potatoes and cucumbers, lettuce and cabbage, beets, broccoli, onions and celery. Truck crops were also ideally produced for places where demand — and profit — was higher.

The Dust Bowl and the boll weevil wreaked havoc on truck farms in the Midwest, Kidd wrote. However, truck farming in the east was not as harshly affected by the Great Depression.

In 1935, *The Washington Post* ran an article about truck farming in east Virginia. Apparently farmers there did not suffer the affects of the Depression as much: *"Mr. Farmer...going about his work...weeding his onions and cultivating his white potato field with a song on his lips and a cheery call for his neighbor...It's kind of funny what a difference a little cash in one's pocket can make, and a farmer — who is one of the most confirmed of gamblers — always gathers hopes for a comfortable price on all his crops when his initial crop sells well."*

Kidd noted that, *"Truck crops were selling well, and truck farmers were doing well enough during the Great Depression to work, at times, with a song on their lips."*

Young son of Frank H. Shurtleff gathering sap from sugar trees for making maple syrup, 1940. Photo by Marion Post Wolcott, via the Library of Congress

It was just the way life was

Al Sanborn

Born 1928 in Sanbornton, New Hampshire

Although I'll be 86 this December, I still have vivid memories of life on a small farm during the Great Depression. We lived in Sanbornton, New Hampshire, a town that was named after my ancestors.

Our farm was about 150 acres with 30 or 40 acres toward hay and a large garden. The rest was wooded with Rock Maple syrup trees.

I was born in 1928 to Howard Sanborn and Elenora (Currier) Sanborn. I was the youngest of four children.

Because I had no life before the Big D I thought that what I was experiencing growing up was perfectly normal although others may have missed the comforts and conveniences to which they had become accustomed.

We were poor, but so was everyone else. We didn't feel poor — it was the way it was. I think my parents were pretty resilient. I hardly knew we were poor even though I didn't have new clothes until I was 15 or 16-years-old. All I'd had were hand-me-downs like everyone else.

We had no electricity; lighting was provided by kerosene lamps and lanterns. Our heat and our cook-stove all ran on wood from our own forest and we had plentiful water piped in from our gravity-fed well up on the hill. Saturday night was bath night and we took turns in the old, round washtub using water heated on the cook-stove. I was the youngest so I was the last one to use that water — it was pretty cool and pretty dirty by then. We bathed in the kitchen where it was nice and warm. There was no such thing as modesty in our home.

Occasionally, we had a shower when it rained. We'd stand under the gutter that was 15 feet up on the barn. It was cold though and because it fell from so high up it pounded on us.

Each year in March we would "tap" over one hundred trees for the maple sap and then we'd boil it in a 6-foot-long flat pan over a hot fire for many hours until the sap had become syrup. This was the magical time when Dad would scoop the pan contents into containers for storage or for sale, and we would produce between 50 and 100 gallons of syrup each year. The syrup sold for $5 per gallon and that constituted a really significant portion of the family income for the year. Weather determined the success of the efforts; sap ran only when there were freezing temperatures at night and melting hot days. When that stopped we had to call it quits.

As soon as the ground was ready to be tilled we were busy plowing, harrowing, and planting corn, potatoes and other vegetables. Then as they grew we had to "cultivate,"

Hired man of Frank H. Shurtleff gathering sap from sugar trees for making maple syrup. North Bridegwater, Vermont, 1940. Library of Congress

or hoe, around the plants depending on how their rows had been planted. And there was always a time when weeds had to be pulled by hand — a really tiring, backbreaking process that I hated.

By mid-June the hay was ready to start the first cutting. In those days, we had no tractor so the horses did the hard work, but the dried hay had to be hand-loaded onto the wagon. Getting the hay from the wagon to the mows up under the roof involved a complicated process involving pulleys, ropes and a "hay-fork" that acted like arms as it opened outward then jabbed down into the hay and it would close on the big forkful as the rope lifted it to the rail that ran the length of the barn's peak. All this mechanical work was powered by a horse on the ground while my dad worked the hay fork and directed the operation.

I recall during summers I went barebacked and barefooted all week and it felt really strange to put on a shirt, socks and shoes for church on Sunday. Speaking of shoes, I recall vividly my first pair of new shoes I ever had. I was probably nine-years-old. My mother fitted me in the store and picked them out two sizes too big. They flopped around for awhile but I grew into them soon — just as Mother knew that I would.

Being poor was nothing really bad; it was just the way life was. And everyone I knew was in the same boat so we weren't ashamed of our hand-me-down clothes. We always had ample food and water, as well as parents who never complained. Well, maybe once when Dad found out the milk company was reducing their payment to 3 cents a quart for our milk. Dad remarked that it was inadequate to even pay for just the grain required by our cattle.

Looking back at the 68 years since high school, or more

appropriately, the 61 years following military service and college, I could never have predicted how my life has gone. My wife, Elaine, and I have been married since 1952, produced four boys, 10 grandkids and three great-grandkids. No divorce anywhere in this whole group — in defiance of the odds.

As for how growing up in the Depression era affected me later, I think that intuitively I chose for a wife a wonderful soul mate who was also a very good planner. She took care of managing funds from our income and held me in check with spending where I may have squandered.

Now we're not worried about having enough funds for the rest of our lives. We've also traveled to all 50 states including Alaska and Hawaii, as well as to Australia, Costa Rica, Ireland and Russia. We are not rich by dollar standards but we are rich in family, memories and health.

I think because of how I was raised I have a better appreciation of money than I would have had. I see the younger generation going into such debt for "things" and it's alarming to me. If we fell into a Depression tomorrow a lot of people would suffer terribly.

Al Sanborn, Massachusetts

Roadside Markets on the Trunk Highways of North Carolina are being Encouraged by agricultural Extension Workers, 1932, "Green 'N' Growing," Special Collections Research Center, North Carolina State University

It took ingenuity

Dwayne Schramm

Born 1927 near Ida Grove, Iowa

My name is Dwayne Schramm, and I am a farm boy — born in the country near Ida Grove, Iowa in 1927. My parents, August Schramm and Carolina Hussong, were German immigrants. I am the youngest of two brothers and two sisters.

We raised corn to feed the hogs that were raised for slaughter, and oats and barley that was mostly used to feed the other animals. We had 10-12 cows that needed to be milked every morning and evening by hand. There were no machines in those days. In addition to milking, it was my job to take the cows out to pasture in the morning and bring them in again at the end of the day.

That time was also pre-tractor days. We used horses to pull all the machinery. We rode the cultivator to bring the corn in, and the grain was threshed the same way. WWII brought quite a change afterward when people could get tractors.

We harvested by using a threshing machine. There were five farm families around us. They helped to bundle it all into shocks then threshed all those bundles to separate the grain from the stems. The stems were used for straw for bedding in the barn and for nests in the chicken house. We didn't waste a thing. If you had it, you grew it.

Mama worked outside the home — in the garden. She grew all sorts of vegetables and raised chickens and geese. We lived off of what we raised. Mother made good use of what we had and we always had a goose for Thanksgiving and Christmas.

There was no money in the bank when the stock markets crashed, so we didn't lose anything. What we ate, we grew in the garden. Mama would can vegetables and store them to get us through the winter. We'd dig up potatoes in the wintertime and we ate eggs — often. Beef was stored in the basement where it was cool. We did our own butchering of hogs, chickens and geese. One of my jobs was to catch a chicken for dinner. I didn't like chopping off the head. But I did catch the chicken.

There was also a disaster in the mid-'30s with the invasion of grasshoppers. It totally destroyed our grain crop. My two older brothers went to Minnesota and worked on farms to earn money to help the family. One of them met his future wife and didn't come back. He sent the money though!

Mama sewed our clothes on a Singer sewing machine that had a pedal. I loved getting under there when she wasn't using it and really making that thing go. We bought overalls but Mama made my shirts. She was quite a seamstress. We did have shoes but when they wore holes in the sole, we put in cardboard. It took ingenuity.

Mondays were wash days. Mama would go outside with a pail and pump water then bring it in to heat the water on a woodstove in the kitchen. She did that four or five times and then dumped the warm water into the washing machine. It was a hand crank with a wringer. Then she did a tub rinse.

I was amazed at the hard labor. They worked from the moment they got up to the moment they went to bed. Hard work went on, on the farm. Everything was manual; there was no electricity. We used kerosene lamps. It wasn't until the mid-'30s that we got a radio. We were so enamored that we could listen to programs like *Amos 'n Andy*.

I loved going to school. The school for primary and elementary grades was just down at the end of our lane, so it was an easy walk. My sister was my teacher in 7th and 8th grades. One of my friends teased me, "Your sister is your teacher? Isn't that awful?" I told him that I like my sister and I like school. I ended up becoming a teacher myself. When I started high school I walked a mile to catch a ride to go the other six miles.

There was such camaraderie in the community; it's hard to explain. Our community worked together to help each other especially in harvesting times. On our farm they would harvest the oats and barley and put them into bundles then haul them on a hayrack to the barn that was ¼ mile away. It was primarily used for food for the animals.

A Model T was our first car. But it was kept in the garage in the winter when we had a lot of snow. We had a team of horses that would pull a sleigh every Saturday when we went to town. That was a lot of fun.

There were good times. I'd wait for my sister to come home from school and I'd jump out from behind a door and yell, "BOO!" That always got her. But I really liked the socializing with the community. Families would get together for dinner. Everyone would bring something — a vegetable, a meat dish, a pie — it didn't cost anything to get together because they'd be cooking something to eat anyway. We had softball games in the summer and sledding on the hills in the winter — boys and girls. We enjoyed sleigh rides too.

Although I worked on the farm, I followed in my sister's footsteps to teach. I went to college and got my certificate but didn't start teaching until after my service in the Navy in WWII.

The war changed a lot. We could get tractors and after WWII we got an electrical toaster. Now when we wanted toast we didn't have to put it into a flat pan and heat it up on top of the stove and use wood for fuel.

We were poor during the Depression but we didn't know we were poor. What we saw was normal — everyone else was in the same position.

I think it affected me later when I raised my own family. We were more thrifty with what we had. We were modest in how we clothed ourselves and spent money. We worked in a garden and grew food. What a blessing to be able to do that. We had fun too, it was not all dull and uneventful. My children and grandchildren love to hear my stories.

Dwayne Schramm, California

Laundry Days

Making Lye Soap

"Do you remember Grandma's lye soap?
Good for everything in the home,
And the secret was in the scrubbing;
It wouldn't suds and couldn't foam

Then let us all sing right out of Grandma's lye soap
Used for everything —
Everything on the place —
For pots and kettles,
The dirty dishes,
And for your hands and for your face."

~ John Standley and Art Thorson, 1952 recorded in the UK for Capitol Records by Horace Heidt & His Musical Knights

During the course of the week, one entire day was dedicated to doing laundry. More often than not, homemade lye soap was used. *"Mondays were wash days. Mama would go outside with a pail and pump water, then bring it in to heat the water on a wood-stove in the kitchen...I was amazed at the hard work."*

~ Dwayne Schramm, California

Clothes were washed and scrubbed with lye soap on the rubbing board then put through a wringer and a rinse. Some children from that era remember their mother scrubbing clothes so long that her hands bled and the soap made them burn. Her hands were not soft but rather red and chapped with broken fingernails.

Here is one recipe for lye soap. Eye protection is essential.

6 pounds grease (lard, fat from animal =chicken, pork or beef)
1 can lye
3 cups water

Put cold water and lye in a large, stainless steel container. Bring it to a boil then cool to lukewarm. Separately melt the fat then let cool to lukewarm. Mix fat into lye water. Stir until it starts to thicken like pudding. Pour into cast-iron pans or moulds to the thickness desired. Cut into bars. Ready for use in about six weeks.

Making Lye

Ashes from the fireplace and cookstove were collected into a big, square box called a hopper. To make lye, two or three gallons of water were collected, depending upon the amount needed.

The hopper was tilted under a spigot or hand pump so the water ran in and dripped out at one side and into a "safe" container such as crockery or glass. The mixture was left to soak for about three days.

A potato thrown in indicated readiness — if it floated about a quarter-size above the water, great. If not, another round of water-leaching was in order. When finished it was stored in a cool, dark place.

Lye was also used to remove the hair and everything off of hides for tanning and to make leather.

And yet...some claim that it worked wonders on hair and skin.

No money in the bank to lose

Esther (Johnson) Tissing

Born 1924 in El Campo, Texas

I was born in 1924 in El Campo, Texas. I celebrated my 90th birthday in 2014. I am number nine of 10 children — two of whom died before I was born.

When I was growing up I didn't know we were in a Depression. We had a farm in the country, about 10 miles out of El Campo. We had cows, calves, pigs, milk, cream, a vegetable garden, eggs and chickens. Mother bought flour and sugar. She baked bread and we shared our vegetables with our neighbors. We took one day at a time.

My parents' names are Adrian and Ruth Johnson. They were Swedish immigrants. My dad grew up in Chicago. When he was 18-years-old he went to Texas for a visit and fell in love with the place. He decided to go back to Chicago and save up enough money to move back. He had a milk route wagon and went door-to-door to earn enough money to get to Texas.

When he got there he sharecropped until he could buy his own farm.

Dad owned himself. He owned his own home and land outright — so there was no money in the bank to lose when the banks closed. Money was used year-to-year to put into the crops.

Dad was a cattleman and a farmer. He grew cotton, corn and rice. He also bid on cattle for sale and if his bid was the highest he would truck them to Houston to the stockyard and sell them for a profit. He preferred to sleep in a park — he never slept in his truck.

There was a time when a bunch of men with money from Dallas showed up to bid on some cattle. My dad didn't know they were going to be there. When he got there, he figured he'd put his bid in anyway because he'd come all that way but figured he wouldn't win. After it was over, he started to leave and the seller asked him where he was going. Dad said, "home," and then found out that he had won! He made quite a profit in Houston — more than he thought he would — and went back to the seller to give some of the money back. He just didn't feel right that he'd made so much money from him. The man said, "Do you think those Dallas men would have come back and offered me money?" He told Dad to keep it because he showed that he was a most honest man.

Dad also raised some cattle for meat and dairy. I milked many a cow. This was mostly for us because we were such a big family and we also fed the field hands and people who came to help us harvest. That was quite a job.

Dad threshed rice with a threshing machine pulled by a tractor. My brother sewed up the bags. Mother stayed busy in the kitchen on those days. I remember that one time some neighbor boys came to work. Mother put up four meatloaves, pinto beans, potatoes, bread. She put the food out on the sacks and brought out water and coffee to drink. She made rice pudding too. We never had trouble getting a threshing crew.

The Mexicans came sometimes to help with crops. They showed mother how to make tortillas by using her flour and showed my brother how to clean a bird that he'd shot, and how to roast it over a fire.

We lived in a four-room house: a living room, a kitchen, two bedrooms and a back porch. All of us kids slept in double beds — all three girls slept in one bed. I loved watching the sun come up and go down from the window. It was beautiful flatland.

On the back porch we had a washbasin with Lava soap for washing up. A ladle and towel were kept out for clean-up. There was also an icebox out there. Dad would buy a big block of ice from town and we'd chop it up to use for cold drinks.

Mom made her own grape juice, lemonade and ice tea. She also made pudding from grapes or strained it to make jelly. At Christmas she mixed tinned pineapple in. And if it was cold enough outside at Christmas, she would make jello and put bananas in for an extra treat. The way she did it was to put it in an open window and shut the door so the room would be cold enough for it to set. Jello was quite a treat.

Mother put meat in jars and sealed them with wax, so we always had meat.

We didn't have a lot of vegetables. We had a garden but our large family used what we planted and we shared what we had with others. For a treat, after Mother made fresh bread she cut the ends off and put butter and sugar on it for us. It was a Swedish treat.

There was also a community meat club. One farmer would butcher a cow or calf and split it up. One family got one part one week — like the kidneys — and another part the next and so on. We always had fresh meat on Sunday.

There was no running water — we got our drinking water from a pump that was close to home. We used the washtubs at night in the kitchen. Mom strung up blankets for the girls. We also had a wood-burning cookstove. I loved sitting around the fire in the evening with Dad while he told ghost stories. There was also no electricity until probably the mid-'30s. I remember cleaning the chimneys of lamps until I was 10 or 12.

We all had jobs to do around the farm. With so many kids we were fortunate to have a two-holer outhouse. We took turns keeping it clean and every Friday it was my job. It wasn't too bad. All of our pets kept all the critters down.

Wash day was all day long. In the washhouse, there was lye soap to soften the water. We'd push the clothes down into it and let 'em boil for awhile. The tub had bluing in it to brighten colors. There were a lot of clothes in our big family. When we ran out of room on the line we hung the overalls on all the fences. We always had egg gravy on bread for dinner on wash days.

Our clothes were always clean. Most of our clothing was made by Mother. Father picked out beautiful feed sacks for play dresses. They made the most wonderful play-clothes; they were so soft. But we did get store-bought Christmas and Easter dresses. Mostly we went barefoot but we did have shoes. Mother would place our foot on paper on the floor, draw around it and send it in to Sears. But I still prefer to go barefooted to this day. I loved to feel the black soil through my toes.

Father cut our hair. He gave us all bangs, shaved the hair up the back and let the tips of our ears show. He cut mine for a school program and mother made a bonnet for me — it was so short. There was a bald man sitting in front of me and I felt sorry for him. So I put my bonnet on his head.

Father also pulled our teeth for us with thread. We never went to the dentist until we were much older.

I liked to visit school so much when I was little that they let me start early — I was five-years-old so that would have been 1929 or 1930. It was called Country Plainview School and it had eight grades with a few teachers.

We went to school in covered wagons. We'd walk a quarter-mile to where families waited in a wagon and they'd take us to school pulled by mules or horses that were kept in a barn near the school. After school, they were hitched up and brought us back home.

Things we did for fun? People talk about sledding in the snow, but we had mud sleds behind a horse. We thought that was grand. We made our own fun. We sat underneath our house that was built up on concrete blocks. We had empty vanilla bottles and built buildings and towns under there. My sisters and I made high heels by putting spools of thread into the heels of our socks. And we made our own paper dolls — we cut them out of the Sears Roebuck catalogs and cut out the outfits. We dressed them according to what time of day it was. We sometimes went to the movies. We rode horses. I had a gentle horse. Most of all, I liked playing with my imagination in the tall weeds in the cow pasture behind the barn. I made "rooms" out of the grasses and pretended I had a big house. I'd just pretend. I did a lot of pretending.

We had our own swimming hole dug out in the place where they would pump out water for the rice fields. I learned to swim by holding onto a one-gallon size bucket and keeping it under my chin. One day it popped out and I learned to swim. We also kept things in the pond to keep cool, including watermelons.

My brother made a pull-toy for me. It was a wood board that he nailed a can onto, made a hole in the end and put a string through it. I pulled it around everywhere; I loved it. I had one doll — I got it for Christmas when I was little.

At Christmas we always had presents — bushels of fruit, baskets of nuts and candy, and we almost always got clothing. The tree had clip-on candles and we always made sure they were out when we went to bed after we listened to Dad tell stories around the cookstove.

One thing we couldn't afford was bicycles. I remember seeing that other children had them.

There was no TV or radio in those days, so we didn't know what was going on in the rest of the country — we didn't see the soup lines. I think we had it easy in the country.

My husband, Robert Tissing, Bob, was from Chicago. He had $17 in the bank when it closed and lost it. He complained about that until the day he died a few years ago. Bob had twisted onions for 10 cents a day to earn that money. One time he went to the movies with a friend after work. They washed themselves with Clorox but everybody knew where they were.

Bob's grandfather walked from Chicago to Wisconsin looking for a job during the Depression. He always said that when bad things happen, you just spit on your hands, rub 'em together and get back to work.

My mother always said the best day of her life was the Fourth of July. Everyone went to the rodeo but she stayed home alone. It was the one time every year that she could do what she wanted — cook, sleep, write, nap — whatever she wanted to do. She was amazing. She had no complaints about her part in life. Her kids were her joy.

The legacy my father left was that to be honest and to be friendly never cost anyone anything. They taught us not to worry; "There is no reason to be worried," they said. They were the most wonderful Christians. People from all over knew that they were good, honest, hard-working people and loved their farm and ranch.

My parents taught us so much by the way they lived. They were loved in the community. I'm still living up to the legacy of my father.

I wouldn't trade my upbringing for 30 millionaire kids. I wouldn't trade it for the world. I had a wonderful life. I was truly, truly, blessed.

Esther Tissing, Texas

Swedish Egg Gravy

Heat 3 cups milk over medium heat. Thoroughly beat 3 eggs. Add 1 tsp salt and 1 Tbsp flour to the beaten eggs stirring until smooth. Stir in 1/2 cup of the hot milk to the egg/flour mixture. Then gradually stir the egg mixture into the hot milk. Stir until it thickens. Overheating will cause curdling.

Cooking with a Depression era stove/oven

"We also had a wood-burning cookstove. I loved sitting around the fire in the evening with Dad while he told ghost stories." ~ Esther Tissing, Texas

Sweltering in summer or comforting in winter; the household revolved around the woodstove in the midst of the kitchen. For Esther Tissing, evenings around the stove created memories that lasted into her 90th year.

Modern electric ovens, ranges and stove tops that we take for granted today would have been beyond the scope of most housewives' imaginations during the 1930s. Kitchens were dominated by boxy, cumbersome cast iron cooking stoves fueled with wood or coal, and later, gas if the family could afford it.

Although gas cooking was popular in England and manufacturers sent their products to America, gas in the United States was still too expensive for many households for it just to be burned for cooking. As a result, most homes in suburban and less-wealthy areas of the nation featured wood or coal burning cookstoves, such as the kind mentioned throughout the recollections in this book.

Most often made of heavy cast iron and sometimes coated with porcelain enameling to pretty up the surfaces in black, white, or grey, that's all there was to cook with during the Depression era. The two-tone color and oven heat regulators for controlled oven temperatures were breakthroughs for convenience and atmosphere.

Cooking or baking with wood and coal required

a different rhythm and different timing than cooking with gas or electricity. Individual stoves are different, so a girl who grew up learning to cook at her mother's oven might find herself with a scorched loaf of bread in her own, new home with a hungry new husband.

Different areas of the stovetop had more or less heat. Finding the right cooking temperature to boil water for beans or to simmer soup all day required intimate knowledge of the kitchen appliance. The area over the firebox was hottest but there were often channels to circulate the heat to the oven and reservoir that got quite warm too.

A thermometer in the oven door let the cook know when a stick or two of wood or a shovelful of coal was needed to keep the heat going at an even temperature.

Like the stovetop, ovens had hot spots. The side next to the firebox had the hottest temperatures and the top rack was hotter because the oven was heated from the top down. Trial and error — knowing what places in the oven resulted in burnt pie crust or golden loaves of bread — showed the cook how to correctly bake in the best spots.

The natural draft Arndt prune dryer is a simple, one-story, wood frame building. The original portion, built for William Arndt in about 1898, measured approximately 14 feet by 15 feet. William's son Fred expanded the building himself in 1920 to 20 feet by 40 feet. The gable-roofed, rectangular building incorporates a partially roofed open loading platform at the southeast corner and a narrow shed-roofed extension on the north elevation. The building remains unpainted both inside and out and presents an appearance virtually unchanged since 1920. The property also has productive, mature prune trees with several trees that were planted in the 1890s. Listed on the National Register of Historic Places in 1979.

Photo from Clark County, WA Community Planning

An Okie boy told me we were rich

Ben Warkentin

Born 1923 in Dallas, Oregon

I was born in 1923 in Dallas, Oregon. Not The Dalles, as everyone seems to want to think. Dallas is about 13 miles west of Salem down the middle of Oregon. I had two older sisters and one younger — I was the only boy. My parents are Henry Warkentin and Elizabeth Euhler.

But I grew up in Shafter, California. My dad got a job as a custodian at Maple School; he was the groundskeeper and bus driver too.

The reason we moved from Dallas to Shafter was that Dad's brother-in-law bought a prune orchard and prune dryers. The crop was very, very good but there was no price for prunes in the beginning of the Depression. They lost the prune orchard and their home.

The first house I remember living in was a clapboard house. It was hot in summer and cold in winter. It was the first building on the schoolyard when the property was bought to be used for a school. It had four rooms and no bath — there was an outhouse. Same with the school. We had no telephone.

At one point Dad wanted to get out of the San Joaquin Valley for some reason and we left for Dallas again. He worked in a lumber mill outside year-round and that was not good for his health. So we moved back to Shafter after a year. Dad was able to get his old job back.

We went back to Dallas every summer to visit my grandparents. When I was in the 6th grade we moved back. Dad got a job working with his brother-in-law at a box factory. But the job wasn't too good or too steady so we moved back to Shafter in 1937 and my dad worked for Maple School again as a janitor.

Mom worked at the hot lunch program at the school too. I didn't notice that there was a Depression going on too much. I did notice in the school yard when we moved back that there were a lot of new people who came from the Midwest: Oklahoma, Texas, Arkansas and Kansas. They were all considered "Okies." Some lived in tents on the school property. They were very thin. We could tell who hadn't eaten as well as we had been eating. Their clothing was worn and most didn't have shoes even when it got cold.

For the hot lunch program farmers donated milk and the butchers donated some meat and bones for soup for the students. I do remember having hot chocolate sometimes.

Every summer Mom and I picked fruit for canning on shares. We got half the fruit we picked — peaches, apricots and figs. It was the only time my mother wore coveralls. She said she was not going to wear a dress while she was climbing trees and picking fruit.

Mom made dresses for my sisters but I had coveralls. I didn't wear shoes most of the time except in the wintertime. When summer was over we needed to wear shoes to church. One year my feet had grown so much over the summer that I couldn't fit into my church shoes. I whined to Mom, "Do I have to wear shoes?" She said that if my feet were clean I didn't have to wear 'em. When I got to be 12-years-old, I had to wear shoes all year-round. Sometimes I wore my sisters' shoes in the summer.

We were Evangelical Mennonites and we always went to church. We are also called The Brethren. So the farmers all around us and the children at school were mostly Mennonites. We considered the people who came from the Midwest as migrants. Because we were out in the country, all we had was our church and we all helped people that we knew.

We often played in the schoolyard when relatives and friends came to visit. We played Red Rover, Last Couple Out and games like that.

At school the girls played jacks and the boys played marbles — but not for keeps. That was out of the question at school. The girls played hopscotch and the boys played foursquare and our own version of hopscotch with a board and elongated squares.

We didn't have a lot of milk and eggs because we weren't on a farm. We had a chicken for a short while — we bought it from the neighbors. But we had three meals a day and never lacked food. It might have been scarce but we children didn't know we were poor. One of my jobs was to clean intestines to make sausages. I didn't think it was a terrible thing. It was a celebration in a way. It's just what we did.

We had a Model T that we moved to Dallas from Shafter in, then we had an Essex, then a Chevy then a Pontiac.

There was an Okie boy who told me we were rich. I hadn't heard that word before and I didn't know what he meant. He also said to me one day, "Are y'all going to church?" I said, "Yes, we are all going to church." He said, "No, are Y'ALL going to church?" I figured it out.

I'm glad I married who I did. We have two daughters. We were of the old school — I didn't want to spend money so I gave my wife the checkbook. I only spent what I had in my pockets.

In later years as I raised my own family, we saved everything. We didn't throw anything away. When we moved into a retirement village I had to get rid of a lot of stuff in my back yard — all the projects I was going to do. I would find a board that was an inch too short for a project but I'd save it just in case because some day I might need it.

We also definitely believe in making Christ the center of our lives. We need to be committed to the Lord and toward helping others.

We have done very good. My wife is from Oklahoma — they had a farm and it was tough. But we're doing okay.

Ben Warkentin, California

The free hot lunch program is born

"Mom worked at the hot lunch program at the school too...For the hot lunch program farmers donated milk and the butchers donated some meat and bones for soup for the students. I do remember having hot chocolate sometimes." ~ Ben Warkentin, California

During the Depression of the 1930s millions of school children were unable to pay for school lunches. Limited family resources meant that boys and girls were also in danger of malnutrition at home. Federal assistance became essential for children and for farmers who couldn't make enough money from their products. Finally, Congress took action in 1935 to help both.

A purchase and distribution program was assigned to the Federal Surplus Commodities Corporation, established in 1933 as the Federal Surplus Relief Corporation in order to distribute surplus pork, dairy products and wheat to the needy. Children who could not pay for their meals would not be identified to their peers.

Destitute families and school lunch programs became outlets for commodities purchased by the USDA. Because of this, poor children ate foods at school that they would not otherwise have. This also helped farmers who were given an outlet for their products at a reasonable price.

In March 1937 more than 342,000 children were served daily in 3,839 schools across the nation. Two years later the number of schools grew to 14,075 and the number of children had risen to more than 892,000.

Following is a sample menu with a few recipes for the first week of school from USDA's book published in 1936, *Menus and Recipes for Lunches at School.*

FIRST WEEK

Cheese bunny.
Grated-carrot sandwich.
Fruit.
Milk.

Peanut butter and tomato soup.
Toast or bread-and-butter sandwich.
Fruit and cookie.
Milk.

Split-pea soup with cured pork.
Bread-and-butter sandwich.
Fruit and cookie.
Milk.

Cracked-wheat chowder.
Bread-and-butter sandwich.
Fruit and raisin cookie.
Milk.

Codfish, spaghetti, and tomato.
Whole-wheat bread-and-butter sandwich.
Fruit.
Milk.

CHEESE BUNNY

5 quarts milk.
1¼ cups melted butter.
1¼ cups flour.
5 teaspoons salt.
5 pounds Cheddar cheese, shaved thin.
1 dozen eggs, well-beaten.
Onion juice and other seasonings as desired.
Crackers.

Make a sauce of the milk, melted butter, flour, and salt. Cover and cook for 15 minutes. Stir in the cheese, and continue stirring until it is thoroughly melted. Add some of this mixture to the beaten eggs, and when well blended, return it to the cheese sauce. Cook about 10 minutes, stirring constantly. Add the onion juice, with other seasonings, such as soy sauce and tabasco, as desired. Serve hot on crisp crackers.

Total measure cooked, about 7 quarts; 56 servings, each one-half cup.

PEANUT BUTTER AND TOMATO SOUP

4 no. 10 cans tomatoes (about 12 quarts).
10 ounces flour (2½ cups).
3 pounds peanut butter.
½ pound peeled onions, chopped.
2 tablespoons salt.

Press the canned tomatoes through a sieve to remove the seeds. Mix 2 quarts of the strained tomato, the flour, and the peanut butter until smooth. Add the onions to the remaining tomato and heat to the boiling point. Add some of the hot tomato to the flour and peanut mixture, then combine with the hot tomato. Add the salt. Cook for about 10 minutes, stirring constantly.

Total measure cooked, about 13 quarts; 52 servings, each 1 cup.

CRACKED WHEAT CHOWDER

2½ pounds cracked wheat.
5 quarts water.
4 pounds scraped carrots, diced.
1½ pounds trimmed celery, cut.
2½ quarts boiling water.
1 pound salt pork, diced.
1 pound peeled onions, chopped.
2 ounces flour (½ cup).
4 quarts milk and, if desired, 9 ounces dried skim milk.
5 tablespoons salt.

Boil the cracked wheat in the 5 quarts of water for 30 minutes. Cook the carrots and celery in the 2½ quarts boiling water until tender. Fry the salt pork until crisp, remove it, and cook the onions in the fat for a few minutes. Stir in the flour and when blended add 1 quart of the milk and cook until the mixture thickens. Add the carrots and celery, including liquid, and combine with other ingredients. Stir constantly until thoroughly heated. (To increase the milk solids in this recipe add the 9 ounces of dried skim milk mixed with the fluid milk.)

Total measure cooked, about 12½ quarts; 50 servings, each 1 cup.

For extra money we sold eggs

Geri (Suderman) Warkentin

Born 1930 in Isabella, Oklahoma

I was born in 1930 in a house on a farm in Isabella, Oklahoma. My father's name is Albert Suderman; my mother is Pauline (Heinrichs) Suderman. I am the oldest child of three; I have two younger brothers.

My grandfather and some of his friends homesteaded in Oklahoma when the government opened land up for settling. When my dad married, Grandfather moved to town and my parents moved onto the homestead.

Dad was a wheat farmer. Sometimes he had oats. He used horses to do all the farming. We had cows for milk, chickens for eating and for eggs, and hogs — that was good eating. We had smoked hams and sausages and used lard to fry chicken and other things in and to make pie crust. We ate a lot of chicken. We never complained and I never got tired of it.

We had a garden too, although it was not a very big

one. Vegetables needed sandier soil than what we had. I do remember that we planted potatoes. Mother's mother shared things from her garden with us and Mother would help her take care of canning all the vegetables. They did a lot of canning. What we couldn't get from our garden we could buy from someplace else — we always knew someone we could buy from so we could can what we needed.

There was a watermelon field a little ways down the road. They were huge watermelons. One time we got 13 for $1. Myself and my two brothers ate a lot of watermelon.

As long as we had our animals we seemed to make it all right. We always had three meals a day.

My dad's salary was once a year because he was a crop farmer. We lived in Grandma and Grandpa's old house for about five years. Then the youngest son married and it was his turn to live in the house. Dad found another house about half a mile away. He bought part of that farm and it had a house on it already — it was about 40 acres. We lived there for years.

Dad did some other work too. He planted in the fall, around September and October, and once the crop was planted all he could do was wait for it to grow. So he got other jobs. One job he had was with the county keeping the dirt roads drivable. He had a grader to smooth out the road.

For extra money we sold eggs in Fairview, a town that was about seven miles away. Sometimes we had too many eggs because we had so many chickens. So we took them to the grocery store and traded them for flour and sugar. We did the same thing with cream when we had extra.

We lost our horses in a storm one year. They were struck by lightning. Dad didn't buy any more because tractors and pickups were available by then. So dad got a car too.

Mother helped in the harvest. My father was very mechanical-minded. He got an old truck and re-wired and fixed it so it would go. He took it out into the field with the combine. Mother would drive that truck following the combine around and when the bin was full she kept up with him while Dad unloaded the wheat into the truck while they were both driving. When it was full Mother drove it back to the elevator. The truck didn't have a door on it so she'd tuck her dress under her legs to keep it from flapping around. Mother didn't want to wear coveralls. There wasn't a seatbelt either.

In between hauling wheat she'd come into the house and show me what to do for the meal. I cooked potatoes. Mother chopped the chickens heads off so I got them plucked and ready to cook.

We fed the threshing crew too. Father and Grandfather and my uncle all bought a threshing machine together. After the wheat and oats were harvested they got a lot of straw and would bale for later use.

The schoolhouse was only half a mile away. We attended the same school that my father had — it was a one-room schoolhouse. All three of us graduated from 8th grade there, then we went to the high school seven miles away in Fairview. The bus came and got us.

Mom made my clothes. The material that chicken feed came in had such pretty colors. We wore a lot of "mash sack" dresses. My underwear was made from flour and sugar sacks. They were cloth bags so we used 'em. Everyone did that.

We knew we were poor — we didn't have the latest equipment. But my dad was such a great mechanic. He made everything go. We were just like everybody else.

When fall came there was a lot of canning and butchering. Mother would go into the cellar to check the shelves and see how much food there was to last all winter. It usually did. We butchered hogs and calves during the day and all the neighbors helped each other.

For fun our families would get together and play. We enjoyed going big shopping to the city 35 miles away where we would go to JC Penney and Sears. There was a really nice park there. We brought a picnic — usually fried chicken and potato salad; we didn't often eat at restaurants. We tried to be in the park to eat at noon. There was a lake and rowboats people could use to go around.

We had a lot of Dad's family living around us. We'd have picnics together someplace where we could go swimming and play outdoor games and table games. Sometimes we had homemade ice cream.

I guess the biggest thing I notice now about how growing up during that time affected me is that I save things. It's hard to throw anything away. And the value of family. We are very close.

Geri Warkentin, California

Fried chicken and potato salad

"Mother chopped the chickens' heads off, so I got them plucked and ready to cook..." ~ Geri Warkentin, California

Fried chicken

2 c. lard
2 small chickens
2 c. flour
1 tsp. salt
1/4 tsp. pepper

Original recipe makes 8

Cut each chicken into 8 pieces, backbone removed. Save livers and gizzards for another use. Wash each piece of chicken. Pat dry.

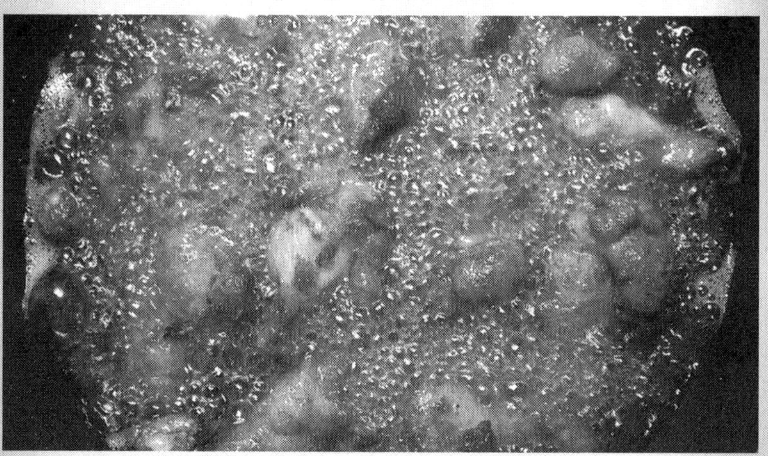

Frying chicken pieces via Creative Commons

Place flour, salt and pepper in a large bowl and mix. Drop the chicken pieces into the bowl and dredge until each piece is thoroughly coated. Shake off excess flour, lay them side by side on waxed paper and place them near the stove so that you can get to them easily when you start frying.

Melt the lard over moderate heat in a heavy 10-12" skillet. The fat should fill the pan to a depth of about 2 inches. Add more lard if necessary. When the fat is hot but not smoking, begin frying chicken.

Put in thighs and legs first and cover the pan at once. Let the chicken fry, lifting the cover occasionally to check the process. When the bottom side is deep brown, turn with a wooden spoon so you don't pierce the skin. Cover and brown the other side.

As each piece is cooked, remove it and put an uncooked piece in its place. Remember that the white meat will take a little less time to cook than the dark pieces.

"We brought a picnic — usually fried chicken and potato salad; we didn't often eat at restaurants…"

~ Geri Warkentin

Potato salad

2 c. diced potatoes
1 T butter
1/4 cup diced onion
1/2 tsp salt
1/8 tsp pepper
2 c. milk
1 T flour

In a large pot, boil potatoes and onion. Cook until potatoes are fork tender. Add butter, salt, pepper and milk. In a separate small container or jar, combine 1 tablespoon flour with 1 tablespoon water and stir well. Add to warm potato salad and mix until thickened, cooking another 5 to 10 minutes. Serve warm or eat cold.

We were always pretty poor

Russell Weikle

Born 1929 near Merrill, Kansas

There's not much of anything there in the northeast corner of Kansas where I was born on March 24, 1929. The nearest town was Merrill. I am number six in a family of seven children. Yes, my parents had quite a few kids during the Depression — six boys and one girl.

My dad, Denny Lee Weikle, was a sharecropper. That's when the landlord owns the land and someone else lives on his property/farm. We split the cost of seed but we harvested and did all the work then split the proceeds in the fall. It wasn't much. We farmed mostly corn but there was some wheat and alfalfa. We had four different homes because we sharecropped on different farms but we stayed mostly in the same vicinity.

When the crops were ready in the fall after we harvested the property we worked on, Dad would make

$1 a day working for other farmers. If they needed his team of horses and wagon and himself, he could make $2.50 a day. He preferred that.

Dad owned horses because there were no tractors or powered equipment. It's how we farmed all through the Depression. We never owned power equipment on the farm. Dad bought a 1929 Studebaker, but mostly had Model Ts before that.

My mother is Ruby (Eisenbise) Weikle. Her dad had a little money and was successful as a farmer. He bought five farms that he was going to leave to his five children, mother included. But he mortgaged them and when the banks closed he lost them.

Dad's family never had much. They always had to sharecrop, because they never could afford their own land.

We never had much, either. We were always pretty poor. But we had a huge garden — a vegetable garden. We raised one calf for beef and raised pigs that were designated for pork. We always butchered in the fall. It was good to have meat and vegetables and some staples set aside for the winter. There wasn't much money for anything else. We did a lot of squirrel and rabbit hunting for extra meat. I could handle a rifle and shoot it at age nine or 10. I always went with my older brother but he didn't let me shoot as much as I wanted to.

Mom baked bread in an old kitchen stove that used wood. We had a heater in the living room that used wood too. There was no electricity, no indoor plumbing, and we had to carry water from the well for all the washing and everything else. Mom was pretty much a housewife. She raised us kids and made sure all our socks were darned and not thrown away. She worked pretty hard. There was

One-room schoolhouses were common.
Courtesy of Franklin D. Roosevelt Presidential Library and Museum

always quite a bit of work at home; there were a lot of chores.

We went to town about once a month. Town was usually about 12 miles from home. We'd go in the Studebaker to get supplies such as condiments, clothing and new coveralls. Mom made some clothing but mostly bought them at the five-and-dime stores like Woolworth's and Newberry in town. Those stores were sort of like Walmart today where you could find a little bit of everything. We got our coveralls there. I still like coveralls.

In summer we went barefoot until school started. We always got a new pair of shoes in the fall for school and we wore them all winter. When the shoes wore out we stuffed newspaper and cardboard in the soles.

We bought all our school supplies at the five-and-dime stores too. You could get used books in dime stores and some were pretty well used. I wanted yellow pencils but they were 5 cents apiece. Mom always bought us penny pencils. They were round with a tiny eraser cut into the top in a hole. I wanted to be extravagant, but they really couldn't afford anything.

Most of my older brothers went through school to the 8th grade. We went to one-room schoolhouses — we moved around quite a bit. Fairview had a brick school with two floors that had several classrooms. But I heard that the best concept is the one-room school because the older kids would be assigned as helpers for the younger grades.

My toys were mostly built by me when I was a child. I did a lot of pretending with a block of wood that became a truck or a car or a threshing machine in the dirt. I remember having a metal truck once and a wind-up tractor that I played with quite a bit.

Christmas presents were usually something that all of us kids could share. We were pretty excited to get a sled one year. And we had a pull-wagon — a Radio Flyer. But it was mostly used to haul split wood from the woodpile to the house. There was always a reason behind a gift; it needed to be useful for chores too.

I was 11-years-old when we left Kansas. My older brother had been working for a farmer who moved to California. Dad had worked for him too, and was enticed. So we moved to Armona in 1941. Dad built a house there for $800. It was a two-bedroom house. My sister got the extra bedroom and us boys slept on a screened-in back porch. We wrapped plastic around it in the winter but it didn't help keep the cold out much.

Pearl Harbor was bombed that December and that opened lots of jobs in the war industry. I'd had about enough of farming. At the end of WWII I was 17 and I joined the Army. I met my wife in Boston and we got married after I was discharged. I started my police career in Boston in 1948. After WWII there were plentiful jobs and I made $25 a week — I thought that was pretty good. It was enough to keep us in shape.

We lived at her and her parents' house because she was helping her mother take care of her grandmother who had suffered a stroke and needed help. We stayed there 10 years.

When I had my own family I found that the way that I grew up during the Depression affected me. I was conservative with money and so forth and tried not to get into debt. I paid cash for most of what we bought. I didn't borrow money except for my first house — that was $9,500 in 1956 in Hanford, California. I didn't do credit.

I do save things, too. I see a nut or a screw or a bolt on the ground and I take it home and put it in a bin in the garage. I save all kinds of string and cords because I might need them some day. You know those kits to build things that come with extra pieces? I can't throw those away, either. It's hard to throw anything away.

Russell Weikle, California

Toys vs Imagination

Simple things such as dolls, finger paints and die-cast model cars were popular in the 1930s. A few board games that made their debut include Monopoly, Scrabble and Sorry!

For families who had money to spare, boys enjoyed Erector sets, toy trains and air rifles. Girls played with a variety of dolls, their clothes and doll houses. The Shirley Temple doll was most popular but hard to come by in the early 1930s because there weren't enough made and they literally flew off the shelves and into little girls' arms.

However, the majority of children who lived and played during the Depression used their imaginations and creativity to pass the time.

"My toys were mostly built by me when I was a child. I did a lot of pretending with a block of wood that became a truck or a car or a threshing machine in the dirt. I remember having a metal truck once and a wind-up tractor that I played with quite a bit. Christmas presents were something that all of us kids could share."

~ Russell Wiekle, California

"We made our own fun," Esther Tissing of Texas said. An older brother made a pull toy for her made out of a tin can nailed to a piece of wood with a string pulled through a hole. *"I pulled it around everywhere. I loved it,"* she said.

Tissing and her sisters played underneath the family home that was built up on cinder blocks. Empty vanilla bottles became buildings in the towns they created. Spools of thread stuffed into socks became high-heels. They cut out and dressed paper dolls for every sea-

These charming, adorable character dolls have been designed and made by clever workers on WPA Toy Repair Projects in various parts of the country. Their colorful dresses and in some instances, even their bodies, have been made largely from WPA Sewing Room scraps, utilizing material which might otherwise be wasted. Besides such playthings made outright on the Project, many discarded toys are received for repair and reconditioning. The majority are then made available to underpriveleged children through WPA Toy Lending Libraries all over the country. Some are placed in WPA Nursery Schools. At Christmas many are given to Santa Claus to distribute to underpriveleged children for their very own.

Franklin D. Roosevelt Presidential Library & Museum

son from the Sears Roebuck catalogue. But most of all, *"I liked playing with my imagination,"* Tissing said. Tall weeds in the cow pasture behind the barn were parted to make grassy rooms in the big house she created: *"I'd just pretend. I did a lot of pretending."*

Unemployed men queued outside a Depression soup kitchen opened in Chicago by Al Capone, 02-1931. Photo in the public domain, via Wikipedia.

I knew things were tight

Jean (McCormack) Wiekle

Born 1929 in Boston, Massachusetts

I am an only child born on May 27, 1929 in Boston, Massachusetts. My dad is Mike McCormack — his parents were Irish immigrants. My mother's name is Emily Guenther. Her daddy owned a bake shop in Boston that did very well.

While I was growing up I didn't know too much about what was going on. I mostly listened to my parents. I knew things were tight. We lived with my grandparents — my mother's parents — in a big house on Ashmont Street.

My dad was out of work like everybody else. I remember seeing lines of people waiting for a free lunch and a free bite to eat while they were waiting for work somewhere. A lot of people were out of work. There were some organizations such as the WPA (Works Progress Administration) and others that helped.

Dad was a vaudeville singer and comedian. He

was especially good at the comedian part. He did different shows and theaters but they all closed when the stock market crashed, which left him out of work because people didn't have the money to go see shows anymore.

Before the Depression, he was part of the *Grand Street Follies of 1929* on Broadway. They went to Chicago and when they closed there, some of them were heading to Los Angeles. A man in the troupe named Jimmy Cagney was my dad's friend. He said, "Come on with us!" But my dad said, "No, my wife's having a baby, I'd better go back to Boston." And that was that. We know how things turned out for Mr. Cagney!

Dad loved to sing. He didn't need to be asked twice; he was a singer anywhere at any time. James Michael Curley was running for Mayor again and always had Dad go out and sing for him at political rallies at Faneuil Hall. The Mayor's favorite song was *Danny Boy*. Dad always got paid for singing and that also helped him get in tight with other politicians which helped him get a job that way.

Because of his work with politicians, he took a few exams, got on a list and got to be a health inspector in Boston. In Faneuil Hall there were cubbyholes where people sold fruits and vegetables and meats. He'd go inspecting on Saturday and then bring home meat and vegetables. He was a very outgoing person and everyone liked him.

Although he was Irish, he learned to speak fluent Italian. He and my mother lived in Italy from 1920-1925 to study music. So he was quite friendly with a lot of the Italians who sold food. They loved him. They would say, "Here! Take this!" and give him food. He never had to stand in the bread line.

My mother was also a vaudeville singer. For a woman,

it was a tricky job. They had to be quite friendly with the producers. She didn't want to go that route, so she got out of it. But she did sing in various performances around the city.

Her dad owned a bake shop. One day my dad came in and she sold him a loaf that was a couple of days old. He came back to complain. That's how they met.

We lived with my mother's parents so she could help take care of my grandmother who had a broken hip. She also took care of the big house. Grandpa sold the bakery in 1932 and moved into the big house on Ashmont Street. He had a few rooms on the second floor converted to a kitchen and apartment, so we had "roomers." But it wasn't room and board, just the apartment. We all shared a bathroom.

Going to the theater was a rare treat.

Courtesy of Franklin D. Roosevelt Presidential Library and Museum

Sometimes we would go to town and as a child, I'd see something I'd like to have but my mother would tell me, "No, you can't have that right now." When you're little, you don't really know how things can change.

Grandmother made all my clothes — she was an accomplished seamstress. Mother directed the American Legion's Glee Club in Dorchester. Dad served in the Navy in WWI. For the singing group, all the women had to have the same dresses. Grandmother made them all. That was quite a project, especially with an old treadle sewing machine.

We had shoes, but if there was a hole in the sole we'd put cardboard in there to make it last a little while longer; then we'd put another piece in. I saw a lot of people without shoes even in the city.

We had a big yard and a big house. Grandfather grew grapes and he made wine. We had several peach, apple and cherry trees. He grew flowers: roses, iris, rhododendrons — just about everything you can think of. He didn't have a vegetable garden although he did have a few tomato plants. Dad brought home the vegetables.

When we wanted to go shopping we walked down the street to catch a subway into the city from the Ashmont station. For 5 cents it would take us all the way into downtown Boston. Filene's Department Store had a basement where there were really good bargains. They'd bring clothes down from upstairs. When I was first married, I could go into Nordstrom's and with $20 buy my kids shoes and little outfits.

Grandfather had a 1929 Buick. It had little shades in the back seat windows that I could pull down. Grandfather passed in 1934 or 1935 and we kept the car a few more years. After that my dad was able to buy his own.

In addition to the Ashmont Street house, Grandpa owned a three-decker house somewhere else and a beach cottage. He was able to keep all these through the Depression. After he died we sold the three-decker house, but a big fire wiped out the beach cottage.

I think my grandfather did so well financially and didn't lose his home or business because he was one of a lot of people who relied on family for money in those days rather than the banks. I think there was an uncle of Grandfather's that lent him money and I know he must have had money from the sale of his bake shop.

The Depression affected me later in that I always wanted my family close at home. My husband worked for the police department and sometimes he was out on call but he always made time to be home for dinner. We are very family-oriented and so is his family.

It is also very hard for me to throw things away. Younger people waste so much food nowadays — that's hard to see. They certainly live more carelessly than we ever did. They think they have to have things and that they have to have them now. They don't know how to save and wait.

Jean Weikle, California

Frank Ducklow and his bride, Jessie, are in the front, 1912.

Free meals at funerals

Tony Ducklow
Father born 1929 in Spring Valley, Wisconsin

As a child there are individuals whom you are not quite sure whether they really exist: Santa Claus, the Tooth Fairy or Paul Bunyan. For me, it was the repairman. I'd seen commercials and television programs about them but not once did a repairman ever visit my house.

The reason is that my dad tried to fix everything. It didn't matter what it was - a freezer, a television, a furnace, a record player or a washing machine. If there were any way it could be repaired, it would be. The amount of time and effort spent on the repair was irrelevant.

All because he was raised during the Great Depression.

My dad, Lyle Ducklow, was born in Spring Valley, Wisconsin the year the stock market crashed — 1929. He was raised during the Depression and it clearly

In this picture, my dad Lyle is the young boy in the front. He appears to be about 8-years-old so that would make this picture from about 1937. I'm pretty sure it was taken in Spring Valley, Wisconsin. His brothers from left to right are Fay, Gerald, Frank Jr. and Alois Ducklow.

had a lasting impact on his life. If one of us seven kids didn't want to eat a sandwich, his response was, "What's wrong with you? Why, when I was kid, the first time I ate store-bought sliced bread I thought it was cake!"

My grandfather is Frank Ducklow. He and my grandmother Jessie raised a family of seven kids as well, with my dad being the youngest. Grandfather owned Ducklow's Bar in Spring Valley and lost a sizeable amount of money when the banks failed. He never got over it. From the stories I've heard, his frugality made my dad look like a spendthrift.

During the Depression money was tight and food was scarce at times. One time a man from the community approached my grandfather and complimented him on what a fine little boy Lyle was. My grandfather thanked the man but asked why he had made that remark. Grandpa Frank was told that Lyle had impressed him with his manners and politeness at a recent funeral. Grandfather was puzzled because they hadn't attended any funerals recently.

It turned out that my dad and a buddy came up with a pretty creative way to fill their sometimes empty stomachs. When they saw that there was a funeral in town they put on their good clothes, paid their respects and got a free meal out of the deal.

Despite my grandfather's legendary thriftiness, this was a step too far even for him. He wasn't too happy to learn of my dad's unusual form of ingenuity. The inadvertent revelation resulted in a trip to the woodshed.

Although this is humorous, hearing stories like this about the effect the Depression had on the both of those men helped me better understand my father and grandfather's fierce desire to protect every hard-earned penny they had ever made.

Near the end of his life my grandfather stayed with us from time to time. There was hardly a day that went by where he didn't ask to be driven to the bank so that he could make sure that his money was still there.

If there was one phrase I dreaded hearing more than any other when I was growing up, it was, "Tony, come here and hold this for a second." That "second" more often than not turned out to be hours or sometimes even days. I can still see my dad hammering away at wheels he'd removed from our cars, trying to get flat tires off a rim. He'd be in the driveway whether it was 90 degrees or -10, with pry bars and crow bars, sweating or freezing for hours. He'd yell at

Frank with his parents and siblings right before the Depression hit in 1926. Frank is in the front middle.

or beg that tire to come off while I helped him. It drove me nuts. I wanted to scream, "Dad, they have a machine for that at the gas station! It'll take that stupid tire off and put a new one on in about two minutes — all for a quarter!"

But that would not have gone over well because I knew his mindset. *Why pay someone when you can do it yourself free?*

Whether I liked it or not, this philosophy evidently influenced me enough so that that when I got married my wife once remarked to my mother, "Tony just hates to spend money. You'd think he was raised during the Depression." My mom replied, "He was. It was called Lyle Ducklow."

Tony Ducklow, Wisconsin

Funeral Food During the Depression era

Even during hard times, traditions continue — such as feeding the grieving and well-wishers at a funeral or wake.

Little Lyle Ducklow of Spring Valley, Wisconsin was probably five or six-years-old when he and a friend got tired of feeling hungry. So they hatched a plan.

"It turned out that my dad and a buddy came up with a creative way to fill their sometimes empty stomachs when they saw there was a funeral in town. They put on their good clothes, paid their respects, and got a free meal out of the deal." ~Tony Ducklow, Wisconsin

Perhaps Lyle and his friend enjoyed this Pennsylvania Dutch staple:

Funeral Pie

Pastry for two-crust pie
1 cup raisins
2 cups water
1 1/2 cups sugar
4 T flour
1 egg, well beaten
2 T vinegar
1/4 teaspoon salt

Wash raisins and soak in cold water for three hours. Drain.

Meanwhile, mix together sugar and flour.

Combine 2 cups water, raisins, and the sugar and flour mixture, add salt, vinegar and egg. Mix thoroughly and cook over hot water in a double boiler for

15 minutes, stirring occasionally. Cool. Pour into pastry-lined pan. Cover with narrow strips of crisscrossed dough. Bake at 450 for 10 minutes. Reduce heat to 350 and bake 30 minutes.

Cool before cutting.

Chicory Coffee and Depression Cake

During the Depression people added chicory to ground coffee to stretch it out for a large gathering. Depression cake was made without eggs, milk or butter, and was popular in the 1930s. Raisins and apples were used to sweeten the cake and eliminated or reduced the need for sugar.

Depression Cake

- 2 cups brown sugar
- 2 cups hot water
- 4 T lard or bacon grease
- 1 pound raisins,
- 1 teaspoon salt (omit if using bacon grease)
- 2 teaspoons cinnamon,
- 1/2 teaspoon cloves, or ¼ teaspoons each ginger and nutmeg
- 3 teaspoons baking soda
- 3 scant cups of flour (a scant cup is minus one tablespoon)

Put brown sugar, hot water, lard or bacon grease, raisins, salt and seasonings into a large saucepan. Boil until lard is melted and well mixed, stirring occasionally. Allow to cool. When ready, add 2 teaspoons of baking soda dissolved in 1 tablespoon of lukewarm water. Add flour; mix well.

Bake in two greased loaf pans at 300 F for 1 3/4 hours

or until a broom straw inserted in the center comes out clean.

Morning funeral meant lunch later

Luncheons typically featured salads made of homegrown vegetables such as tomatoes, cucumbers, radishes and onions. Dandelion-leaf salad was common. Dressing was a simple combination of salt, pepper, oil and lemon. Chili, macaroni and cheese, and sliced hot dogs mixed with potatoes and onions served as a hearty main dish. Homemade Italian ice was a refreshing, inexpensive and easy-to-make summer dessert. Baked apples or pears were popular in winter.

Lemon Ice

1 cup sugar
4 cups boiling water

Dissolve the sugar in the water, cool.

Add 3/4 cup lemon juice and 1 Tablespoon grated rind if handy. Do not grate the pith, or it will be bitter. Freeze in a tray, stirring crystals occasionally lest the ice freeze rock solid. When frozen, scoop into little cups.

Government gets involved: "Hard-Luck Pot-Lucks"

The U.S. Department of Agriculture officials and those from other federal aid agencies encouraged people to attend large gatherings, such as funerals, in potluck-style to reduce costs. This food was served, then leftovers used by the family in the days following the funeral.

Bean casseroles were popular at large gatherings during the Depression because they were filling and went a long way. Hard times called for preparing simpler recipes, substituting traditional ingredients with economical ones, using home-grown vegetables, and serving bread or pasta to stretch a meal.

Casseroles and other one-dish meals such as soups and stews also became staple dinners during the Depression and offered a way to use leftovers — if there were any. Because these dishes only needed one pot for preparation and cooking they were a good way to feed a large crowd. Stews were made with meat ends and homegrown vegetables. Soups could be stretched out over a few meals by adding noodles, potatoes and more vegetables.

Depression Casserole

1 1/2 lbs. ground beef
2 cups kidney beans
5 sliced, raw potatoes
3 sliced, raw onions
1 can tomato soup
Salt, pepper and garlic powder

Brown ground beef and flavor with salt, pepper and garlic powder. In a casserole pan, layer kidney beans, potatoes, onion, and top with meat. Cover with tomato soup. Repeat with a second layer in same order. Cover and bake at 375 degrees for about 1 1/2 hours. Uncover during the last 15 minutes of baking. (May need to add small amount of water if too dry.)

Only the wealthy used hospitals

Susan Elfers-Warren
Grandfather born 1895 in Reading, Ohio
Grandmother born 1896 in Reading, Ohio

My grandparents, John Wilhelm Elfers, Sr. and his wife, Ursula (Weis) Elfers, moved into a duplex on Jefferson Ave in Reading, Ohio in 1918 — shortly after their marriage and before they started their large family.

Grandpa John was born in Reading, Ohio in 1895. His father, John William Elfers, immigrated from the Netherlands. Grandma Ursula Marie was born in Reading also, in 1896. Her parents, Frank Weis and Mary Ann Merkle, came from Germany. When I was little Grandma cursed at me in German when I misbehaved. I always laughed because it sounded funny.

Grandpa John was employed at Procter and Gamble in Cincinnati at age 14. Amazingly, he kept this job throughout the Depression. He worked there for 50 years and retired at age 64. They had nine children and raised them all in that duplex on Jefferson Avenue: Mary Lee born in 1919, Ralph (Whitey) in 1921, Louis 1922, Jack (Chick) 1924 [my dad], Pauline 1926, William (Bill) 1929, Jean 1932, and twins Lorraine and Laverne 1933.

All nine Elfers children were born at home — only the wealthy used hospitals at that time. My Grandma had three babies sleeping in one crib because they couldn't afford a bed or crib for each child. When the twins Lorraine and Laverne were born, Laverne was very blue. The doctor turned the kitchen oven on low and placed Laverne in a roasting pan then set her in the oven to warm her up.

Grandfather played the piano and organ. He left his job at Proctor and Gable for a short time before those lean years and pursued the hope of making a living as a musician. He gave lessons, played in a band and also performed for silent movies in theaters before the era of talking movies. But he didn't make enough money so he went back to his job at P&G.

Grandfather made each of his four boys learn to play an instrument in order to help feed their 11-member family. Grandpa formed a band and named them The Cotton Tops because all the boys had blonde hair. The Cotton Tops played in the German beer gardens in Reading and surrounding communities and also at wedding receptions and other occasions. At age nine, my father was given a set of drums because Grandpa needed a percussionist. My dad took the bus every week to downtown Cincinnati for drum lessons from a Jewish man who played in the Cincinnati Symphony. Lessons were 50 cents for 30 minutes. That was a lot of money during the Depression.

Grandma did not work outside the home. But as the

The Cotton Tops - 1934

children grew, they contributed to the family income when they weren't in school. The oldest, Mary Lee, quit school in the 8th grade to help care for the family. Clothing was handed down from child to child. All the children attended Saints Peter and Paul Catholic School through the 8th grade then went on to high school. The two oldest boys attended Roger Bacon High School, but my dad and the rest of the younger children attended Reading High School because tuition was an extra $5 per child to attend Roger Bacon.

As difficult as life was during those years, my dad and his siblings found ways to have fun. One story in particular is one of his favorites: he and some neighborhood boys hiked up to West Chester to swim in a pond. No one could afford bathing suits so the boys all swam nude. The pond

Ursula and Johnny

was near railroad tracks. Whenever a passenger train went by, the boys would stand up and "shoot the moon" to the passengers and laugh at their horrified expressions.

It seems the Depression era forged peace between the Germans in Reading and the Irish in nearby Lockland, too. Reading had a saloon or tavern on nearly every corner. Every night the Irish would visit, then scuffle with the Germans in the street after imbibing too many beers. At some point a truce was called and they erected a sign over the bridge that spanned Mill Creek between the towns that read, "Reading-Lockland, Where Friends Meet." The sign stayed until 1994 when the bridge was remodeled.

After the Japanese bombed Pearl Harbor, my dad's brother Louis was drafted to the Navy, Ralph to the Air Force, and then in 1943 Dad went to the Army and was given a letter of referral by his Jewish drum instructor to join the Army Military Band, Dixie Division. He was sent to perform in the South Pacific.

My dad married my mom, Dois *[sic]* Loraine Berry on April 30, 1949 at Saints Peter and Paul Catholic Church in Reading. They moved into the upstairs apartment at my grandparents' place until they could afford their own home. They raised four children: Janis, John, Julie and me.

Dad worked at Richardson-Merrell 10 hours per day, five days per week and four hours on Saturdays. He'd come home, take a nap and play in his band every Saturday night. He also played for wedding receptions and anniversary parties. After Mass on Sundays he played softball with a team from the American Legion Post 69 — losers had to buy beer. Dad's band money paid for our two-week vacation every summer at Indian Lake when the rest of the Elfers clan rented cabins there. In later years Mom worked at AAA in Cincinnati and wrote TripTiks.

Being Dutch, my dad passed on his tightness on spending money and both of my parents taught us the value of hard work. But the biggest thing that our parents passed on to us from growing up during the Depression was a sense of humor. Our family loves to laugh, joke and tease, but all in playful fun, never putting someone else down. Humor helped deal with the hardships of that time. Our Catholic faith played a big part too, and the sense of family. We are a large family — I have 25 cousins and their spouses. We grew up together, share the same heritage and are still very close.

Susan Elfers-Warren, Ohio

Laughter kept worry away

Black and white photographs from the Depression era show suffering etched on faces from careworn farmers to mothers and skinny children dressed in rags.

Despite the hardships Americans faced, they found ways to keep their spirits up and distract themselves. Entertainment was one way to leave behind worries about crops, weather and money.

The cost to attend a "new" talkie movie was roughly 10 cents; for an hour or so people escaped their personal adversities with a peek into high-society life, musicals and gangster movies. Shirley Temple overcame trouble with her cheery disposition, audiences were dazzled by Disney's first full-length animated movie, *Snow White*, and those who lost their jobs related to *My Man Godfrey* – a man who lost his fortune in the stock market crash and became a butler for a rich family, and saved them from ruin.

Radio was also popular – and free after the initial purchase -- offering programs from sermons to sports to mysteries and soap operas. President Roosevelt endeared himself to Americans with his *Fireside Chats*, and family time at the end of the day consisted of sitting around the radio for a variety of programs.

In the 1930s, big bands, jazz and swing music were popular, with Duke Ellington, Benny Goodman and Glenn Miller keeping people moving -- even on homemade, portable dance floors.

"Grandfather made each of his boys learn to play an instrument in order to help feed their 11-member family. Grandpa formed a band and named them the Cotton Tops because all the boys had blonde hair… [they]

Movie theatre night in Ohio circa 1938. Library of Congress

played in the German beer bars in Reading and surrounding communities and also at wedding receptions and other occasions." ~ Susan Elfers Warren, Ohio

Neighbors played cards and other games. Church socials and school programs were popular. Inexpensive dates at soda fountains and local dances gave young people a chance to spend time with friends. Action comics were popular with the adventures of Superman, Flash Gordon and detective Dick Tracy.

"People here are funny. They work so hard at living they forget how to live." ~ Mr. Deeds Goes to Town (1936)

Families on the move often covered the backs of trucks and wagons with canvas to protect all their worldly goods inside.

Franklin D. Roosevelt Presidential Library & Museum

What you face is just a challenge

E.R. Kingsbury II

Father born 1915 on the plains of Oklahoma

My dad, Ray Kingsbury, was born October 27, 1915 in the back of a horse-drawn wagon in the middle of "nowhere" Oklahoma but close to Cousa. His parents were camp followers who provided a soup kitchen while the railroads were built from Missouri into Oklahoma. Dad was born in the kitchen of that wagon on the side of a hill facing the railroad construction.

When Dad was eight or nine-years-old, his parents and three sisters settled down in Houston. By the time the Great Depression came around he was barely a teenager living on the west side of Houston near a bayou where he liked to swim.

One of his contributions to family life before and after school during the Depression was to milk the family's only Holstein and deliver milk to neighbors in either a cart or shoulder box. At that time, Houston was just a sleepy cow town that was just getting into the "oil" thing.

His dad, Edward Robinson Kingsbury, hailed from northwest Kansas and held several jobs to get the family through. A house painter by trade, Edward painted mostly businesses and did anything else he could find. Dad's mom, Ruby Culbertson Kingsbury, was a seamstress and made clothes for all the family and anyone else who could pay.

Ray Kingsbury and Dorothy Jean Ziegler on their wedding day, 1942.

My dad also helped out by working with his dad as a house painter. It seemed that the only institutions that could afford to have their buildings painted in Houston were banks and whorehouses. My teenage dad got an early education as to where money was made and where it was spent in his town.

They were painting a house one day and he told his dad that he wanted to go to college. He didn't know what he wanted to study — he'd figure that out once he got there.

His dad, a contemplative man, simply said, "Go ahead, but clean up your paintbrush first."

So at 17, my dad packed up his few clothes and left for the University of Texas, Austin. He got to Austin and into school and worked three jobs: parking cars, kitchen helper, and waiter in a sorority house — breakfast, lunch and dinner. He especially loved that job.

But Dad never graduated. He had to quit during his second year in 1931 or 1932 when his dad, mom, and sisters Estelle and Julia were in a bad car accident. Somehow they'd gone off the side of the road and hit a tree — they were all seriously injured, but mostly his dad and Julia. They were hospitalized for quite some time and subsequently without his dad's or mom's regular income.

So my dad came home from college and did whatever he could. He delivered milk, parked cars for rich people at the hotels in Houston and took up his father's business of house painting along with odd jobs. His older sister Jeanette quit her job in Port Arthur to come home and help the family, too. It was a full year before they really recovered.

Shortly after that, somewhere between 1934-1940, Dad's parents divorced and went their separate ways. By 1941, Dad was working in the Hamilton-Standard propeller plant in Pittsburgh, Pennsylvania, and Jeanette worked nearby. She was a smart cookie who graduated from high school in Houston at age 15. She made pretty good money and got her hair done weekly at a beauty salon where Dorothy Jean Zeigler of Zellenople worked alongside her sister. Jeanette played matchmaker, and Dorothy and Dad married in 1942 the day after he graduated from the US Army Air Corps Flight School in San Angelo, Texas. (In an aside, he flew nearly every airplane the AAC and

Kingsbury children from left, Julia, Ray and Jeanette in 1916.

USAF had in his 26-year career — ending by flying the largest bomber ever flown — the B-52.)

The Depression generation, "The Greatest Generation," was dealt many bad hands: the Depression, World War II, and other obstacles. One of my proudest moments in life was when Dad told me and my older sister, Betty, that he was proud of both of us for never giving up on anything.

That may be the one thing that the Depression taught him and his generation — that quitting is not an option — what you face is just a challenge. He taught me many things: honor, tell the truth, never give up, how to fix anything, always keep the safety on with my rifle, how to love and give love to a woman, how to fly an airplane and that war and flying have many hours of sheer boredom combined with seconds of stark terror — I was a helicopter pilot in Vietnam.

I have nothing but love, respect and gratitude for being the son of two of the most wonderful, loving parents a kid could ever have. What a guy! What a dad! What a hero he was to me.

Erdie Ray Kingsbury II, Florida

The humble hot dog

The man most responsible for popularizing the hot dog in the United States is Nathan Handwerker, a Jewish immigrant from Poland. In 1916 he worked at a hot dog stand at Coney Island and made a whopping $11 a week slicing buns.

The hardworking Handwerker lived entirely on hot dogs for a year until he'd saved $300 to start his own stand using his wife's recipe. A savvy businessman, Handwerker charged only 5 cents apiece to his former boss's 10 cents for each dog. Of course, customers flocked, his competitor went out of business, and Nathan's Famous was born.

By the Depression era Nathan's hot dogs were consumed throughout the United States. In fact, when President Franklin Roosevelt and First Lady Eleanor hosted England's King George VI and Queen Mary at a picnic in Hyde Park in 1939, Mrs. Roosevelt added grilled hot dogs to the menu. Despite the press's dubious predictions, the King enjoyed them so much he asked for seconds.

Nathan's popularity reached to Al Capone, Eddie Cantor, Jimmy Durante and Cary Grant, who made special visits to his New York establishment. Later, Roosevelt had Nathan's hot dogs sent to Yalta in February 1945 when he met with Winston Churchill and Joseph Stalin.

In Ohio in 1932 regular wieners were 8 cents per pound — a bit more affordable for a Depression era budget.

Poor Man's Meal

4 T oil
3 large potatoes, peeled and cubed
1 large onion, diced
Water as needed
4 hot dogs, sliced into rounds
3 T ketchup

Poor the oil into a frying pan and place over medium heat. Add potatoes and onions. Stir occasionally, adding a little water until the potatoes are browned to keep them from sticking to the pan. When the potatoes are crisp and golden brown on all sides, add the hot dogs and let simmer with potatoes and a little more water for about 5 minutes or until they begin to curl. Add ketchup and turn off the heat. Let stand 5 - 10 minutes. Serve immediately.

Hot Dog, Potato and Onion Casserole

1 package hot dogs
1 large onion
6 or 7 potatoes
2 cans tomato soup
1 cup milk

In large casserole dish make two layers of sliced potatoes, onions, hot dogs. Mix soup and milk, pour over mixture. Bake at 350 about 1 hour or until potatoes are done.

Father had a glum look

Norman S. Reed

Born 1923 in Newton Upper Falls, Massachusetts

I was born in Newton Upper Falls, Massachusetts on July 18, 1923. My parents, Warren and Marjorie May Reed, my older brother Warren and two sisters Priscilla and Lillian, lived in a few different towns in our early years before deciding to make our home in Stoneham, Massachusetts.

I recall that it was a sunny day in 1928 when we left 72 Clewley Road in West Medford for 46 Maple Street in Stoneham. I was five-years-old. A friend of my father's who worked with him at Rever Sugar Refinery in Charlestown drove all of us to Stoneham in some kind of van or large automobile with a few sticks of furniture wedged in amongst us.

When we arrived at the little gray-shingled bungalow on the corner of Maple and Ledge, I noticed the largest pine tree that I'd ever seen just to the right of the wide front steps in our yard. I raced up a narrow pathway leading off the street that had been made through a stone wall that had once encompassed the Cowdrey Estate years before.

I swung open an old screen door that was in disrepair and entered the small back porch in front of the kitchen door. I waited impatiently for my father to come and unlock it. When we were finally all inside, we hurried about choosing our bedrooms. I ended up with the attic to myself, surrounded by ancient suitcases and rusty old trunks that had been handed down to my parents from my grandparents over the years or bought at secondhand shops. As we settled in, some pieces of our furniture ended up at the large thrift shop facing Main Street next to what we decided was the best bakery in Stoneham — Treacy's Bakery.

As I opened the door that led to the attic, I spied an old piece of string hanging down from a bare light bulb high above the staircase. I pulled it and the staircase came down. I made my way upstairs and noticed that the unfinished floor had planks missing from where it butted up along the edge of the roof, and that there were old dingy rugs on the floor. My iron bed was put in and faced one of the windows where I could look out over the street.

Without a slightest doubt, the single most important impression made upon me in the earliest years of my youth was the value of what we refer to today as security. Money was a scarce commodity at that time, and any extra dollar that could be made in any way could be stretched a long way.

Employment was hard to come by. But usually something that wasn't very appealing could be found for a certain length of time, such as odd jobs. To a young boy, the only way that I could come by a bit of change was to cut lawns in the summer and shovel snow in the winter.

At one time I had a paper route but getting up at such an early hour to be at Schaefer's Store where they sorted the bundles was too much for me. At that tender age I was not an early bird! Added to this was the fact that I inherited the route from a boy just after Christmas and the weather at that hour of the morning was more than I could bear. The papers sold for 3 cents. The price had just gone up 1 cent and I made 2 cents to a nickel per customer per week. I had no quarrel with the profit; it was that early rising and cold weather that made me reluctantly leave my first job.

Sometime in the early 1930s when I came home from school I heard mumbling as I entered through the screen door leading to the porch. My father had a glum look and his eyes looked like he'd been weeping. I was just happy to be home and asked what had been going on. My mother said that my father's salary had been cut from $50 a week to $38.

In those formative years before my teens, especially after my father's salary had been cut, I came to realize that these were far from prosperous times. An uneasy feeling came over me, and I blurted out to my father as he sat by the back door, "Don't feel bad, Dad. I know that we are poor." He looked at me as if momentarily stunned, half-embarrassed, and I suddenly realized what a terrible blow I had struck him. I hadn't meant to hurt his feelings, but that was exactly what I had managed to do and I could have bitten off my tongue at that moment.

From that day forward, life took on a different meaning and I made a silent vow that anything that came my way would be utilized to the best advantage.

My father started doing odd jobs in Winchester. One

day he asked me if I would like to take the bus with him to help with a lawn and to change storm windows and put up screens on a house. At one house where he had regular work there were small thorn bushes around part of the property that slanted down to the sidewalk. It was hard work with my bare hands reaching in to pull out rotted leaves and getting stuck with little barbs.

At my young age, raking lawns wasn't as difficult as trying to clean panes of glass in windows and trying to hold storm windows in place long enough for my father to get two screws lined up in the screw eyes so that I could relax my grip. With him on the stepladder and me on the ground trying to brace that window between the ladder and the side of the house while a cold, bitter wind blew and my fingers numbing, it wasn't the easiest job. But for 60 cents an hour he didn't complain.

As I got older I could take the bus by myself to cut the lawn and rake leaves and occasionally clean someone's cellar. My mother sometimes made extra money by babysitting for one of the prominent Boston dentists.

Sometimes when I went with my dad, I brought my fishing tackle to use at Wedge Pond. Luckily for us I was a good fisherman. I caught bluegills, crappies, pickerel and other types of pan-fish and brought them home for meals. They were quickly devoured. This went on for several years until, with occasional raises in pay, it became less and less of a chore.

Those various jobs that my father tackled with zest bordered on desperation. What can be said of raking a lawn, putting up storm windows or cleaning a dusty cellar? It was just a monotonous number of steps until the job was completed and two or three extra dollars found their way into his pocket.

But that extra income during those lean years served a useful purpose in many ways, such as food on the table, or another sorely needed pair of shoes for one of the children while he went about his business with strips of cardboard in his own shoes. We didn't forge ahead but we were able to hold on until better days came our way.

Years have passed by, but those times are crystal clear as if it was yesterday. I can still remember quite vividly, gazing out of the attic window overlooking Maple Street or from the front porch, seeing people making their way to the Stoneham Theatre for the double-feature plus the serial thriller such as *Flash Gordon* and other coming attractions. It was considered a good deal for 15 cents. Haircuts were 25 cents. The best tasting bread at Treacy's was 12 cents per loaf and hamburger at McDonough's was 35 cents for 2 pounds, or 3 pounds for 50 cents. Fish-haddock was 5 cents per pound, or 19 cents if you bought 4 pounds. Sometimes we walked down Park Street to the corner of Maple to take a 20-minute bus ride to a drug store in Winchester Square for a dip of ice cream sprinkled with chocolate jimmies for a dime.

They were difficult times but we persevered. They were happy days because we were a loving family.

Norman S. Reed, Martha's Vineyard, Massachusetts
Includes excerpts from "Forty-Six Maple Street"
by Norman S. Reed, with permission

Fishing for food

Those who were fortunate enough to live near lakes, rivers, ponds and other bodies of water supplemented diets with a variety of fish. Sometimes a license was required, but the cost was often prohibitive, so poaching -- not the cooking process – was rampant.

Clara Wanner Lacy's family moved from North Dakota to Portland, Oregon. Along the way, her father provided their evening meal from streams: *"One time in Montana just past Billings we camped by a river. My sisters and I were playing by the woods and heard Mama honking the horn. A game warden was there and Mama was trying to warn Daddy, who was fishing. Now, he didn't have a license for fishing and he couldn't get his rod and reel put away fast enough. They were going to take him to jail, but he asked, 'What are you going to do with my family?' They confiscated his fishing gear instead… so there was no fish for dinner that night."*

As an adolescent, Norman S. Reed of Massachusetts helped provide food on the table for his family: *"Sometimes when I went [to work] with my dad, I brought my fishing tackle to use at Wedge Pond. Luckily for us I was a good fisherman. I caught bluegills, crappies, pickerel and other types of pan-fish and brought them home for meals. They were quickly devoured."*

Pan-fried bluegill

2 lbs. dressed and filleted bluegill
1 1/2 tsp. salt
Dash pepper
1/4 c. milk
1/2 c. flour

1/4 c. cornmeal
Vegetable oil for frying

Clean fresh-caught fish, then fillet. Add salt and pepper to milk. Mix flour and cornmeal. Dip fish fillets into milk mix and roll in flour mixture. Fry in hot oil at moderate heat for 4 to 5 minutes or until golden brown on one side.

Turn carefully and fry 4 to 5 minutes longer - or until other side is golden brown and fish flakes easily when tested with a fork. Drain on paper.

Pan-fried pickerel (pike) steaks

Wash pickerel steaks thoroughly under cold running water.

Place pickerel in salt water and let soak for 10-15 minutes.

Rinse well under cold running water, drain well.

Melt butter in a frying pan, add onions and fry until they begin to brown.

Push cooked onions to the edge of the pan and place pickerel steaks in the center.

Fry the steaks for 2-3 minutes on each side, until the flesh starts to come away from the bone.

Finally add lemon juice, season generously and serve immediately.

Charles Asa Stauffer using his invention, the hydrospear.

Everyone was thin; everyone had crooked teeth

Lynn Frank

Father born 1924 in Honey Brook, Pennsylvania

My father, Dr. Charles L. Hosler, Professor Emeritus of Meteorology, Senior Vice President for Research, and Dean of the Graduate School Emeritus for Pennsylvania State University, lives in State College, Pennsylvania. A meteorology scholarship there bears his name.

As a child of the Depression era, he's come a long way.

Dad was born June 3, 1924 in Honey Brook, Pennsylvania to Charles L. Hosler Sr., and Miriam Deichley Stauffer. Even at age 91, Dad's mind is remarkable and his memory is impeccable. I could sit for days just

Miriam and Charles L. Hosler

listening to stories about his life during the Depression and WWII eras. He and his parents struggled hard then.

Before the Depression his dad, mother's brother Alfred, and his mother's father went into business together. They owned a machine shop and built or repaired whatever people needed them to, including fire escapes, farm machinery, and did welding projects.

But during the Depression, farmers didn't have money for much of the work they were doing, so the business floundered. My father and his parents worked a variety of jobs to make ends meet. Grandfather worked for farmers and was paid with potatoes. He did odd jobs on farms. He helped the town undertaker bleed corpses, sold Fuller Brushes, installed electricity and running water for those who didn't have any, fixed windmills that charged the batteries for electricity, and various plumbing including pump installations. At a young age my dad helped bring in income by digging ditches, holding pipe wrenches and whatever else he could do to help his dad. My grandmother sold Avon, raised flowers, made cookies to sell and worked in dress factories.

It is interesting to note that President Roosevelt had a Works Project Administration in place where people were paid to "lean on shovels." But they wouldn't employ anyone who wasn't a registered Democrat so that left my grandfather — and many others — out. Workers were paid 25 cents per hour to build things no one needed in order to put people to work. They built a tennis court in my dad's town but there were no racquets to play with.

The 1920s and 1930s were indeed depressing. Dad's parents argued a lot. His mom's brother Uncle Alfred was a crook. Money disappeared. Alfred and his mother would take cash out of the money drawer in the machine shop. Alfred also ran up big debts through the business by paying thousands of dollars for figure-skating lessons for his daughter — Sonia Henning was making a big splash as a figure-skater at that time.

Because Alfred was a partner in the business with my grandparents, the business went bankrupt because of his improprieties. My grandfather had to mortgage the house to pay the debts and ended up losing the house to the bank. However, a kind woman bought the house and rented it back to them for $25 per month. He also had stock in a local savings and loan that went belly-up.

There were only two people in my dad's hometown of Honey Brook who had money. Everyone else was thin, everyone had crooked teeth and everyone wore the same clothes for years on end. My dad had one pair of pants. His mom unraveled leftover WWI socks to knit a sweater for him, and she also made his one shirt.

When Dad was seven or eight-years-old, he gathered dandelions and watercress from a nearby stream to sell to neighbors for 5 cents a basket. The only time they had meat was every couple of weeks when an aunt would get an old hen that couldn't lay eggs from a local Amish farm and bring it home to share.

Cereal was out of the question. Breakfast usually consisted of a broken-up loaf of bread with sugar and milk on it. Through a relative they had credit with a bread company, so they got bread for 5 cents a loaf.

The family grew their own potatoes and tomatoes. After harvest-time the family picked up soybeans and tomatoes that got left behind in fields. Dad also went to local carnival grounds to hunt for dropped Popsicle sticks that had the word FREE on them so that he could get a free Popsicle.

During the Depression, farmers couldn't afford to farm because the market prices were so low. President Roosevelt started a program to destroy food. While people starved, farmers were killing and burying cattle and pigs and pouring milk on the ground.

Other strange memories come to mind: my dad's house was heated with wood or coal. Every night at 10, an unknown man from the local Mafia knocked on the door and sold them a truckload of coal for a few dollars. Garment factories from New York came to Honey Brook to set up sewing machines and pay people a "learners" rate of 15 cents per hour to hem skirts, repair buttons and the like with the understanding that after a determined period they would get a 10 cent per hour raise to 25 cents an hour. But the night before the rate increase was to take effect, the

Charles Hosler Sr. and Miriam, with their three children, Barbara (left), Suzanne (right), and Lynn.

machines were pulled out and taken to a different town to avoid paying the increase.

After awhile things started looking up. In 1938 Pennsylvania elected Republican Governor Arthur James. After that, my father's dad got jobs: he worked as a road inspector and determined where to put white lines in the road, he collected overdue taxes in Harrisburg for the state, was an inspector at a Luken Steel plant in Coatsville to inspect plates used to build battleships, and he worked in offices in Lancaster and in Reading where they made parachutes.

In high school, my dad worked summers on Mennonite farms. At 16 he got a driver's license. After school he picked mushrooms to sell to restaurants. During his last high school summer he was put in charge of 16 employees who ran a quarry in Downington. He worked 10 hours every day, six days a week for 25 cents an hour. During the Depression and the beginning of WWII, there were no real career choices or counselors. There were no bugle lessons, gym classes or after-school activities. But Dad was never envious. Everyone was poor.

Dad joined the Navy in November 1942 and got out in 1946. He went on to study Meteorology at Penn State University. He worked hard to become an important part of the Earth and Mineral Sciences department at PSU and beyond. He rose from tough circumstances and poverty to become an important and popular administrator at Penn State: from Professor to Dean to Vice President of Research to Provost, as well as a national and worldwide consultant.

In those days, every man, woman and child had to contribute — everyone was a wage earner. There weren't many choices. People simply did what was possible and within reach to get things done. Perhaps the most poignant memory about those times is how much responsibility one had at a very young age and how it shaped and molded people into the strong, intelligent, diligent and accomplished generation they became.

Lynn Frank, Pennsylvania

Living off the wild land

Depending upon the region, families who lived on farms mostly fared better than city-dwellers during the Great Depression when it came to providing food for their loved ones.

Throughout this book, several contributors refer to eating dandelions plucked fresh out of their yards and put into a salad. They remember foraging in wooded areas, community parks and their own lawns for ways to stretch a meal.

"When Dad was seven or eight-years-old, he gathered dandelions and watercress from a nearby stream to sell to neighbors for 5 cents a basket." ~ Lynn Frank, Pennsylvania

Dandelion Salad

Dig up dandelions and discard flowers, roots and dead leaves. Soak in clean water and rinse three times. Repeat twice more if necessary. Once they are clean, let them dry. Arrange leaves in bowl and pour lemon juice and olive oil over, sprinkle with a little salt. Mix up the salad with a spoon or your hands.

"Daddy gleaned watercress, sassafrass root, black walnuts and horseradish from the woods at the end of town...Mom made the best salad out of that watercress combined with the dandelion greens that grew in our yard." ~ Nina Stitt Gilfert, Florida

Watercress

A member of the mustard family, watercress is eaten raw in salads or as a cooked green. It is a common water plant found in shallow running water where it forms dense mats. Stems grow 4 to 10 inches high and have small oval leaves. Watercress is rich in calcium, beta carotene and iron, and vitamins C, B1, B2 and E. An added benefit is that watercress is used to treat coughs, gout and arthritis. It's a diuretic, so it helps to relieve fluid retention.

Pokeweed

Pokeweed: Phytolacca americana, appearance of the full herbaceous perennial plant, late in annual season, showing stems, leaves green and red, and flower/fruit structures (dark masses in the leaf clusters). Creative Commons

Pokeweed grows in a variety of soils and in open places — in fields, along roadsides and in the woods. The plants are poisonous after purple berries form, but in the springtime when the plants are short, the large, pointy leaves are safe to eat and great in salad, or cooked up like collards, spinach or turnip greens. The taste is similar to spinach and in some parts of the country is referred to as wild spinach.

"My parents' survival skills kept us alive by foraging on wild plants and nuts, eating pokeweed and dandelions for greens and hunting wild game and fish for meat."

~ Juanita Reid, Ohio

Moonshine whiskey for food money

Ginger (Gill) Brown

Father born 1891 in Dallas County, Arkansas

My dad, James Ervin Gill, was born November 14, 1891 in Dallas County, Arkansas. He married his first wife, Maggie Speer, in 1916 and had seven children. The early 1900s and the Depression years were hard for them. Dad moved his family in with his in-laws to help run their 131-acre land grant farm in Ramsey, Arkansas about eight miles from Bucksnort. Yes. Bucksnort.

After Dad and his family moved in, the log house had to be expanded to accommodate all the kids. The house had a dog-trot separating the bedrooms from the other living quarters. Each bedroom had a fireplace. The living room had two beds also. Did I mention there were lots of kids? All of the beds had rope bottoms to support mattresses.

My dad was quite talented at making furniture and working with wood. He made the dining room table and benches from rough-cut pine to accommodate the large family, and hickory-bottomed chairs that he fashioned by cutting the bark off hickory trees, cutting them into strips and weaving the strips back and forth to make the bottoms strong.

As he expanded the log house, he made the floors of tongue-and-groove 1 x 4 pine. The walls were 1 x 6 boards with canvas nailed over them and then wallpapered. The kitchen had a Home Comfort cook stove with a 10-gallon reservoir and two warming doors. There was also a pie safe and flour bin.

In later years, Dad had the kids help roof the house. He cut his own shingles using a splitting maul and a froe — an L-shaped tool used to cleave wood and split it along the grain — to shave Cyprus shingles to the size needed. Any left over was used for the barn.

Education was important, so the children went to school. The only school nearby in the 1920s was in Princeton, nine miles away. It was a converted old church house with a partition down the middle; four grades were on each side of the partition. Wood heaters kept the building warm; some days it was so cold that the smaller kids would be crying by the time they got to school. The bigger boys drew drinking water from a deep well. Only one dipper was used for the entire school. All the kids brought their lunches with them, which usually consisted of a biscuit and a piece of ham wrapped in newspaper.

A few years later, a brick schoolhouse was built for all 12 grades. It had a Delco Generator for electricity. The only bathroom was an outhouse and it had to be limed to keep the smell down. The new school had a lunchroom and hot lunches were 25 cents. Dad didn't have lunch money to spare for all of his children, so they took a sack of potatoes to eat. By the time the children got home from school, usually around 5:30-6:00 p.m., they felt starved. Their after-school snack was cornbread and onion before they did their chores. After supper, homework was done by the light of a coal oil lamp.

Washday wasn't easy. Water was drawn from the deep well and put into the wash pot. Once the water boiled, the clothes were put in and homemade lye soap was used to clean the clothes. The clothes were dipped into and out of the hot water with a big stick and carried to a rubbing board. The clothes were rinsed twice in large washtubs and then hung on a clothesline. Sometimes the clothes were rinsed in starch water for ironing later. An old, flat-iron that was heated on the wood stove pressed the clothes for church.

In 1933, Dad's first wife was killed in an accident. The oldest child, Maggie, was 14. From then on, all the kids worked from sunup until sundown when not in school, and on Sundays. In 1936, Dad remarried Idella O'Mary and had six more children. I am the youngest.

Because times were hard, Dad made and sold moonshine whiskey so that he could feed his family. The whiskey was stored in gallon jugs under the chicken house. Sometimes the children were scared because they feared Dad would be caught by the revenuers.

Food wasn't fancy. On special occasions there was dessert: usually teacakes, plain cakes, and Dad's favorite molasses cookies. We had plenty of pork because Dad had wild hogs. Sorghum was grown to make our own molasses. If the sweet potato crop was good, Dad made sweet potato biscuits. He allowed us to use plenty of butter from the ole Guernsey cow's milk because we churned our own milk to make butter. Boy was that a treat. Once, one of the older boys went to town with our oldest sister. They stayed in town for lunch and he got a Coke and a hamburger for 10 cents. He told everyone it was too much money, but it was the best food he had ever eaten.

We had a large garden and vegetables were plentiful. Dad used a turning plow to break up the dirt and a Georgia Stock (a plow beam with handles) to lay out the garden rows. Fertilizer came from the chicken house or barnyard, and sand was carted in with a shovel. After summer, the turnips were left in the field and covered with straw to keep from freezing. After all the vegetables that we were going to use were gathered, we left some on the vine to dry for seed for the next year. We did the same thing with watermelons, cantaloupes, and pumpkins.

In 1935, Dad leased two farms to grow more cotton. It was 5 cents per lb., or about $425 per bale. He needed help working the cotton because the kids couldn't pick fast enough. The farm produced about five bales of cotton per year if the boll weevils didn't cause too much harm. Dad used flour sacks to spread cotton poison over the rows of cotton and to cover his and the horses' noses so they wouldn't breathe it.

Once the crop came in we could usually talk Dad into going to the creek to cool off. We'd pile into the wagon with fishing poles cut from cane, and a coffee can with red wigglers. We also brought along a few quilts to nap on if the mosquitoes didn't eat us alive. Sometimes we looked like we had measles we had so many bites. But if any fish were caught, they were cooked on the creek bank.

The local general store allowed Dad credit for necessities until his crops produced. We mostly got sugar, coffee, soap and kerosene. Kerosene was 12 cents per gallon. When the bill was paid and there was enough left over, all of us kids got haircuts for 10 cents each. The boys got a new pair of brogans (a heavy, ankle-high shoe or boot), two pairs of overalls, two union suits (one-piece long underwear), two shirts and a warm coat. The girls got new shoes, two new dresses and a coat. They were mail-ordered from the Sears and Roebuck catalogue.

After harvest, the weather turned cold and it was hog-killing time. Neighbors gathered and all the men hunted until they had six to eight hogs to share. Water was heated in the wash pot and when it was hot enough, put into big, 55-gallon barrels that were put into the ground at a 25-degree angle. The dead hogs were dipped in the hot water; then the kids scraped all the hair off. After that, the hogs were hung by their hind legs on a gamble stick so they could be drained and cleaned. All parts except the entrails were saved. Even the bladders were used for fun for the kids; a cane stick was used to fill the bladders with air so they could play ball when chores were done.

Lard from the hogs was cooked out in the wash pot and stored in crocks in the cellar. All the hams, shoulders and pork loin and chops were cured with burning hickory chips in the smokehouse. The kids were responsible for keeping the fire going and keeping the sugar cure and salt on the meat. The hogs' heads were used for souse (pickling) and hogshead cheese. The smoking took about a month. Afterward, the shoulders and hams were hung with bear grass to keep the nails from rusting from the salt. The shoulders, hams, sausage and bacon were hung in cloth sacks to prevent flies from getting to the meat and laying eggs. It was cold enough, so no refrigeration was needed. The carcasses hung in the smokehouse until ready for use. Red-eye gravy was made once the hams were cured, and served with homemade biscuits and sorghum molasses.

For fun, the community held square dances. Each family brought potluck and a good time was had by all. A "log rolling" event to build a cabin or a barn called for all friends, relatives and neighbors' help. Each family brought their own team of horses, wagons, axes, saws and tools. They helped clear the land of trees, brush and rocks. Women brought food and cooked over campfires. It took several days to build and finish a cabin.

Christmas was special, although there wasn't much money. A big hoop of cheese and a surprise coconut was a treat. To this day, I buy a coconut each Christmas to remind myself how poor my family was during that time and hope to never be that poor again. But at the time we did not know we were that poor. Everyone had a pretty hard time during those years.

Ginger Brown, Louisiana

Lunches and snacks were sandwiches and garden fare

Packed into metal lunch pails, sandwiches made with thick slices of homemade bread were wrapped in waxed paper, greased brown paper or newspaper and taken to work, out in the fields and to school.

"All the kids brought their lunches with them, which usually consisted of a biscuit and a piece of ham wrapped in a newspaper."

~ Ginger Gill Brown, Louisiana

Sandwiches during the Depression were made with a variety of ingredients. Mayonnaise was not common – most likely lard or bacon fat, also known as "pig butter," was smeared on slices before adding anything else — if anything else was added.

Fried egg sandwich from Wikipedia

Care to try any of these?

Fried egg sandwich, slice of raw onion optional

Raw onion sandwich – with mustard if available, or salt sprinkled between slices

Tomato and onion sandwich — add cheese if handy

Molasses and honey sandwich

Lettuce with bacon fat

Cucumber, with or without raw onion

Bread and butter pickle sandwich

Lard spread thickly on slices of homemade bread

Baked bean sandwiches

Toasted bread buttered and slathered with yellow mustard

Alfred Farris, who grew up in Alabama, remembers often going hungry after school and doing chores until the evening meal: *"We'd be hungry when we got home from school, but there were no snacks to tide us over until supper."*

However, more often than not after-school or work snacks consisted of grabbing a biscuit or a slice of corn bread from the stove drawer, or pulling an onion, bell pepper, radishes and turnips from the garden and eating them raw after the dirt was brushed off.

"I remember picking a radish out of the ground, washing the dirt off of it and eating it."

~ Katherine Sigera Dillon, California

The Depression vanquished father

Chet Hanson

Father born 1896 in Oakland, California

Chester William, "Red" Hanson, my dad, was born in Oakland, California in 1896. He had hair so red they called him Red. He had a fighting spirit to match. As it turned out, his life required all the fight he could muster — and then a bit more than he had.

When Dad was about 11, his father contracted Tuberculosis. During the prolonged illness, his father was quarantined to a small, converted shack behind their home. My dad's mother loved and missed her husband so much that she snuck out to the shack to be with him. Unfortunately, she contracted TB herself. Both of his parents died, leaving his mother's mother as the last surviving adult to care for him and his two younger siblings. But she got it too, and died when Red was 14.

One of his most vivid memories were the two times ambulances came to take his mother and grandmother

"Red" Hanson, bottom front.

to a sanitarium for their last days on earth. His mother fought death, ripping the cloth ceiling of the vehicle with her fingernails. On the other hand, his grandmother wore a peaceful smile.

When my dad was fully orphaned, he was in the second semester of 7th grade. His choices were to turn his younger brother and sister over to an orphanage or try to support them by himself. He chose the latter. He may not have been able to finish his education then, but he had a lot of skill in his hands and an engineer-like mind. Over time, other families absorbed his younger siblings.

When the Great Depression hit, it did not affect him much at first. He was single and had money in his pocket from commercial fishing in California. In fact, in 1930 he set out in his snazzy 1928 Auburn automobile see what the rest of America looked like.

His needs were simple. Being a capable, hardworking man, Red was only responsible for himself. By 1938 he was a fisherman on the Mississippi and lived in a houseboat. He loved his freedom and was doing well in spite of the national economic plight.

But he also had a lot of heart. A neighbor died in the middle of the Depression. Red married his neighbor's widow, Marie Pillow, and took her children to raise. He knew he could love her, and her children were near starvation. Two of her five children were twin boys, Leo and Theo. Theo died of ptomaine poisoning because he was so hungry he ate from a can of spoiled food.

Eventually my father came to know what most every man with a family knew: the Depression created want. What had been more than enough for one was not nearly enough for six.

As the Depression deepened across America, stories about California as the last bastion of hope swirled. But there were also stories about how brutal the agricultural work was, and what job-seekers had to endure.

Red was a skilled fisherman and already had experience angling for albacore tuna out of San Diego. He knew some boat owners and they knew him; he believed that gave him an edge. The family, all except 13-year-old Roy who had hitchhiked on ahead, crammed themselves and all they could carry into his car.

But the Auburn died en-route. The auto manufacturer had gone out of business, so there were no parts to fix it. He parked his family with a Pastor in Phoenix and hitchhiked to San Diego.

Red met up with Roy and managed to get them both

jobs on a fishing boat. He finally sent for his family. The only place they could afford was beyond their ability to clean well enough to get rid of rats and other vermin. It wasn't until they had their first child together that they opted to leave that structure and live in a tent. This was my first home for nearly a year.

Red saved every penny. He managed to buy a small tuna fishing boat of his own; it was small, but it was his. He christened her *Capitao,* which is Portuguese for Captain. He also acquired two other tuna boats. When he had lived in San Diego before, Red built a pier and beam fishing shack so he could have a place to stow gear and to bunk down as a single man when he was in port. He'd sold it when he left.

One day while walking with my mother, he pointed it out. She fell in love with the humble shack. She had been so poor she had never had a home of her own and wanted Red to buy it back. The man he sold it to didn't use it much and was in need of money. It was an easy trade.

The place — only 18-feet by 18-feet — was one room, had no plumbing, running water or electricity. Red, Leo, and Roy brought in utilities and divided the shack into four rooms: a kitchen, a bathroom, one bedroom and a tiny living room. They added a screened-in back porch for the two girls, Grace and Sydney, to sleep in and a front porch to use as a family closet. The boys slept on bunk beds in the living room while Red, Marie and I slept in a tiny double bed in the only bedroom.

Finally, life seemed to be righting itself and they started to feel as if they were doing well. But Red's life was not meant to be easy.

While Red fished one dark night, *Capitao* ran into an

unlit naval tender — a big, floating, steel buoy off Catalina Island. The collision put a hole into *Capitao*'s hull big enough to drive a small car into and it all but sank. Only the cork insulation of the fish hole kept her afloat while my dad took refuge atop the cabin until the Coast Guard spotted him at dawn.

The Navy apologized and the Coast Guard towed the half-sunken craft back to San Diego. Red repaired it himself in the back yard and got back to business. The cannery that he worked for noted his hard work and good results and offered to finance the fishing boat of his dreams. It could make four times the money the dinky *Capitao* could.

It looked like he had finally fought his way into the good life by the early 1940s. But that was not to be his lot. Before Red could sail his 38-foot, diesel driven, refrigerated live-bait boat out of the harbor for the first time, he was diagnosed with Tuberculosis.

Before antibiotics, this was a death sentence. Red could not help but note that TB took his father, his mother and finally his grandmother. When his strength was back his boat was gone. The cannery was not willing to replace the money-maker Red had lost, but they helped him get what fisherman called a "little stink pot," and off he went.

On a blue-sky day nearly 300 miles off the coast of San Diego in August 1946, he received news that knocked him permanently off-kilter. He already had a little over two tons of albacore tuna on ice and just landed close to 30 more fish. Two more days like that and he could navigate back to port, to his beloved Marie and now a new daughter, Bobby Jean. When he scoured the sky back to the east he saw the first glimpse of a plane. A few minutes later he saw the plane had not left the area. *Unusual,* he thought, *must be searching for something*. Ten minutes later that same plane was so close and so low he could see the face of a Coast Guard member looking at his boat through binoculars.

They flew over twice more and dipped their wings to be sure they had his attention. On the third pass the man threw something from the side door of the airplane. It was an orange buoy, suspended by a small parachute.

Red fished it out and opened it up. The message was straightforward and simple, "Your wife is dead. Your children need you. Return to port."

I was four at the time and remember that day vividly. My father stored all his fishing gear under the pier and beam house. No stranger to hard work, my 34-year-old mother decided to take out much of his equipment and make it orderly. In the process, she lost control of a large, heavy anchor and it fell on her arm. The bruise was substantial enough that she saw a doctor who told her to keep it in a sling. But she was impatient and went about her work. Our house was small, and during the course of a normal day we children were in and out of her bedroom. During one of these sorties, my 14-year-old sister realized that our mom was dead. All four of us ran next door to the neighbors' home because they had a phone. The Death Certificate says, "heart attack."

Red came home, put all of us children into foster care and continued to fish. He visited us often but for many years we wondered why he didn't leave fishing, take a job on shore and raise his family instead. Later, we realized that he had no fight left in him. The cards that life had dealt — especially the Great Depression with all of its losses — rubbed out his spirit like a sentence written in pencil.

Disillusioned, Red was drawn to promises made by Communism. He embraced it for decades. Just before his death at 86, he confided to me that he still thought it the best form of government imaginable but no longer believed that man is capable of living under it or governing by it.

The Great Depression caused some to leap from buildings or to find other ways to quickly end their tribulations. Some even prospered. And some, including Red Hanson my beloved father, found that their fighting spirit couldn't fight anymore and were vanquished.

My father was a crushed man. I did not realize this until much later in life. He had given up on all but subsistence living. He did not think that Capitalism was fair. He was very frugal, yet unabashedly generous. He respected money.

I should have learned to be frugal, but did not. I did inherit his spirit of generosity. I have embraced freedom and know it can only exist when you have a free market system. My father was a man of quiet love. He did not come from a generation of men that hugged. But he was always there for me. I guess the most important lesson that my dad passed on to me is that love, no matter how you are capable of expressing it, is the most essential element to life.

Chet Hanson, California

Alfred Farris

Two choices: Eat it or leave it

Alfred Farris
Born 1931 near Margerum, Alabama

My story is about a sharecropping family living in near-poverty on a hardscrabble farm in rural Alabama. My mother, Hester, died when I was five-years-old, leaving my father, Frank "Cook" Farris, to be both father and surrogate mother to my brother Gene and me.

I was born in 1931 at the onset of the Great Depression near Margerum, in the west end of Colbert County, Alabama. The world was a much different world then than it is today; poverty was rampant, people were of little worth financially and many wealthy people lost their money in the stock market crash of 1929. This was the world I was born into.

Our house was built of logs. There were two large rooms separated by an open hallway (dog trot), and a kitchen attached to the backside of one of the rooms. The countrymen of that era knew how to use a broad-

Alfred Father Gene

ax and crosscut saw and how to hew pine logs and dovetail the ends to build a house, and how to build a bush-arbor for summer camp meetings.

We had no electricity and got our water from a well. The house was hot in summer and cold in winter, and would never appear in *Better Homes and Garden* magazine. In cold winters the dipper froze in the water bucket. Our homestead consisted of a large barn, log smokehouse, cottonseed house, a yard full of clucking chickens and a corncrib where I spent many Saturdays shooting rats. Our only form of entertainment was the AM radio. We didn't need an alarm clock because the sun could never slip past our roosters as it rose in the morning.

We lived a mile from the main road. After I started to school I had to walk that mile every morning to catch the bus. The scene as I walked that gravel road displayed a landscape of poverty and despair. Our chief mode of transportation was walking. We walked everywhere.

The school had three rooms with two classes taught in each room. There was no janitor, so in winter the boys had to build a fire in the wood heater. By the time the rooms were warm it was time to go home. Discipline was never a problem because of the implied threat of the wooden paddle beside the teacher's desk. There was no class envy because we were all poor.

The boys played baseball with homemade bats and string wound into balls. The girls played jacks and skipped rope. All of us played Ring-around-the-Rosy.

We would be hungry when we got home from school, but there were no snacks to tide us over until supper. Although we lived in "cholesterol country" with lard, butter, and whole milk, there were hardly any fat boys, because we had to work hard and only ate at mealtimes.

We would work all week and on Saturday go to the "picture show," which cost a dime until you reached the age of 12. Hamburgers and sodas cost a nickel. This was during the heart of the Depression and most families existed on the barest of necessities. Some of the poorer ones had living standards that were hardly civilized. It was a time and place where menu choices were few and many families left the table with their hunger pangs not fully satisfied. The slogan then was, "Use it up, wear it out, make do or do without."

I spent the first 10 years of my life where many families had only two meal choices: eat it or leave it. Children were admonished to clean their plates. Although families were dirt poor, they were rich in pride and spirit, and most families lived in clean houses and kept their dignity.

In cities I saw proud men bow their heads so no one would recognize them while they stood in bread lines to get subsistence for their hungry families. Day after day they walked the streets looking for work. Families who had relatives in the country moved back home. It wasn't unusual for two or three families to share the same house.

Many homeless in cities resorted to living in groups of shacks called "Hoovervilles." People sold apples or pencils on the street or begged for their minimum intake of nourishment, driven day and night for a slight hope of charity. Small rural towns weren't infested with beggars like the large cities were, but I saw a man who had lost both legs in WWI sitting on a cushion selling pencils on the street of my hometown.

Many hobos could be seen in the doorways of boxcars of almost every freight-train that passed by, or encamped in freight yards known as "hobo jungles." The tramp, ragged, emaciated by hunger with his meager belongings slung in a bag across his back, was a common sight. Daddy often quoted a poem that seemed to emphasize the plight of these people:

I saw a wayward stranger, in tattered garments clad, struggling up the mountain, it seemed that he was sad. I saw him in the evening, the sun was bending low, he had overtopped the mountain and reached the dale below.

Where we lived there was very little criminal activity, which might be surprising because times were so hard. Everyone struggled and people were willing to work for what they got. Most men were humbled by their situation, but if a wife had no food to set on a table where hungry children were seated, a good man might be led astray to crime by absolute want.

The South during this period was primarily agricultural, essentially third-world. Everybody worked. Women stayed busy. When not helping on the farm, they were doing household chores or picking and canning vegetables and berries. Quilting Bees were social events where women got together in a joint effort to make quilts for their beds, gossip and socialize.

By living in the country and raising our vegetables, meat, and having milk-cows, my family was self-sufficient, although we seldom had sumptuous meals. We always had a big garden and an orchard of apples and peaches. We lived on a high hill out of a frost pocket so our trees produced abundant crops every year. Daddy had "truck-patches" of corn, peas and potatoes, so our table was set with the most basic of foods but we never went to bed hungry. In some of the poorer homes kitchens reeked from the smell of boiled cabbage for a cheap meal.

Cars were few in the country, so people's primary universe was about an eight-mile radius. Local stores sprang up to accommodate them. Five stores were near my home that was little more than a crossroads. These were general stores that stocked groceries, dry goods and hardware. They were not models of neatness, but among the assorted clutter, shoppers could find most anything needed.

Every store had a roller that held white paper to wrap sliced bologna, cheese and other foodstuffs. The wrapped paper was tied with a cotton string from a spool fastened to a fixed post on the counter. Sacks or "pokes" were used to sack other items. The cats that lay curled in the store were permanent and necessary fixtures to keep mice from damaging the sacks of feed and other things that were not under glass.

After selling our prime bottomland to the Tennessee Valley Authority in 1936 for the Flood Control Act, Daddy became a sharecropper. I accompanied him on bone-jarring trips to his rented fields in our old mule-drawn wagon with iron-strapped tires that jolted with every turn of the wheel. In the springtime the woods were filled with blooming dogwoods and the smell of honeysuckle mingled with the scent of freshly turned earth from the fields.

The amount of land a sharecropper rented depended upon the size of his family and placed a premium on each family member. Poor whites and blacks were subsistence-level farmers, eking a living from working someone else's land.

I was embarrassed riding in that mule-drawn wagon as we passed classmates from school whose fathers worked hourly jobs. It seemed as if my dad and I were on a pedestal and every eye was upon us as we passed.

My father worked every day when it wasn't raining. After the crops were laid-by, he and his brother hewed crossties for $1 per tie or worked cutting timber for sawmills. He never worked on Sunday — that was God's day.

The first cold weather signaled hog-killing time. We would kill two hogs then salt and smoke the shoulders and hams in the smokehouse. Instead of using the middlings for bacon, we used them to make lard. The tenderloin, ribs and backbone were "fresh meat," and weren't salted down for later use. Sausage was bagged and hung in the smokehouse. It was wonderful to come home from school hungry and find a big plate of tenderloin or fried spareribs. We're talking *soul food*. Some people used the lard mixed with lye to make lye soap. Some used the small intestines of the hog to make chitterlings.

Farmers often made their children work in the fields from a very early age. The wives worked too, bringing the smaller children to tend to the babies that were placed on a pallet in the shade while the women toiled.

People where we lived had never known jasmine-scented mansions, the popular imagined view of the Old South. My ancestors never saw a mint julep or even knew what it was, but did know the weight of a cotton packsack against their shoulder and hands callused from pulling a crosscut saw. In those days men wore frayed bib overalls and straw hats, and women donned their weekday tattered housedresses and bonnets. Both were shackled to a lifetime of toil with very little reward.

In the fall we dragged cotton packsacks to gather our meager harvest under a blistering sun. The harvest depended upon the weather and the boll weevil. This little unwelcome visitor from Mexico could devastate a cotton crop and sent more than one farmer to the poorhouse. Some fields were infested with Johnson grass that had to be dug up by the roots, making it very hard to control. If left alone, it would choke out the cotton plants. A day's work was not set by the clock, but by the sun.

When I was about eight-years-old there was a government program to assist families in making their own mattresses. The government furnished part or all of the material and the families had to make their own mattresses, which were of good quality. This sounds like a trivial thing, but many people used mattresses stuffed with corn shucks.

During the Depression, Roosevelt instituted programs for shovel-ready, make-work projects. Typical of these were the Civilian Conservation Corps, Works Progress Administration and Tennessee Valley Authority. Some were controversial, but they did put food in hungry mouths while roads were upgraded and schools were built.

The Depression wasn't about a falling stock market and the catastrophe of the Dust Bowl — it was about people and how they handled the tragedy inflicted upon them. As the Depression dragged on, people held on to the elusive phantom of hope that next week, next month or next year things would get better. But, as Alroy Jones wrote:

The days rolled by and the weeks became years, but our coffers were empty still. Coin was so rare that the treasuries quaked if a dollar dropped into the till.

Two of the most popular Depression era songs were, *Brother, Can You Spare a Dime?* and *Wait 'til The Sun Shines Nellie.*

We never fully realized how poor we were because poverty was all around us. We were better off than most because we owned our own home and had money in the bank from the sale of our farmland to the Tennessee Valley Authority. I guess seeing others around us in worse circumstances than ourselves silenced any complaining before it started, similar to the story about the man who complained that he had no shoes until he saw a man who had no feet.

The millions of poor people during this period were not dumb, lazy slobs to be pitied. These were people who were willing to work for what they got, and did not expect wealth without sacrifice. The hearty souls of that era who lived with hope, determination and the gift of survival lived to see a better day. Pen and ink cannot convey the reality of what it was like to live through the dark hours of those years.

Alfred Farris, Alabama

Cabbage public domain

Boiled cabbage and chitterlings

"In some of the poorer homes kitchens reeked from the smell of boiled cabbage...some used the small intestines of the hog to make chitterlings..."

~ Alfred Farris, Alabama

Southern Boiled Cabbage

1 head of cabbage
2 T butter or lard
2 T olive oil
½ teaspoon salt
½ teaspoon black pepper
1½- 2 cups water or chicken broth if handy

Cut cabbage into quarters, removing the hard stem. Slice each quarter into 1-inch wide strips. In a large pot, add butter, olive oil, salt, pepper and cabbage. Add water or chicken broth and toss.

Bring to a boil over medium-high heat. Cover and reduce heat to medium low. Simmer for 12-15 minutes, stirring occasionally until cabbage is tender. Do not overcook.

Chitterlings

1 red pepper, cut up
1 clove garlic, minced
1 onion, cut up
10 lbs. chitterlings (hog intestines)
1 T salt
1 T pepper

Wash chitterlings thoroughly. Trim fat, leaving small amount on chitterlings for seasoning. In large saucepan cover chitterlings with water. Add red pepper, onion and garlic, 1 tablespoon salt and 1 tablespoon pepper. Cook until tender, about 5 hours or until done. Drain and cut in serving size pieces. Serve at once. Makes 6 to 8 servings

Food in lieu of rent money

Barbara (Liebmann) Lodge

Mother born 1923 in St Louis, Missouri
Father born 1921 in St. Louis, Missouri

My parents were both "Depression Babies."

My father, Lester Liebmann, is the only son of Loretta Witte and Edwin Liebmann, and brother to Marcella. He was born in 1921 in St. Louis, Missouri.

In a time when divorce was rare, especially among Catholics, my grandmother Loretta divorced my grandfather Edwin because he was a scoundrel and ended up in prison. As a result, she became the single mother of two children and moved back home with her father and brothers. Not much is known about her mother — I assume she passed away before these events.

We grew up calling her Grandma Retta. She worked in a bakery that was owned by an extended relative in the south-side of St. Louis — an area that was populated by the "Scrubby Dutch," who were from Germany. They were called that because they cleaned everything, and "Deutsch" was pronounced "Dutch."

Dad grew up poor. Nevertheless, Grandma Retta told me more than once of her gratefulness to God for providing income for her and her family. At least one of her brothers was always employed so they kept a roof over their heads and food on the table during the Depression era. But sometimes the food was a little hard to stomach. My father said that meat frequently consisted of something really disgusting, such as beef heart, because that was all they could afford. He got physically ill when forced to eat it.

When Dad was 12-years-old he got appendicitis and almost died when it ruptured. He was hospitalized for six weeks. Because he was literally incapacitated during an important growth period he turned to books. He went to the neighborhood library weekly and eventually read every book in the children's section. At that point he had to get permission from his mother to begin reading "adult" books. He read everything he could get his hands on. Reading became his lifelong passion.

Although Dad was never overly athletic he actually became good at fencing. There was an aunt who was on the Olympic fencing team. He was the captain of his Catholic high school's fencing team. He eventually won a full-ride scholarship to St. Louis University where he graduated after three years — in 1940. Afterward, he joined the Army and ended up in France, serving under Patton.

My dad wasn't perfect, but the Great Depression and his mother taught him that the most important attribute a person can have is integrity. His scoundrel of a father used to steal his and his sister's lunch money. This was a major deciding factor in who he became later in life, having suffered at the hands of someone who should have been trustworthy.

I also think that his Catholic faith was a large part of his family's background. He had a real relationship with the Lord at an early age; when he was in the hospital for so long during the appendicitis episode, nuns came into his room, knelt around his bed and prayed for him daily. That affected him deeply. Dad also had a direct experience with a touch from God when he received the Confirmation sacrament. After a bishop prayed for him, the presence of God surrounded him.

Growing up fatherless left scars in my Dad and kept him emotionally distant most of my young life. Many years later in the mid-1970s, my father received Jesus Christ as his Lord and Savior and received the baptism of the Holy Spirit. This change healed him of many old, emotional wounds. When he looked upon the Lord as his Father, Dad became affectionate, often telling me he loved me and hugging me.

Dad continued to hold integrity as his highest ideal until he passed away.

My mother had a vastly different upbringing. Natalie Federer Liebmann was a vivacious, cheerful person. She was the second oldest of five children born to William and Marie Federer in St Louis in 1921. I called them "Pawpaw" and "Grandmarie." They were Catholic also and stayed married throughout their lives — but their marriage was not a happy one.

My Pawpaw was a rather selfish man and a philanderer. Grandmarie was a small-minded woman who was given to emotions and tantrums. Pawpaw was also an unscrupulous businessman and could make money.

While Mom was in elementary school they lived well. All the kids went to a Catholic parochial school, and they had horses and learned to ride. Pawpaw made money. Lots of money. And Gram spent it liberally.

By 1929, Pawpaw was a millionaire. They built a huge Tudor-style home in a fashionable area of south St. Louis across the street from a large park. In fact, Pawpaw had his own real estate firm and it was his firm that built that whole area. The home featured a sunken living room with high ceilings, five bedrooms, servants' quarters, a two-car garage with a large family room above it, a swimming pool and more. It was impressive.

They moved into the fancy house in 1929 and promptly lost most of their money in the stock market crash that same year. Pawpaw managed to hang on to two pieces of property: the house and a building that housed a grocery store. He made a bargain with the grocer to provide food for his family in lieu of rent money so that his family wouldn't starve. All Pawpaw and Grandmarie had now was a big, fancy house and a bunch of kids.

Mom remembers cutting cardboard to put in their shoes when the soles wore out. They had a maid from "out in the country" who cooked for them in return for living in the maid's quarters — neither Grandmarie nor Mom ever really learned to cook. Mom wore hand-me-downs and shared a room with her sister who was a "slob." Mom would clean a lot. She became the maid for most of her growing-up life because they couldn't afford one and she was the oldest girl.

I think Mom always felt sorry for herself for having to keep house. I remember her weeping when she ironed our clothes — like she shouldn't be made to do such menial work. Mom grew up behaving like she was rich even though she wasn't.

Appearances became very important to Mom. There was something about that big, fancy house being in the family. To this day, keeping up appearances seems to be a trait of all the Federer children. One of my aunts and an uncle battled over who got that monster after Grandmarie ended up in a nursing home.

Growing up during the Depression affected Mom's entire personality, which seemed to revolve around the desire to give the impression to everyone that we were wealthy — but we never were. I always felt sorry for her about that. That being said, Mom also learned to love people and "little things" through the Depression years. If there was no "fun" around, she knew how to create it. People were drawn to her by this characteristic.

The Depression era brought out something in Mom that might not have surfaced. When you don't have money as a child, you develop your imagination — and Mom had oodles of it! She was an artist and could create something out of nothing.

Barbara Lodge, Missouri

No meat wasted

When you're hungry, you'll eat.

Farmers who raised cattle and pigs in the 1930s didn't waste anything that could be consumed. Those who didn't live on farms were often part of community meat clubs where families took turns taking different parts of the animal each week.

"Families often joined together in their fight to make it through. One example was the beef club. Through the first years of the Depression, cattle had no market. To overcome this, families joined together every Saturday to butcher fresh meat. The Kramers were one of twenty-four families who banded together in their joint effort to survive." ~ Maedell Dillon, Texas

Esther Tissing's father raised dairy cattle, and her family was part of a community beef club in Texas: *"There was also a community meat club. One farmer-would butcher a cow or calf and split it up. One family got one part one week – like the kidneys – and another part the next and so on. We always had fresh meat on Sunday."*

Sometimes the offerings weren't appetizing, as Barbara Lodge from Missouri recounts: *"Sometimes the food was a little hard to stomach. My father [Lester Liebmann] said that meat frequently consisted of something really disgusting such as beef heart, because that was all they could afford. He got physically ill when forced to eat it."*

Ginger Brown's family in Arkansas used every part of the pigs they raised, including the head: *"The hogs' heads were used for souse [pickling] and hog's head cheese."*

Braised stuffed heart

Wash and slit the hearts, remove gristle and blood vessels.

For the stuffing, chop an onion and a stalk of celery into two tablespoons of fat and cook for a few minutes.

Add two to three cups of soft bread crumbs and season to taste with salt and pepper. Thyme goes well with heart - add a pinch to the stuffing.

Fill hearts with stuffing and sew up the slit with coarse thread.

Brown the hearts on all sides in fat, then place in a covered baking dish or casserole.

Add a half of cup of water, cover closely and cook

Two men handling beef carcasses in butcher shop.

Adams, Ansel, 1902-1984, photographer, Library of Congress collection.

until tender in a very moderate oven, about 300F.

Calf hearts require about one and a half hours, beef hearts will require much longer, about four to five hours.

Make gravy of the pan drippings and serve the hearts piping hot, garnished with crisp greens. Beef or calf hearts are rich in iron and vitamin B

Hog's Head Cheese

Start with two fresh hog heads washed, with eyes cut out.

Cover the heads with water and add 1/3 cup pepper corns, 10 bay leaves, 1/2 cup salt and 2 cups apple cider vinegar.

Bring to a boil, cover and simmer for 4 hours.

Remove heads from liquid and let cool. Pick out all the meat.

Take a few quarts of saved liquid and add 2 large chopped onions, several chopped celery stalks and several chopped garlic cloves.

Boil until tender.

Remove vegetables from broth, add to meat and mix.

Add 1/2 cup vinegar and mix well.

Pack in 1-pound bread tins.

Cover with plastic and refrigerate overnight.

Makes about six pans of head cheese.

A butcher shop window. Norwich, Connecticut.

Jack Delano, photographer, Library of Congress collection

TD Crockett worked as a soda jerk in a drugstore that sold the most Coca-Cola in the country at the time. He entertained children on their way home from school by flipping ice cream from the scoop.

Poverty meets prosperity in Pennsylvania

Lynn (Pitcairn) Genzlinger
Grandfather born 1883 in Alabama
Grandmother born 1888

My grandfather, TD Crockett, was no stranger to poverty. He was born in 1883, the son of a poor family in Alabama. In fact, the Crocketts were so poverty-stricken that Grandpa secretly whisked his family away to Georgia, leaving a 12-year-old son behind to work off his father's debt at the local grocery store — with no hope to pay.

But before all that, TD met his wife, my grandmother, Florence Frost, who was born in 1888, but I'm not sure where, while working as a deliveryman at Nunnally Candy Company in Atlanta where she also worked. He delivered messages and they got to know each other. They eloped on November 11, 1908, the same day that my grandfather's sister ran away to get married — neither knowing what the other was doing.

TD said that he and Florence were too poor for a honeymoon so they went to the station, sat on a bench and watched the trains come and go. We were never sure if this was the truth or if it was just one more way our grandfather "pulled our legs." In any case, he got his point across — they had empty pockets but hearts full of love.

Florence and TD raised their growing family of eight children in Atlanta during the Great Depression. My mother, Geneva Crockett, was the second-to-youngest, born in 1922. During this time my grandmother Florence became known among the very poorest people as someone who always had food to share. My mother remembers men showing up at their back door for whatever food Florence could spare.

TD worked different jobs during these years. He worked as a soda jerk in a drugstore that sold the most Coca-Cola in the country at the time. He entertained children on their way home from school by flipping ice cream from the scoop he held in one hand to the cone in his other. But he was chastised by his boss — "There'll be no more tossin', Mr. Crockett." However, when the boss wasn't around he'd do it anyway. At his counter he served Oliver Hardy and took refreshment to Margaret Mitchell in her apartment while she wrote *Gone With the Wind*.

In later years, TD taught his children to be frugal during the Depression. For example, he told them to use both sides of one square of toilet paper. He insisted that they turn off lights when leaving a room. He taught by example when he walked miles to work rather than spend a dime for trolley fare. He saved up for my mother's graduation dress by collecting nickels and putting them in his top dresser drawer.

However, TD had his pride too. He was embarrassed and upset when his family received a basket of food at Christmastime from a local charity. He worked hard to make sure his family had food to eat and a roof over their heads, even when they lost the only home they owned during this time.

Florence stayed at home to raise their children. One of her greatest joys was having a minister of her faith travel to Atlanta to preach to families there. His visits were infrequent but Florence waited eagerly to discuss the teachings of the New Church, a Christian-based religion founded on the Bible along with the writings of Emanuel Swedenborg.

In 1930, Florence traveled to Bryn Athyn, Pennsylvania, headquarters of the New Church, for a church assembly. While there she learned more about the Academy of the New Church, the educational arm of the religion she held dear. Being too poor to send her older children away to Bryn Athyn, she vowed upon her return to Atlanta that one of her children would one day attend this particular school for college.

That day finally came in the fall of 1940 when she sent her youngest daughter, Geneva, to Bryn Athyn. Geneva did not want to leave home and told her mother, "I will only embarrass you." Florence responded, "I will take that chance." The first night in Bryn Athyn, Geneva attended a garden party put on for the students by a couple in the community. Geneva's future began to unfold that night when a shy young man named Michael Pitcairn introduced himself to her under a rose arbor in the garden.

Michael had grown up in a home in Bryn Athyn that was

a world away from Geneva's childhood. Michael's grandfather, John Pitcairn, had been a "captain of industry" in the mid-to-late 1800s. Some would have called him one of the Robber Barons except for the life he chose to lead which was according to his religious beliefs set in the New Church. He attended Sunday school in the Pittsburgh area with a young Andrew Carnegie.

In John's teen years he was employed with the Pennsylvania Railroad. He rose through the ranks of the railroad system, with many of his travels taking him back and forth to Philadelphia. At one time, John accompanied Abraham Lincoln in a blacked-out train when the Pinkerton Agency discovered a plot to assassinate the President. With his railroad earnings, John invested in oil and later co-founded Pittsburgh Plate Glass, now known as PPG Industries.

It was his strong belief in New Church teachings that made John, and subsequently his children and many descendants, the people they would become. He was a peer of Andrew Carnegie, Andrew W. Mellon, Henry Clay Frick and John D. Rockefeller. His name is not a household word because he chose to be modestly useful to his fellow man as a devout husband and father and strong member of his faith. He was known for his honesty and integrity.

It is the common thread of the New Church that brought these two disparate families together. The Crockett family in the south had a common experience of living through the poverty of the Depression. The Pitcairn family lived a life of comfort and ease because of the wealth that John Pitcairn had created. Otherwise, my parents might not have met.

Raymond Pitcairn, John's oldest son, helped those less fortunate during the Depression when he constructed a

Gothic/Romanesque-style cathedral in Bryn Athyn, which was funded by his Industrialist father. He also employed workers from 1928-1939 to build the elaborate Gothic-style Glencairn, his home nearby. The home is now a museum of religious art from around the world.

Many workers were European craftsmen — immigrants with the talents Raymond needed to implement his specific building plans modelled after 12th and 13th century designs. As the Great Depression deepened, Raymond was faced with a decision. His resources, challenged by the stock market crash, were not enough to continue at the pace he had set. He could halt construction entirely, putting men out of work at a terrible time, or ask if they would accept lower wages so that he could keep them employed. The workers chose the latter.

Once the economic climate improved, these men showed their appreciation by giving a special lamp and a letter to Raymond to thank him for helping them to take care of their families during the Depression. The shade on the lamp depicts all the different occupations that were used to build Glencairn.

Appreciation lamp

My father, Michael Pitcairn, married my mother, Geneva Crockett, on November 17, 1945 in Bryn Athyn where he grew up, one month after he arrived home from his service in the Pacific Theater. They were married in the Bryn Athyn Cathedral. They raised eight children together in Bryn Athyn.

Blending the two families from such diverse backgrounds wasn't as difficult as one might think. The Crockett side was thrifty, but so were the Pitcairns who were of Scottish descent and naturally frugal.

TD was thrifty even after the Depression and into his old age. He was wary of the banking system and didn't have a bank account, so he kept his cash wrapped with a rubber band and called that his wallet. He kept this in the pocket of an old pair of pants that hung on a hook inside the closet door of the spare bedroom. He saved rubber bands from the newspaper delivered to his door each morning in a side table drawer in the living room. When a rubber band around his cash broke, he would say, "Time to get a new wallet," and go to the drawer.

When my mother lived at Glencairn with her future in-laws during the war waiting for my father to come home, she would go around turning lights off. Her father had taught her to never leave a room without turning off the lights. So by habit she continued this behavior at Glencairn until someone took her aside and gently told her she needn't do that there. The values instilled in the Pitcairn family were influenced by their strong religious beliefs rather than from results of the Depression, but it served them and future generations well.

Lynn Genzlinger, Pennsylvania

Coca-Cola: "The Pause that Refreshes" during the Depression – did it have cocaine?

Civil War veteran and Atlanta pharmacist "Doc" John S. Pemberton created Coca-Cola in 1886 as a way to relieve aches and pains — and take advantage of the growing soda fountain industry which sold mostly unflavored soda water, other non-carbonated beverages and ice cream.

Pemberton brewed the first mix of his drink in his backyard using a modest three-legged kettle. He created flavored syrup mixed with carbonated water; those who sampled it deemed it "excellent."

Rumors of cocaine as an ingredient dog the soft drink. According to *For God, Country & Coca-Cola* author Mark Pendergrast, the syrup was meant to go along with the culture of the times as a "nerve tonic" to calm people down. The drink naturally used coca leaves, which mixed different sorts of alkaloids. In comparison, cocaine is a pure alkaloid. It would take about 30 glasses of Coca-Cola to produce an actual dose.

On May 29, 1886 the first Coca-Cola ad appeared in the Atlanta Journal on the patent medicine page: *"Coca-Cola. Delicious! Refreshing! Exhilarating! Invigorating! The New and Popular Soda Fountain Drink, containing the properties of the wonderful Coca plant and the famous Cola nuts. For sale by Willis Venable and Nunnally & Rawson."*

The "cocaine" content of Coca-Cola remained until 1903 and made the drink very controversial — which contributed to its success.

After Pemberton died in 1888, part owner and Atlanta businessman Asa Griggs Candler rescued the business and in 1891 became the sole owner. His first controversial move was to sell Coca-Cola syrup itself as a patent medicine, claiming it would get rid of fatigue and headaches.

Candler launched an innovative marketing technique: he hired traveling salesmen in the Atlanta area to hand out coupons for a free Coke. His goal was for people to try the drink, like it, and buy it.

In addition to coupons, Candler spread the word by plastering the "handwritten" Coca-Cola logo on calendars, posters, notebooks and bookmarks to reach customers on a large scale. It was a step toward making Coca-Cola a national brand rather than just regional to Georgia.

After the free marketing campaign, Coca-Cola was sold for 5 cents per glass. During the first year, sales averaged a modest nine servings per day in Atlanta. Around the world today, 1.9 billion daily servings are sold.

After the Spanish-American War, Congress passed a tax on all medicines. As a result, Candler decided to sell Coca-Cola as a beverage only and didn't sell the syrup as medicine. After a court battle, Coca-Cola was no longer sold as a drug.

Impressed by the growing demand for Coca-Cola, Mississippi soda fountain owner Joseph Biedenharn installed bottling machinery in 1894 in the rear of his shop, making the beverage portable. Five years later, large-scale bottling was made possible when three

Tennessee businessmen secured exclusive rights to bottle and sell the soft drink. Asa Candler sold them bottling rights for $1.

On September 12, 1919, the Candler family sold Coca-Cola Co. for $25 million to a group of investors led by Ernest Woodruff, president of the Trust Company of Georgia. The business was moved to Delaware with the headquarters remaining in Atlanta. The new company issued 500,000 shares of stock to the public for $40 a share. Coca-Cola's stock not only survived the stock market crisis in October 1929, it made new highs within two years of the crash.

One of the most famous advertising slogans in Coca-Cola history, "The Pause That Refreshes," first appeared in the Saturday Evening Post in 1929. Ads drawn by Norman Rockwell followed every year for several years.

"Office Boy - 4 p.m. - The Pause That Refreshes" is one of three Rockwell paintings originally done for Coca-Cola that are currently missing. The company is seeking to return the original oil paintings to their colliection.

American women are rapidly taking their places on the industrial front. Here in this small midwest factory, the owner's wife operates one of the machines making dies for incendiary bombs.

Franklin D. Roosevelt Presidential Library & Museum

Times were tough, but she was tougher

Mary (Smiley) Sweeney

Mother born 1926 in Chicago, Illinois

My mother, Shirley Wolff Smiley, was born in 1926 in Chicago, Illinois. She was the eldest of two children. Living in the south side of the city in the heart of downtown Chicago, her family deeply felt the effects of the Depression. Despite bread lines and people looking for work in those difficult, challenging days, Chicago remained a busy, bustling city with many people and tall buildings.

City life with its hustle and noise was all that my mom knew as a child except for an occasional family trip to her aunt and uncle's farm in Missouri. There were a few cows and horses and my mom and her younger brother enjoyed eating fresh produce from the large garden. The country air was much fresher than the stagnant atmosphere of the city.

One of my mom's favorite memories of visiting the farm were the times when her uncle placed several large water barrels on an old, rickety wagon and invited her to come along for the ride. His two sturdy horses slowly pulled the wagon to the farm's water source, then filled the barrels with water and carted them back for the animals. It was something so different than what she was used to in the city with cars, subways and trolleys.

Another difference she enjoyed at the farm was the feather bed she slept in. Mom dreamed of her favorite story, *Heidi,* and imagined herself at a little cabin in the Alps surrounded by tall mountain peaks.

In the 1930s times were challenging and there wasn't much extra money. My grandmother walked a mile or more just to save a penny. My grandfather job-shared at a downtown men's department store — two men could work one job to provide for their families.

My mom remembers that even at eight-years-old in 1934, her impression of the Great Depression was that those days were hard for her parents. She knew that Franklin D. Roosevelt was President, and that there was a big war going on in another part of the world. She realized that most of the money her father earned went toward rent and that not much money was left over for food.

My mom had very few toys. She played with paper dolls and colored their clothing with crayons. She mostly spent her days playing outside. On a typical summer day she was outdoors as long as there was daylight. The neighborhood kids played baseball in the alley, Kick the Can and Red Rover. She'd come home hot, tired and dirty around 5:00 p.m. in order to be on time for dinner. After dinner nearly every night the family listened to *Little Orphan Annie* on the radio. She looked forward to that after-dinner-time and used her imagination to picture the scenes of the stories they listened to on the radio.

On rainy days Mom played school inside the house with a deck of playing cards. She pretended that the cards were students and that she was the teacher. The Queen of Hearts became Mary Miller, who was asked to stand up and read to the class, then placed back into the "class row" of cards.

Mom and her friends learned the value of a penny and of sharing. If any of her friends were given a penny to spend, they would all run several blocks to the candy store to buy a red or black licorice rope. She never had an extra penny, so unless someone offered to share a bit of his or her rope, she had to watch the others enjoy the yummy treat. More often than not, a friend offered to share by tearing the rope into small pieces so that everyone could have a bite.

One memorable Christmas season during the Depression years, my mom asked Santa for a hugely popular Shirley Temple doll. Most children of that era loved and admired the little actress. My grandmother searched high and low for the doll because Mom wanted it so badly. She finally left her name on a waiting list at Marshall Fields in Chicago, begging for them to call her if a doll happened to be returned to the store. As it turned out, one was returned just before Christmas Day. My grandfather raced over to the store and grabbed the doll right away. Even then, Mom knew how hard it was for her folks to get that doll and how difficult it was for them to pay for it. She had another special doll given to her by her aunt and uncle when she was three-years-old. She named it Mary Lou; her aunt made clothes for it. Mom still has both of those dolls.

Shirley Temple dolls were popular. public domain

Mom graduated from high school in 1944. She didn't have money for college, so she went to work for Chambers Gasket using the typing and shorthand she learned during secretarial courses in high school. But it was an hour-long commute each way on the elevated train from her home on the south side and it was too much. My grandmother found a job listing for Wilson and Company — a meatpackers business located near their home at the stockyards. At the time of Mom's interview the workers were on strike, but she crossed the picket line in the pouring rain and was hired for $45 per week.

Mom had always longed to travel and had taken short jaunts, but in the 1950s she found herself living in the Blackfeet Indian Reservation town of Browning, Montana, near Glacier National Park. She taught basic reading, writing and math skills to second grade students and in turn learned the history of the Blackfeet Tribe and gained an understanding of their many traditions passed down from generation to generation.

While fueling up her car in East Glacier one day she met Glenn Smiley — the operator of the Standard Service station and an avid Chicago White Sox fan. They married on June 3, 1959, and had one daughter — me — born in 1961.

In 1967 tragedy struck. My dad suddenly passed away due to a serious heart condition. Mom found herself all alone in a wild, unforgiving country where she had put down roots and called home. She had no family in the area, had a daughter to raise, a business to deal with and the responsibility of earning money on her own.

She was alone, yet because of her upbringing during the Depression years she was strong, resourceful, and prepared to do what needed to be done. While growing up, she learned lessons that enforced being grateful for what little she was blessed with and she learned to be frugal and save. She didn't know any other way — it's how she was raised and the experience she lived. If she couldn't afford it, she couldn't have it — plain and simple. She learned the power of patience.

Living life during the Depression era strengthened my mom. She grew up without things and didn't know she was missing them. During the years surrounding World War II, food-rationing coupons were issued to people for items such as sugar, meat, butter and gasoline. But, as my mom often said, she was happy. Times were tough, but she was tougher. Those experiences shaped and formed her.

Mary Sweeney, Michigan

The Shirley Temple phenomenon

Was it only 80 years ago that there were no televisions, computers, electric stoves or lights — and that having a stiff drink at the end of a long workday was federally forbidden? Add to that, nearly half of America's banks had literally gone bust and one in four people were unemployed.

It's no wonder that people needed an entertainment diversion. The cost to see a movie with refreshments was 30 cents for an adult; a children's admission ticket was 5 cents. Although not every family could afford to go, it was within reach of most.

The first feature film originally presented as a talkie was *The Jazz Singer*, released in October 1927. Up until then, silent movies dominated theaters, but only those who could read enjoyed them. Speech with sound opened up the cinematic world to everyone.

Throughout the 1930s, talkies were a global phenomenon — and little Shirley Temple rode high as the number one box office star from 1935 through 1938, beating out established screen stars such as Clark Gable and Bing Crosby. Her charming, childlike appeal offered an escape from the harsh reality of Depression-era life — if only for 90 minutes.

Biographer Anne Edwards wrote, "This was mid-Depression, and schemes proliferated for the care of the needy and the regeneration of the fallen. But they all required endless paperwork and demeaning, hours-long queues, at the end of which an

Shirley Temple in *Glad Rags to Riches*, 1933

public domain

exhausted, nettled social worker dealt with each person as a faceless number. Shirley offered a natural solution: to open one's heart."

At the tender age of three, Shirley Temple began her career. Her mother, Gertrude, enrolled her in singing, dancing and acting lessons at Meglin's Dance School in Los Angeles in 1931. Shirley's father was a banker. Gertrude was a fan of Mary Pickford and styled her daughter's hair in ringlets similar to what the silent movie film star wore.

Although Temple was discovered hiding behind a piano by a casting director in 1932, it wasn't until she starred in *Stand Up and Cheer!* in 1933 that she became a hit. At the end of the year she signed a $150/week contract with a seven-year option; her mother was hired at $25/week as hairdresser and personal coach. A year later, Temple's contract was raised to $1,000 a week and her mother's salary was raised to $250 a week, with an additional $15,000 bonus for each movie completed. By the end of 1935 the six-year-old raked in $2,500 a week. Temple was among highest paid actors in 1937, at $307,000. She reportedly made 15 times that amount in endorsements and licensing that same year.

Temple received a special Juvenile Academy Award (Oscar) in February 1935 for her outstanding contribution as a juvenile performer to motion pictures. She was the epitome of wholesome family entertainment — everyone's daughter, every girl and boy's friend, a lovable, parentless, waif whose charm and sweetness mellowed gruff, older men. Her characters changed the lives of the cold, the hardened, and even the criminal with positive results; her capacity for love was uncritical, extending to pinched misers and common hobos. Whether she played the precocious Cupid or the good fairy, reuniting her estranged parents or smoothing out young couples' wrinkled romances, she was beloved. Temple was often motherless, sometimes fatherless or an orphan confined to a dreary asylum. Wholesome goodness triumphed over meanness – wealth over poverty, marriage over divorce, and a booming economy over a depressed one.

Even President Franklin D. Roosevelt said, "It is a splendid thing that for just 15 cents an American can go to a movie and look at the smiling face of a baby and forget his troubles."

In 1934, Temple filmed nine shorts, appeared on the cover of 14 magazines and was the subject of dozens of articles. By the end of the year, Shirley Temple merchandise —dolls, books, paper dolls, dishes, and clothing modeled after her film characters flew off the shelves. She had difficulty going out in public for fear of being mobbed or kidnapped.

In the late 1930s a bartender at Chasen's in Beverly Hills reportedly mixed ginger ale and grenadine garnished with a maraschino cherry and served it to the young actress. Forever after known as the "Shirley Temple," the sweet, pink concoction became the mock cocktail for generations of kids.

After the release of *Stand up and Cheer!* and because of its popularity, a Shirley Temple Doll came out in time for Christmas 1934. One problem is that no one anticipated how popular the doll would be, so supplies quickly ran short.

For a whopping $1.98, (for some, this was more than a week's wages) the doll came with rolling eyes and curlers, a Shirley Temple book, movie badge and an autographed photo.

Mary Sweeney's mother, Shirley Wolff, was eight-years-old and living in near poverty in Chicago and wanted that doll. She knew her parents couldn't afford one. But nothing was impossible for Santa Claus. So she asked him and told her parents about it.

"One memorable Christmas season…my mom asked Santa for a hugely popular Shirley Temple doll. Most children of that era loved and admired the little actress. My grandmother searched high and low for the doll because Mom wanted it so badly...she finally left her name on a waiting list… one was returned just before Christmas Day."

~ Mary Sweeney, Michigan

City and County Building SLC by Charles Roscoe Savage.

He suffered a nervous breakdown

Joan Compagno-Wright

Grandfather born 1891 in Salt Lake City, Utah

My grandfather Chester Young is the grandson of Brigham Young, Jr., and the son of John Washington Young. My mother, JoAn Young, is Chester's daughter.

Publicity still for Chester Young, entertainer.

January and early February of 1901 was tragic for the Young family — Chester was 10-years-old when his little sister Liberty died from a case of diphtheria on January 21. Nine days later his mother, Anna Sears Young, also passed from diphtheria. Three days later his two-month-old brother John Washington Jr. died of pneumonia. Chester's father became an alcoholic in his inconsolable grief. Although John wasn't violent, Chester couldn't stand being around him when he was drunk. In later years he never took a drink and abhorred anyone who did.

As a result of his father's alcoholism, Chester ran away from his home in Salt Lake City in 1905 when he was 14-years-old and headed for Portland, Oregon in the Great Northwest.

Chester thrived in Portland and soon found work as an elevator operator at one of the downtown hotels. By 1916 he relocated to San Francisco and married Mildred Noonan. By the early 1920s he worked summers as a Golf Pro at the Lake Arrowhead Golf Club and provided the same services in Palm Springs during the winter months. Golf was a game he enjoyed until he died at age 93.

Chester was a self-taught man. Now a father of two little girls, (JoAn born in 1923, Rose Marie in 1921), he had elevated his skills and found employment as a civil engineer for Richfield Oil Company in Southern California. He and his family lived in Pasadena and he commuted to work in downtown Los Angeles to a beautiful black and gold building. Then the financial crash hit America. In the Depression that followed, Chester not only lost his job, he suffered a nervous breakdown.

Family came to their rescue in 1929. Mildred's sister Bea had steady employment at the State Legislature; she and her husband, Oscar McShane, beckoned the family north to the town of Carmichael. At that time it was nothing more than a farming community in Northern California.

Chester learned to grow vegetables and various flowering plants while recuperating at their farm. Chickens and rabbits were also raised as a source of protein through those tough years. However, rabbit meat was something that Rose Marie and Bea forsook the rest of their lives.

Chester and his family thrived in this new environment. They remained with Auntie Bea and Uncle Oscar for three years. The summer months provided respite from so many mouths to feed when JoAn and Rose Marie, now aged six and eight, spent time in Dunsmuir, a magical little railroad town near Mt. Shasta, with Auntie Edna, another of Mildred's sisters.

There was only one bathroom in the Carmichael home, so Chester took it upon himself to build an outdoor shower made from wood pilings and an oil drum that held water above the unit. He was very good at architectural design. The hot San Joaquin Valley sun heated the water during the day, making it the perfect temperature for a quick soap-up and rinse in the evening. A drawback was an abundance of toads that hopped between the floorboard slats!

In 1933, Chester was hired by Standard Oil and the family moved back to San Francisco. Ever the penny-pincher, Chester walked four miles round-trip each day from the top of California Street to the Standard Oil building in the Financial District. Dressed in his suit, hat and leather shoes, Chester never complained about scaling those hills as long as he was able to avoid paying that 5-cent trolley fare. He was also part of the planning of the Bay Bridge stretching from San Francisco to Oakland. Some of his blueprints have been preserved by the family as a reminder of how things used to be done – *by hand.* His drawings and penmanship are as precise as any a modern day device could produce.

In 1934, San Francisco commerce was further paralyzed

by a Longshoremen's strike that saw 40,000 men walk off their jobs at ports up and down the Pacific Coast. Teamsters walked in solidarity with the longshoremen by also refusing to unload shipped cargo. It was months before the dock-workers' demands were met and they went back to work.

Chester was an enthusiastic inventor, a consummate storyteller and a singer who often serenaded audiences with his beautiful tenor voice while accompanied by Mildred on a piano. There is a black and white publicity photo of him for a live performance at KFWB in Los Angeles. He was quite an entertainer. He resembled Jimmy Gleason, a character actor/playwright/screenwriter of the 1930s. For fun, Chester often signed autographs in Gleason's name.

Chester and his family survived the Depression. Shortly after Pearl Harbor was attacked in December 1941, he enlisted in the US Navy. He was 50-years-old. He served with the SeaBees in Dutch Harbor, Alaska and retired as a Chief Warrant Officer. Later, he spent two years in Saudi Arabia and one year in Venezuela as a representative of Standard Oil Company.

He reconciled with his father later in life. John had remarried and moved to Los Angeles around the same time that Chester married in San Francisco, and was a regular visitor when the family relocated to the Los Angeles area.

Chester retained an unstoppable optimism all his life. He never stopped believing in himself. If we learned anything from him, it was his boundless enthusiasm and belief that you could be anything you wanted to be in life.

Joan Compagno-Wright, Californi

Father earned dimes and quarters

Gerald Walpin
Father born 1894 in New York City

My father, Michael Walpin, was born in New York City a few years before the 1900s, into what seemed to be a wonderful family. He was the eldest and shortly after he was born, the family increased with a brother and sister.

Their world collapsed around them in 1904 when their mother suddenly died and their father quickly deserted them by leaving them at an orphanage. My father was about 10-years-old.

Although he was extremely intelligent, he was not permitted to seek to attend college and was offered only vocational training instead. The orphanage limited the number of residents who could go to higher education, and he was not chosen. He left when he

Children lined up to board an orphan train about 1920.
Patrick-Sheets-Trickel Collection

was 18. He was drafted for WWI but was soon released because his eyesight was so weak.

My mother, Mary Gordon Walpin, was born in 1897 in New York City. She never had a college education but had vocational training to be a bookkeeper. She learned from her mother about strength and fortitude in the face of adversity and was creative in getting our family through the Depression years and supplementing our father's income.

Her mother, Rae Kainer, was born in a little village in western Russia. She was the 13th child after 12 preceding boys. All of the boys, one or two at a time, left Russia for America or Canada. Rae was scheduled to go to Canada, but the outbreak of World War I left her as the sole member of the family living with her mother.

Starvation during that time was rampant in Russia. Rae and her mother's meals were limited to sharing one boiled potato per day that a Russian landowner allowed the villagers to pick from his fields in the Fall. They created a soup by boiling the potato. At the end of the war Rae's mother died of starvation. So Rae, a young woman in her teens by then, literally walked into and across Poland with a band of refugees into Antwerp. With the help of HIAS [Hebrew Immigrant Aid Society], she was reunited with her brothers in Canada. She later came to the United States, married and started a family of her own.

Her example inspired her daughter and my father. During the Depression years my father had no work. Through odd jobs and such he infrequently earned a few dollars – more correctly, dimes and quarters. I recall my parents' sacrifices to allow their three children to eat and attend school. There were many days when Mother and Father went without dinner, leaving the limited pickings to us children. They sacrificed to ensure the strength of their new generation.

We lived in a fourth-floor walk-up apartment in The Bronx. I vividly recall various times that the doorbell rang and my mother rushed to shush her children and did not answer the bell. I later learned that the visitor was usually a representative from the electricity or gas company who wanted to shut off the utility because of non-payment.

But my mother figured out a way to save enough pennies to pay the utility bills. She took in work at home to help out my father's meager income. For several hours after dinner and late into the night she did piecework for a button store; she methodically created and pasted buttons together for ladies' clothing. She never complained. Her view was that she was working as a partner with her husband to keep the family together.

Father corresponded with Herbert Hoover and considered him his hero. My father believed that FDR was the worst President because he had instituted a "gimme" philosophy and expectation to the country's citizens that he believed was inconsistent with the hard work and enterprise mentality that had made this country great.

The deprivation he experienced during his childhood and the Depression likely would have caused many people to sour on America and good principles - but not my father. He had a never-reduced love for this country and the opportunities it allowed for all to be successful.

My parents were always in the lowest economic category until the time I finished my education and military service. After that, I was able to help them out. They recognized that they had little as compared to those in the top 10 percent, but they remained Republicans until their death, believing that freedom and self-initiative is the best for them and the country.

Rae developed Multiple Sclerosis as a young woman. Within a few years she was unable to walk and was eventually totally bedridden. But she never voiced any self-pity or dissatisfaction with life. She taught her children and all who would listen that she was most fortunate to live in the United States and have her two children live in freedom.

I believe that my father, my mother, and my grandmother's spirits are what helped make America great.

Gerald Walpin, New York

Orphanage populations soared in the 1930s

Thousands of schools operated on reduced hours or were closed down entirely during the Depression. Some three million children of all ages had to leave school and at least 200,000 of them took to riding the rails either with their parents or as orphans. Many were nomads traveling the highways with hobos on foot and railways by boxcar.

Countless children were left truly orphaned when parents succumbed to disease or starved. By the mid-1930s, the number of children in orphanages rose to a peak of 144,000 and 249,000 children were in the foster care system.

There was also a large population of "half-orphans." These were children who had one surviving parent who could not — or would not — care for them. Government benefits for unemployment, Social Security and disability did not exist. Sometimes children were left at orphanages temporarily; sometimes they were altogether abandoned. Michael Walpin of New York City was 10-years-old when his mother died leaving him behind with a younger brother and sister. Michael's father deserted them at an orphanage in New York State. Michael left there when he turned 18.

Children under 12 were more desirable for placement. The orphanages of New York became so overcrowded that private aid groups sought ways of dispersing orphans to families willing to take them. Children were sometimes placed on an Orphan Train with a one-way ticket headed west. Rural areas had families who could use extra hands at farms and were willing to take orphans. As the train stopped along the route, youngsters were cleaned up and paraded on makeshift stages before crowds of prospective parents. Some farmers saw the children as nothing more than a source of cheap labor for rigorous farm work in exchange for room and board.

John Brummer recalled seeing the trains in Kansas. His daughter K.E. Wass remembered, "Perhaps one of the saddest things was the orphan train that stopped frequently in Osborne. Only farmers without children took an orphan — they wanted older ragamuffins as labor for their farms...my grandfather used their existence as a reminder to his own children that things could always be worse."

When the drought and Depression deepened into the 1930s, farmers could no longer afford to take in extra mouths to feed, so the Orphan Train program essentially dried up.

Lillie May Heathman became a widow with six children in Missouri. After she underwent surgery to provide skin grafts for one of her daughters who had been badly burned at a birthday party, she couldn't work and subsequently wasn't able to house and feed her children. She sent them to a nearby orphanage. Her daughter, Doris Heathman House, who was five-years-old at the time, didn't mind too much. She had her siblings with her and food to eat and had occasional weekend visits home. In fact, she remembered: "We had a pretty good life at the orphanage — churches helped support it. We always had donated clothes to wear, and the Brown Shoe Company would use us to test their shoes."

Hobos...we kept our distance

Jack Bolkovac

Born 1935 in Youngstown, Ohio

When I look back on the years 1929 to 1939, I can clearly see that it was a time of hardship. But to many of us who were born and raised during that time, we did not realize then the significance of the era.

My father, John Bolkovac, was an immigrant; he came to America as a teenager from Croatia. My mother, Catherine Subasic, is the daughter of Frank and Barbara Subasic who were also immigrants from Croatia.

I was born in 1935, the youngest of four boys, during the middle of the Great Depression in Youngstown, Ohio. Youngstown was a growing steel town then. I believe the area was the third largest steel producer in the nation.

My family lived in a two bedroom, four-room home with no bathroom on Brittain Street. The street was half concrete and half cinder, and two blocks long with a dead end at both extremities.

We lived on the concrete part. Most families on my end of the street had parents who were immigrants from southeastern Europe — mostly Slavic, Croats, Slovaks, Slovenians and Poles. Black families who migrated from the South rented homes on the cindered half.

In my family we were lucky that there were four boys so we did not have any problem sharing one bedroom. Our room had two double beds and two wardrobes — no closet — and a dresser. I am the youngest: my oldest brother John is 10 years older, Nick is eight years older and Al is a year and a half older.

Dad worked in the Republic Steel mill and was an active member of the new CIO Steelworkers Union. He also worked part-time as a bartender for my uncle who owned Jack's Café in town. My mom also worked at the cafe as a cook, waitress, and housekeeper. In those days it was common to operate a business downstairs and have rooms for boarders upstairs. My aunt and uncle had a couple of rental houses in the neighborhood. Ours was one and he owned two others. They also had a couple of boarders staying above the bar, which doubled as my aunt and uncle's living quarters.

Near our neighborhood was a large wooded area. Tucked into those woods was a big shack built by "hobos" — men who were down and out. They lived on what they could beg, borrow or steal, and we kept our distance.

As I look back, I can see that my family was not deprived of any necessities of life like the hobos that I saw and knew about, but I understand now that we had not much else than bare necessities. I believe that we were more fortunate than most because our father was actually able to provide for us by working as a barber, a bartender and when possible, in the steel mill. There was a small steel strike in 1937 — father was an active participant and involved in the confrontation with the National Guard in Youngstown.

We had food, clothing, shelter, and a loving family. That was all we needed. Our breakfast was usually toast and coffee, maybe cereal, but not often. Sunday dinner was always the big weekly meal and was most often roast chicken or chicken soup. The chickens were ours and egg gathering was one of my first chores.

Dad was a hunter. He had two beagles, Queenie and Shorty. In those days one did not have to travel far to find a place to hunt. Dad and a friend often went out and came home with a rabbit or two, sometimes a pheasant, which not only helped give us a variety of food, but also a desire to hunt and enjoy the outdoors into our adult lives.

For the most part our clothes were handed down, so by the time they came to me all the pockets had holes and several patches had been added. The same thing for shoes that were usually repaired at the local shoemaker and kept in the family for a long time.

There were families around who were more needy than us. Neighbors often took food or clothes and other things to them. For the most part they were appreciative, but at the same time not happy to be in that condition and have to accept handouts.

Jobs were scarce, pay was small and local grocery stores usually had a tab for families that would be settled on payday. For many, the grocery store was a daily visit because refrigerators were not common. Every day or two an ice truck delivered ice to people who had an ice box. In the summertime we kids picked up chunks of ice off the truck when there was a delivery — that was a real treat.

Deliveries were also made for several needed items. Heating was mostly from coal and all homes had a coal cellar, so coal was delivered in the winter. Milk was delivered every morning, a ragman with horse and wagon came collecting, and men with knife sharpeners and grinders called in at homes — peddlers of all types were common.

Every neighborhood had many shops that were owned by individuals: the grocery store, shoemaker, barber, beer garden, gas station, pool room, candy store or whatever, were all owned by people who lived in rooms over their shop. Most of them operated the same way — hoping tabs or bills would be paid on payday.

An interesting memory is of the quarantine signs posted on our house when one of us got the measles, mumps and other diseases which kept us kids in for the duration. However, our parents were free to go about their lives. Looking back, that was kind of strange. I am sure the bugs did not just stay inside the house with us.

Most folks seldom saw doctors those days. Home remedies, home first aid and midwives were mostly used. On a few occasions I had some more serious wounds that were cared for by Mom or a neighbor, washed out, then peroxide or iodine dabbed on and a tight bandage around the injury was common treatment. I only had two trips to a doctor: one was for my vaccinations and the other for a leg wound that was too severe for home care. My first trip to the dentist was probably at six or seven-years-old and was not a good experience.

We had neighborhood "gangs" such as those depicted in the old *Our Gang* movies. Older boys dominated the groups and we younger kids tagged along. Most of what we learned was from those older brothers. Sports and games were our activities and the street was our playground. That worked out well because it was a dead end street and there were very few cars. But for the most part, our days were filled with school and play. I did not start school until 1941.

The main entertainment was the radio — a fairly new invention that was the center of most living rooms. Our favorite programs were kids' shows, mom liked soap operas and dad enjoyed baseball, boxing and sometimes football. In the evening the entire family would enjoy half-hour sitcoms or mysteries. I remember listening to President Roosevelt. On Saturday we might go to a movie, which was 5 or 10 cents.

My dad owned a car so we were fortunate to enjoy a more mobile life than others. We took Sunday trips to our grandfather's farm near Sharon, Pennsylvania or a ride in the country. That was the major family-shared activity for us.

My wife of 53 years, Joan Pavlov, was born in nearby Struthers, Ohio, which was downriver from Youngstown and part of "Steel Valley." I believe that our childhoods helped make us more appreciative of things that we had later, and we tried to instill that value in our own family.

Joan's dad, John Pavlov, was a steelworker and her mom, Mary, worked as a housekeeper for a wealthy family in Youngstown. Joan lived on the outskirts of town near a large open area that was used by many in the community to keep farm animals. They had a cow for milk, chickens and a goose or two at times. In those days, many people had chickens in their back yards. Sometimes a cow or pigs could be found within the city limits.

Joan came from a similar background as mine because

she is a daughter of the Depression. However, she was the oldest of four, not the youngest. She also has a sister, Shirley, and two brothers, John and Don, which made her family dynamics a bit different than mine.

Her dad was also adept at many other jobs. He made several additions to improve their home. Her life was similar in many ways to mine, and she also managed to get through those times not realizing how tough they were because her parents, like mine and most others, provided love and protection which was the main role of parents at that time.

Life in Youngstown and Struthers was very much the same for those of us born during the Depression. There weren't too many frills but we managed to have a good life. We learned values and depended a great deal upon our faith in God to get us through. The Church was the backbone of most communities. In time of need it provided support and counsel to help families through. As children, we were expected to be part of that community and to fulfill the steps and obligations of our religion. I believe that was a very important part of our lives and gave us a foundation to build our families and instill those same qualities in our own children.

The Depression was a tough time. But it was a great beginning to life. It taught us that life is not easy, and to appreciate all that you have. It taught that respect and honor are important, but family is most important. The saying, "A family that prays together stays together," in good times and bad, is certainly true.

Jack Bolkovac, Ohio

Living as Hobos

In 1924 15-year-old Les Wallenborn left his divorced mother's home in Chicago, Illinois and "rode the rails" to Los Angeles, California looking for work. His uncle Edward lived there; it wasn't long before Les used his carpenter skills to build homes in the flourishing community.

Like so many young men at the onset of the Great Depression at the end of October 1929, Les felt the pinch of lost income and joined the Army for "three hots and a cot." A single man, he couldn't believe his luck when he was sent to the Hawaii base to ride out the Depression. In 1937 he was sent back to the mainland at Fort Lewis in chilly Washington State.

As a 15-year-old, Les joined countless old and young men who were either shiftless or down-and-out and looking for whatever work they could find — they were hobos.

Hobo is a phrase coined during post-Civil War days when returning soldiers couldn't find work. They put their meager belongings in a sack, tied it to a hoe and perched it on their shoulders while walking and looking for work. They were called "hoe boys" because they were usually employed to hoe crops.

During the depths of the Depression, people who were forced off of farms heard about work hundreds of miles away. Most often, the only way they could get there was by illegally hopping boxcars on freight trains. It is estimated that more than two million men and perhaps 8,000 women became hobos. Riding the rails was dangerous. "Bulls," or brutal guards hired

From Wikipedia

by railroad companies, kept hobos off trains starting in the early 1930s. A hobo couldn't just go to a railroad yard and climb onto a boxcar anymore.

Hobos hid along tracks outside the yard. As a train gained speed they'd run along, grab hold and jump into open boxcars. Sometimes they missed. Many lost legs and sometimes their lives. When the train neared its destination, hobos jumped off before a new set of "bulls" could arrest them or beat them up.

In 1933, about 6,500 hobos were killed either in accidents or by the guards. It was easy to get trapped between cars, and one could freeze to death in bad weather. When freezer cars were loaded at an ice factory, any hobo inside was likely to be killed.

No amount of clubbing or shooting or accidents could keep all of the hobos off trains. Desperate to feed their families, many had no choice but to hop a freight train to look for work.

Walter Ballard, a displaced farm worker photographed by Dorothea Lange in 1937 in Hardeman County, Texas, couldn't find a job. He rode the rails across the Great Plains before getting work with Roosevelt's WPA. He vividly remembers encountering "bulls" during an interview for Wessels Living History Farm in York, Nebraska. Walter and his brother-in-law were hijacked while going down through the railroad yards among everyone else prowling around. A "big guard, mean as could be" stepped out between the cars, and asked where they were going. He told them to catch a boxcar at a certain point when it would be going 50 mph. "He knew we couldn't catch that train a-going that fast," Walter said. "But he meant it. He meant stay out of that yard."

In Cheyenne, Wyoming guards riding horses and firing pistols in the air ran them all out, Walter said. "There was so many [hobos]. They just couldn't let you congregate in one town."

Another time in Chadron, Nebraska there were so many people on the freight train that "It looked like blackbirds all over it," Walter said. "We was scared to death to ride it, afraid we'd get throwed off or beat up. And believe it or not, when we got ready to go, that old brakeman hollered, 'All aboard!' Just like it was a passenger train. Well, then we felt at ease."

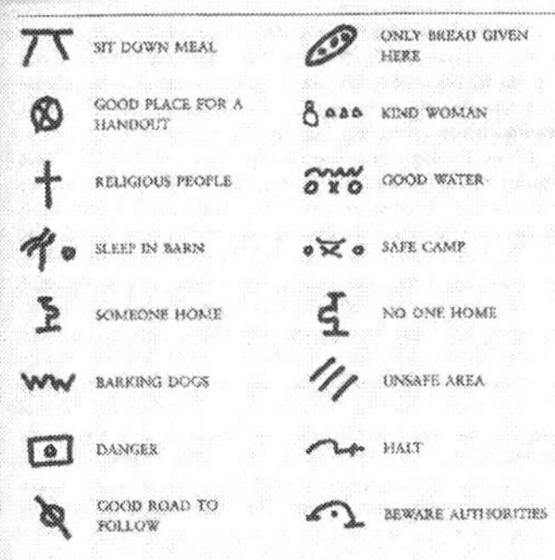

One of various samples viewed on the Internet, believed to be public domain.

Finding food was a constant problem. Hobos often begged for food from local farmhouses. If the farmer was generous, the hobo marked the lane so that other hobos would know "here" was a good place to beg. They left "signs" that other hobos could "read." Most were left on fences, lampposts, or mailboxes just outside the place. Some places would only give bread; others would give out food and clothes. Hobos were usually thought of as more than bums. People knew they were down on their luck and tried to help them.

"Hobos came to our door to work for a meal. We lived close to the train tracks that were hidden by a small hill. Mom said our house must be 'marked,' likely with chalk, because there were quite a few hobos who came by." ~Lynn Rohde, Washington

American hobos who later became famous include: Dust Bowl troubadour and country-western singer Woodie Guthrie, novelist Louis L'Amour, TV host Art Linkletter, oil billionaire H. L. Hunt, journalist Eric Sevareid, actor Robert Mitchum, and Supreme Court Justice William O. Douglas.

Hobo's Dinner

1 can tomatoes poured into a small saucepan.
Tear about 6 slices of bread into large pieces and add to the pan.
Stir gently so the bread doesn't entirely melt.
Add about 1 T butter or lard.
Salt to taste.
Heat thoroughly and serve over rice or a potato.

Mulligan Stew

Combining into a pot whatever food hobos had to share.

A boy's life consisted of working

Carol Byers

Father born 1925 Naola, Virginia

My Dad, Bernard Byers, grew up in a large family in Naola, Virginia, almost 15 miles southwest of Lynchburg. His father, Marshall Dillon Byers, and his mother, Annie Ruth Noel Byers, had nine children — six boys and three girls. Bernard was four-years-old when the Depression Era came on.

Granddaddy Byers grew up in Noala as did Granny. He was a confirmed bachelor but married Granny when he was 39 and she was only 16. They started a family right away: Hilton, Hubert, Frank, Daddy, Billy, Wesley, Pearl, Emma Lorine and Geneva. Granddaddy chopped wood and worked at the sawmill, and worked on building Route 501, laying rock for drainage.

"Little girl by radio." Rural Electrification Administration. Courtesy Franklin D. Roosevelt Presidential Library & Museum

The family lived on a small homestead with a main house, barn, chicken coop, hog pen and vegetable garden. They did not have electricity until 1935 when President Franklin D. Roosevelt instituted the Rural Electrification Administration to bring electricity to rural areas of the country. Before that, they used oil lamps. They didn't have a telephone and had to walk about two miles to use one at the general store when necessary. They had a radio with spotty reception to listen to news.

Every winter Granddaddy had ulcerated legs and kept his feet up because they were painful. Dad thought it was caused from the years of chopping wood. Although he never drank a drop of alcohol in his life, Granddaddy had a foul temper and if the situation called for it, he would hit you with anything he had in his hand such as a belt, a stick or even a piece of stove wood.

A tragedy struck in the fall of 1930. A 21-year-old neighbor loaned a .22 rifle to my five-year-old dad and his older brothers Hilton and Hubert. The rifle had a broken hammer spring held in place with a large rubber band. The boys were too young to purchase such a gun on their own, and they were glad to borrow it. They had shot their last round and Hubert bent to pick up the empty shells. The rubber band holding the hammer spring slipped out of Hilton's hand and a bullet pierced Hubert in the chest just below the heart. Hilton and Frank ran to get a doctor, but there was no car. The boys got into a boat and crossed the James River to get the doctor, but Hubert was dead by the time the doctor got there.

Despite that tragedy, Dad was interested in becoming a good marksman so he could shoot deer, rabbits and squirrels to add to the cast iron skillet on the wood stove for dinner.

The children all had chores, whether it was taking the cows out to pasture, feeding chickens, slopping hogs, planting vegetables, berry picking or whatever else was needed while waiting for harvest time. Everyone lived off the land, eating fruits and vegetables and relying upon hogs and chickens to feed their families. But there were fun times too. Living in a rural area, the children were accustomed to playing in fields, woods and streams, surrounded by horses, cows, chickens and pigs, as well as the usual cats and dogs. The children also rode horses, went fishing and canoeing and hunted small prey.

My father grew up without running water or indoor plumbing. They got water from either a well or a mountain spring and had to tote it back to the house in buckets for cooking and bathing. During fall and winter, the house was heated by a wood stove. Windows were opened in the summer.

Because there was no refrigeration, they had to can, preserve, pickle or dry fruits and vegetables for use later. They also had to salt meat after slaughter to keep it from spoiling; ham, bacon and sausages were put into jars along with hog fat. Unlike today, a boy's life consisted of working to help put food on the table. Occasionally, Dad was paid a few cents to take care of his Uncle Renzi's mule which was kept in their stable when he went away for the weekend. He hid the money until he could walk to the general store.

During the Depression, my granddaddy would take whatever work he could get, but it wasn't enough to feed a family of 11. The Byers family had no assets to fall back on, so the children were eventually farmed out to different families for a while. Alice Davis, a good friend and neighbor, made their clothes from material Granny bought at the dry goods store.

Dad attended first and second grades, but when the Depression hit, almost everyone was out of work and the Byers children didn't get to go to school at all. In the 1930s, a woman named Miss Grant from the Government visited house to house and found that the Byers family had fallen on bad times. She took everyone to Lynchburg, bought them new clothes and enrolled the children in school. To get to school in Pleasant View from the homestead, they rode 20 miles by bus.

When Dad was nine-years-old he stayed with Aunt Lily and his cousin Daisy for a year. Then he went to stay with the Bailey family for two to three years: Walter Bailey was 75 and his wife, Delia, was 66. Dad took care of their livestock. Although they were well-to-do, they did not send Dad to school. After he returned from the Baileys he skipped the 3rd grade and went to the 4th grade. Because he was way behind with children his age, he failed and had to retake 4th grade. He turned 15-years-old while he was in the 5th grade.

Toward the end of the Depression when World War II broke out, Dad went to stay with George Burks, who was caretaker of the Waugh estate in Waugh, Virginia across the river from Naola in Amherst County. The house had 12 bedrooms and 12 fireplaces, but only four chimneys. Keeping up with cutting wood for those 12 fireplaces was a full-time job.

Dad and his friend Junior Burford, who lived on a farm above the Waugh plantation, raised watermelons to sell — but everyone else had the same idea so they didn't sell many. Meanwhile, Dad got a job working on the railroad for seven months until he was called up into the Army. When he was 18 he registered for the draft and one month later he was called up and sent to the South Pacific.

Dad met Mom at a rooming house after WWII where Mom worked as a housekeeper and helped with cooking. People there asked if he had met Lillie. He said that he hadn't, and they remarked, "Don't worry, she'll be on you like a Junebug on a leaf." My parents married, had seven children — four boys and three girls — one of whom died three days after her birth due to pneumonia. We lived in a three-bedroom house with one bathroom in the Pimmit Hills area of Falls Church, Virginia all our lives. In the summer, Dad kept a garden in the back yard filled with all kinds of vegetables such as tomatoes, radishes, cucumbers, onions, squash, green peppers and sometimes a watermelon.

Dad taught us that work ethic is very important, and to be careful with money and not squander it. He wanted us to experience nature — picking our own apples, oranges, melons and berries. He taught us to take care of our things. He taught us not to be wasteful. He is an honest man.

Dad grew up in an impoverished region and, despite the hardships as a youngster, persevered in seeking a better life. He went from the homestead as a teen, traveled the country during World War II and went to the foreign shores of the South Pacific Islands. With death all around him, he never lost his moral compass. I am at a loss to understand how a young boy and teenager processed the hardship of the Depression and the brutal calamities and uncertainties of war without being scarred by them.

All of my life, I have known my dad as a man of integrity — he is an honest, principled, sensitive, loving and hard-working man who loves his family. He tried to appreciate life and always do what was right every day. I can see why Mom fell in love with him and wanted to be with him for life. Knowing so much about my dad's life helped me to understand why he never took it for granted. He is now the sole survivor of his nuclear family and has passed the mantle of integrity to his sons and daughters.

Carol Byers, Virginia

Radio brought the nation together

"[Dad] didn't understand all that was going on in large cities, but he heard enough on their Zenith radio to know that men all over the country were out of work and families were going hungry… Listening to the radio was a nightly ritual." ~ K.E. Wass, California

During the 1930s spending money on outside entertainment such as talking movies or theater productions was a rare treat. Radio was the nation's first mass medium that linked the country and made rural residents less isolated.

Above all, the radio provided a way to communicate

Roosevelt shortly after giving one of his famous fireside chats.

public domain

like never before. President Franklin D. Roosevelt's *Fireside Chats* helped people from country to city feel closer to their leader and fostered trust that he would get the nation out of the deepening Depression.

According to information from Zenith, the Great Depression drove down the average price of a radio from $139 in 1929 down to about $47 just four years later: "But the brutal market forces of the early Depression did not stop Americans from buying radios; by the end of the 1920s, one-third of US households owned a radio and by 1933 that number climbed close to 60 percent."

Despite the fact that using credit was part of the reason so many families were in dire straits, radio sales in the early 1930s were mostly on credit. According to Zenith, 75 percent of all radios were sold on installment payments in 1931 with the average radio buyer putting 20 percent down.

However, radio was of priceless value as people struggled to pay rent and put food on the table. It was a way to leave worries behind for a little while. Jack Bolkovac of Ohio said the radio was the center of family entertainment in his household, especially in the evening. *"I remember listening to President Roosevelt,"* he said.

Seabiscuit winning the Santa Anita Handicap in 1940. The match race between "the Biscuit" and War Admiral was in 1938. public domain

Having a radio for news and entertainment was so important that the 1930 Census included a question asking if the household had one.

Electricity didn't reach much of the country until the late 1930s so most radios were "wireless," or ran on batteries. Radio towers transmitted radio waves over mountains and were set up to reach far away radio sites. Some homes had "farm radios" — special radios made to run on DC power that were powered/recharged by wind. The earliest farm radios used A, B, and C batteries.

"Also, we got to listen to the radio if the wind had blown enough to charge the battery. We liked to listen to 'Inner Sanctum Mysteries' *and* 'The Lone Ranger.' *It was the only way the folks had to hear the news."* ~ Donna Abbott, Oklahoma

An advertisement for *Inner Sanctum*
from Wikipedia, fair use

Baseball stars Joe DiMaggio and Lou Gehrig were cheered on, boxing matches between Joe Louis and Germany's Max Schmeling in 1936 and 1938 had men talking, and nearly 40 million people listened to the horse race between Seabiscuit and War Admiral in Maryland in 1938.

Walter Winchell and Lowell Thomas were popular news commentators. Families laughed at comedians Jack Benny, Fred Allen, George Burns and Gracie Allen, Amos and Andy, and Fibber McGee and Molly. In the evening the Lone Ranger, Green Hornet, The Shadow, and Jack Armstrong entertained along with singers

"Oh the humanity!" The Zeppelin LZ 129 Hindenburg catching fire on May 6, 1937 at Lakehurst Naval Air Station in New Jersey. pubic domain

Bing Crosby and the Mills Brothers, Guy Lombardo's orchestra and the Grand Ole Opry.

In news coverage, the German airship *Hindenburg* caught fire in 1937 when landing in New Jersey. Thousands of people across the country heard newscaster Herb Morrison describe the terrifying scene on live radio and crying, "Oh the humanity!" Orson Welles famously broadcasted *War of the Worlds*, a radio play about Martians landing on Earth. Millions of people who didn't understand that the story was fiction panicked and tried to leave town. ~ *LivingHistoryFarm.org*

You cannot buy love — only stuff

Muriel (Salganek) Campbell

Father's birthdate unknown in Fastov, Ukraine

My father's family's Great Depression story began before 1929.

The Salganeks are Jewish immigrants who fled from Fastov, Ukraine to America around 1908. The story is that my grandfather was an abusive alcoholic and his children begged my grandmother Goldie, a strict Orthodox Jewish woman, to leave him. She was penniless with five children when she arrived; they came through Ellis Island and settled in Fall River, Massachusetts. My dad doesn't know his birthdate because his mother only knew that he was born during a blizzard. So the agents at Ellis Island gave him one.

Because they were in such dire straits, my dad, Louis Salganek, quit school in 5th grade at his mother's request. When he was 11-years-old in 1913, he traveled to the Midwest to find work. He hopped a freight train and found seasonal work — raking leaves in au-

Second Ellis Island Immigration Station, opened on December 17, 1900, as seen in 1905. Courtesy Wikipedia

tumn, shoveling snow in winter, helping with gardening and lawn mowing during spring and summer. He slept in fields when it was warm and movie theaters in the winter unless someone let him sleep in a barn. He sent just about every penny home to his mother. By then, she was taking in the neighbor's washing for pay. My father's two sisters quit school to work in factories as seamstresses when they reached age 12.

When Dad turned 14 he lied about his age to join the U.S. Cavalry in WWI just to get "three hots and a cot." After the war he moved back to the East Coast. A friend arranged a job for him in New York to deliver bread in a truck. By the time the Great Depression came around he was lucky to still have a job. Although he was bored and hated it, he didn't leave. He was happy to be working.

My mom, Florence, grew up in Brooklyn, and then Boston. Her parents were immigrants from Germany and Russia. Her mother died when she was 12, so she was in charge of cooking for her father and siblings. She was so busy writing shopping lists that she got in trouble for not studying for school.

My parents met at a mutual friend's home after he returned to Fall River. Dad's friend Marcy who had gotten the bread truck job for him in New York was married to Ida — one of my mom's friends. They met at their home and married sometime later. It was not a fancy wedding because they didn't have money. There weren't any wedding photos either, just one from their honeymoon in Atlantic City.

It wasn't long before Mom and Dad were expecting twins, but my sister was stillborn. I am an only child.

I think people with small families or without a family had a much more difficult time. Two sets of aunts and uncles moved into one large apartment with my grandmother Goldie to save money and keep a roof over their heads. She died when I was four-years-old. She loved me and I loved her. She would peel an apple 'round and 'round and then slice it and give me a tiny piece. She drank hot tea in a glass and liked to pinch my cheeks.

Mom was great at handling the little money we had. She had envelopes for food, rent and entertainment, which included carfare to the free beaches of New York or a movie on Saturday night and occasionally a babysitter. Movies back then were only 25 cents. Mom also had an envelope with about $10 that was to be used at month's end. She hounded department stores looking for a bargain to buy one of us a gift after it had been marked down three or four times.

Mom always told me that money for rent was most important; other things could wait. We did not have a lot of extras. A car was too expensive. We rarely went downtown or uptown on the subway, except to shop for a monthly treat at the month's end if she still had that leftover money.

Because we had little money to spend, we all talked to each other. Dad read the funny papers and all of the news stories to me that were in the nine or so New York City newspapers. We didn't have many books. I recall two children's books, *The Pokey Little Puppy*, and *Peter Pan*. I only had one doll at a time — when one wore out I would get another but had to wait a long time.

I had something that many of my friends who were much wealthier did not have — the time and attention of my parents. Every Sunday my dad gave my mom the day off and took me to either walk up the hill to my grandma and aunt's apartment or take the trolley. We stopped at a free public park and my dad put me in the swing and pushed it, then he'd sit on the seesaw with me and pretend to be a big baby. I so loved him. A day with my dad is what I had — and that was often more than other kids who had new dresses and a family car.

Despite the hardship of our lives, my best days were spent with my parents. We never went away to the country like other kids did or to the seashore because we could not afford it.

A lot of immigrants in the city worked for pauper wages and lived with large families in crowded tenements. On days off they headed to the beach with bathing clothes under their everyday wear, brought their own food and had spare change jingling in their pockets for a bathhouse to change clothes in, food and entertainment. Then there was the cost to get there.

But sometimes when we could afford the travel, we went to the free beaches at either Coney Island or Brighton Beach in New York City. We'd meet all of my aunts and uncles at the seashore. Dad came straight from work in his Ward's Baking Company uniform. He'd stand on the beach and peel his suit off to reveal his red wool bathing suit, then jump in the ocean for a swim. He'd come back and take a giggling me into the water, 'way over my head, but I trusted him to be a man of his word and not drop me. He never let me down.

My favorite time was going to the movies and sitting with my parents in the dark eating Good and Plentys and Sno-Caps which are chocolate drops covered with white sprinkles. My parents could not afford a babysitter so they took me with them.

Some sacrifices Mom made during the Depression years weren't apparent to me until years later. Sometimes at dinner she ate cereal, saying she was not hungry while my dad and I ate steak or lamb chops. She later confessed that she only had enough money to feed two people well, so she ate cereal and a banana instead. If she was ill, which wasn't often, she didn't call a doctor. It only cost $4 for our wonderful Dr. Jacobs to come to the house to take care of me when I had the Measles and Chicken Pox — and fix the broken ashtray for the same fee — Mom put that $4 away for a rainy day rather than spend it on herself.

I enjoyed dinnertime too because of the conversations I had with Dad, even as young as four-years-old. He would read an article to me about a political topic. He was a Democrat but would first argue it from the Republican position, then tell me to argue from the Democrat's position. Then he would say, "Switch," and I had to argue from the Republican's position and vice versa. He taught me that good men may have good ideas on both sides of the aisle and to respect people of all beliefs even if I did not agree.

Dad also taught me hateful, ethnic slurs and made me repeat them. Then came the threat: if he ever caught me saying any of these words or calling anyone by an ethnic or religious slur he would wash my mouth out with soap, and that if I used them I would have no right to complain if someone called me by an ethnic slur.

Dad read the Constitution and talked about it with me. He taught me to stick up for people who had a handicap and always to be honest. I actually got rewarded for coming home from a friend's house because her parents had the radio on and my punishment was to not be allowed to listen. My parents were so proud of me for coming home and remembering my punishment that they lifted it.

Had my dad not had his low-paying job during the Depression I'm not sure what would have happened. But I do know that we would have all been together wherever we were. For me as a kid having two loving parents was all that mattered. I learned that truthfully, the best things in life are free. You cannot buy love, only stuff.

Muriel Campbell, New York

What little he had was for his family

Nina (Stitt) Gilfert
Born 1927, North Apollo, Pennsylvania

I was born in 1927 just after my parents purchased a little bungalow with a mortgage of $900 in North Apollo, Pennsylvania. They already had two children and had another little girl a year and a half later. They struggled to make ends meet even before the Depression hit.

My mom and daddy are Frances and Roy Stitt. Their four children were under the age of 10 when the steel mill where Daddy worked came to a screeching halt and incomes in our small town dried up.

But we had a roof over our heads, thanks to Mr. Wallace who held the mortgage on most of the houses in the valley. Mr. Wallace very wisely told his mortgage holders they could stay in their homes if they paid at least the interest until times got better.

My parents were resilient and inventive. They were also unselfish and willing to do whatever it took to take good care of us. Our home was a happy place, not a depressive place. They played with us and kept us supplied with toys that they made out of whatever was handy.

Daddy was full of surprises. He made us stilts, skis, toy guns that shot rubber jar rings, tire swings, scooters, and cars out of wooden crates. Mom made doll clothes, paper dolls, cradles out of empty, round oatmeal boxes and all of our clothes. If we had to wear shoes we had outgrown because there was no money for new ones, Daddy took a razor blade and cut the toe out so they wouldn't hurt our feet. He also resoled them for us with glue and tacks. Sometimes they had cardboard liners to keep the tacks from sticking in our feet. Often the glue came loose and the soles flapped as we walked. But that was nothing, because all our friends had the same problems.

I remember that school children were given a pint of milk a day by some kind of charity. I was sent to school when I was five — maybe so that I could get that pint of milk. I remember waking up early in the morning and looking out the window to watch our local dairyman Mr. Heckman park his horse and buggy by the curb and bring our milk up to the kitchen porch. In the winter the milk froze before we brought it in and the cardboard top was standing up from the mouth of the jar.

Keeping six people fed on a little bit of unemployment insurance was a challenge, but a challenge my parents were up to. Mom grew a vegetable garden in the back yard that kept us in tomatoes, cucumbers, lettuce, onions, beans and potatoes. Daddy turned his clubhouse into a chicken coop and built rabbit hutches to provide us with eggs and meat. We also had cherry, peach and plum trees and a grape arbour. Mom canned whatever was left over to see us through the winter. My sister Jean and I helped.

Daddy gleaned watercress, sassafras root, black walnuts and horseradish from the woods at the edge of town. He also picked raspberries and apples at his uncle's farm. Mom made the best salads out of that watercress combined with the dandelion greens that grew in our own yard.

The hardest thing our family endured during those days was my brother Herb's illness. Herb suffered from asthma. In those days it was an illness without much treatment. It kept him weak and unable to play games with the other boys.

I came home from school one day and saw the doctor's car outside the house. I rushed inside to find Herb, pale and languid, propped up with pillows on the couch. Dr. Lewis told my strain-faced mother that he'd done everything he could and that the rest was up to God. Thank goodness God is good and let us keep our brother, although he never was very strong. His health issue was another strain on my parents' meagre income.

Despite all of our family challenges, there were others even less fortunate. Mom saved every little leftover bit of food so that she could feed hungry travelers who came to our door. They were honest men traveling the countryside looking for any work. In the wintertime these leftovers were kept in a wooden crate nailed to the kitchen windowsill because we didn't have an icebox. The crate also held whatever milk, meat and eggs we garnered.

Those hungry travelers marked our house with chalk to let others know they could get food there. Mom wouldn't let us wipe off the chalk because she wanted them to know she would feed them from whatever she had.

But my parents found humor in little things. I remember my mother sitting at her mending. She laughed and tossed Daddy a sock and said, "Roy, there is not enough sock left here to mend." I know what she meant because it was my job to hang the laundry and I was embarrassed to hang Daddy's worn-out socks and underwear. He never bought a thing for himself. What little he had was for his family.

Through it all, my mother never lost her sense of pride. She taught us how to set a table correctly and insisted that we do so every day. The whole family sat down in the dining room at the table for our evening meal with cracked and broken tableware set properly on a mended white cloth. Good manners were always enforced.

Tom Brokaw has called my generation, "The Greatest Generation." Maybe we learned selfless duty by the example set us by the generation that raised us.

Nina Stitt Gilfert, Florida

Every school child got milk

"I remember that school children were given a pint of milk a day by some kind of charity. I was sent to school when I was five – maybe so I could get that pint of milk. I remember waking up early in the morning and looking out the window to watch our local dairyman Mr. Heckman park his horse and buggy by the curb and bring our milk up to the kitchen porch. In the winter, the milk froze before we brought it in and the cardboard top was standing up from the mouth of the jar."

~ Nina Stitt Gilfert, grew up in Pennsylvania

In 1933 when Congress established the Federal Surplus Relief Corporation in order to distribute surplus pork, dairy products and wheat to the needy, Nina Stitt Gilfert, her siblings, and children across America benefitted.

A Kentucky boy benefits from a school milk program in 1930.

Library of Congress collection

The USDA declared that at school, "Each child should have a full glass – one-half pint of milk -- to drink at each meal in addition to any milk used in the preparation of the main dish. This milk may be served as cocoa occasionally if there is time and equipment to prepare it."

Ben Warkentin grew up in Shafter, California. He said, *"I do remember having hot chocolate sometimes."*

With the USDA involved, milk for school children came under strict regulations, despite the fact that many children across the country lived on farms and probably had a dairy cow at one time or another.

Officials decreed that " ...[milk] should be delivered in bottles stoppered with tight-fitting caps, preferably the kind of cap that fits down around the sides of the rim. Loose milk, or milk carried in large cans to be dipped out for the children is unsafe because of the many possibilities of contamination in handling. Also, such milk may lack cream and it is more subject to adulteration than bottled milk."

USDA officials also didn't like for children to drink milk from straws because, "Experiments show that when children drink milk from a bottle through a straw they often leave a considerable quantity and this milk that is left contains nearly 16 percent of the original amount of fat in the bottle. This means a loss of vitamin A as well as of fat."

Information taken from "Menus and Recipes for Lunches at School" published in 1936 by the USDA.

Heated discussions about what to do with the children

Cindy Phillips
Father born May 1929 Springfield, Ohio

My dad, Richard Phillips, was born May 26, 1929 to Margaret (Slentz) and Robert Phillips just a few months prior to the stock market crash. His older brother Robert was born in February 1928, and his sister Barbara was born in July 1930. They were like triplets and remained close throughout their lives.

My dad's father committed suicide when Dad was two-years-old in April 1931. He was a tenant farmer in Clark County, Ohio near South Vienna. I think they raised hogs and chickens, cows for milk and meat, and corn or wheat.

He knew that the Sheriff of Clark County was coming to arrest him for passing bad checks. Grandma Phillips said they came and got her instead. She sat for hours in the basement of the Security National Bank and Trust Company in downtown Springfield writing his name over and over again. They were trying to implicate her so that they could charge someone and make them liable. Uncle Howard Garst, her mother's brother, was a known businessman as part owner of Yost Superior Co. in Springfield and was able to stop that.

There were heated discussions about what to do with the children after their father's suicide and what would happen to their mother. The paternal side wanted my dad and his siblings raised Catholic — the maternal side didn't. But Robert's family wouldn't take the children to help Margaret out. They were going to be sent to a children's home, except for the only girl whom another relative wanted to adopt.

However, Margaret's dad, John Slentz, declared that the kids weren't going to be separated, so they went to live with him and his wife, Grandma Nellie, on a farm several miles from North Hampton. He lived by the Golden Rule but didn't go to church.

Grandpa Slentz lost a larger farm of about 50 acres at the beginning of the Depression. He was forced to rent a smaller one of about 15 acres doing the same thing — raising corn, and Holsteins for milking, beef cows, hogs, chickens and geese. They raised what they needed to eat then sold or traded for other things. Grandpa paid the same monthly amount for the smaller farm that he did for the larger one. When Dad was old enough to understand that, it really bothered him — especially because the landlord was strict about things being on time.

His mom, my grandma Phillips, was extremely fortunate. Uncle Howard knew people at Collier's Weekly magazine in Springfield, Ohio. A married woman in the subscription department offered to give up her job for a widow or a woman with children who had been abandoned. Grandma got that job and remained with the company until they closed in 1956. They were the world's largest publishing house at one time and were an important employer during the Depression era.

Grandma rented a room in town and worked at Bangart's Market as well, which was owned by her sister Mary's husband, Ivan Bangart. Grandma ran the register, stocked shelves and swept floors.

In those days, gasoline was rationed unless you worked on a farm, so Grandma rarely made it out to see my dad and her two other children. Not only was gas scarce, she didn't have a car and worked six days per week. There was no bus that went that far out into the country — 10 miles away or more. So her relationship with her children during the Depression years became more like an aunt — someone who came to visit occasionally and brought gifts. She just didn't make enough to support them all or even give her parents money to help. As a result, they looked upon their grandparents as parents, calling Grandpa "Dad," although they still called Nellie Grandma, or Grandma Slentz when speaking to others.

Dad always said they were fortunate because they lived on a farm and grew their own food. Grandpa Slentz was also fortunate enough to work for International Harvester hauling gravel when Citizen's Dairy in Springfield was being built. Later, he worked in the dairy's bottling plant and stayed even after the economy started to recover. The company sent lame milk-truck horses out to their farm to heal up. Because of that, Dad had a love of big draft horses throughout his entire life.

As they got older Dad and his brother, Bob, worked for money to help the family. One job was down the road baling hay for a Dunkard Brethren man. They worked sunup to sundown for two days and all the religious man gave them in payment was an ice cream cone. Grandpa Slentz, who wasn't an angry man, went down and had words with him about that. Ice cream wasn't a fair wage for boys who worked for two days, sunrise to sunset.

Dad and Bob raised and sold geese for Christmas dinners one year. He was never so sick of feathers and plucking them in all his life. They bought candy as a treat and gave the rest of the money to the household. The duo also went to work sweeping floors for Uncle Howard's business after school when they were teens.

There were good times too. Uncle Howard got tickets to professional baseball's first-ever night game on May 24, 1935 — Cincinnati Reds against the Philadelphia Phillies. He took Dad, Bob and Grandpa Slentz. Of course, there were no Interstates back then, so it was a long trip from Springfield to Cincinnatti and back. They got home in time for Grandpa to get ready to go to work, while Dad and Bob milked the cows and did morning chores.

One Christmas, Dad, Bob and Barbara shared a huge gift — a Radio Flyer red wagon with slat sides. They took turns riding in it while the other two pushed it around the house — it was laid out such that they could go in a circle through several rooms. They kept hitting the side of the doorway. Grandpa Slentz warned them, "One more time," and it would go into the barn until spring. Well they did, and it did. There was no whining or pleading or begging. The wagon was gone.

The farmhouse didn't have central heat. The kids ran downstairs in the morning to the coal-fueled stove to get warm before running to the outhouse. They were in high school before indoor plumbing was installed, which included a toilet. One spring day the kids came home from work and saw the neighbor's Billy goat in front of the outhouse. He had trapped Grandma Slentz in there all afternoon. Every time she opened the door to see if he was gone, he charged!

As I grew up, I noticed the way that my parents (Mom, Barbara Jean Flannery, born in 1932 lived with relatives on a Kentucky farm during the Depression) kept and reused everything. Dad and Mom saved everything because, "You never know when you might need it."

As a result of growing up during the Depression, Dad was quite handy. He helped to build my younger brother's home and helped with various things in my own home and my older brother's as well. He could fix almost anything or at least jury-rig it. He often went into the basement to find the thing he needed to fix something. Dad and a few other men also designed and built the baseball field in Northridge, the community we lived in. He coached teen boys in baseball before he had children.

Growing up without a father really affected Dad. He always wanted to be a father. When Mom had her third miscarriage he was the one who suggested adoption. They adopted my older brother and me. Later, as medical science caught up, they were able to have my younger brother on their own.

The Depression had a profound affect on both parents.

Giving of oneself, working toward the "good of the order" and sacrificing for family and country was as much part of them as breathing.

They volunteered in the community, helped others and instilled in us a love of our country, family and faith. They were founding members of Christ Lutheran church, now called Faith in Christ; they served on the counsel, sang in the choir and were Altar Guild members. Mom also made things for their annual Christmas sale.

Dad was a founder of the credit union where he worked. He was also elected treasurer at the initial meeting of the Boosters Club, a position he held until three months before his death in 2011. Throughout the years they raised money for indoor visitor bleachers and all of the outdoor athletic fields. As a tribute they named the football field after him. But he believed that it should be named Volunteer Field in honor of everyone who had volunteered.

I think "The Rest of the Story," as Paul Harvey would say, is the carry-over of those difficult Depression years and how they played out in the lives of people like my parents who then instilled the same values into their children. While probably almost all of those people would think their lives ordinary, they were truly extraordinary from lessons learned in a time when hope was in short supply. It is a legacy that will endure.

Cindy Phillips, Ohio

Christmas geese for sale

From Wikipedia

One thing the Depression era brought out in nearly everyone was the ability to make money in variety of ways – or at least try.

When Cindy Phillips' dad, Richard Phillips, and his brother were fairly young adolescents, they decided to try their skill as entrepreneurs in geese for Christmas dinners: *"Dad and Bob raised and sold geese for Christmas dinner one year. He was never so sick of feathers and plucking them in all his life."*

Following are instructions for how to prepare and cook a Christmas goose the old-fashioned way:

The most time-consuming step is plucking the bird. Large feathers are fairly easy to grasp and remove, but it's difficult to remove every last one of the finer down feathers closest to the skin. Scalding water helps loosen them up.

After stripping the feathers away from the torso, string up the goose by its feet to help in removing the neck, head and wings. Remove the feet.

Remove the internal organs and set them aside to use later with the carcass bones for stock or for gravy.

Slice off the neck skin about one-half inch in front of the body.

Remove excess fat from the goose and save it in a pot with about ½ cup water. Grab the fat inside the body cavity and add it to the pot. Slice off the wide belly flaps covering the body cavity if the bird is not going to be stuffed. Remove the tail. Put all of this into the pot and put over low heat to render out to make goose fat spread.

Prick the goose's skin all over with a needle without piercing to the muscle so the bird crisps up as it bakes.

To bake: Preheat the oven to 325F. Baking time is about 2 ½ hours total

Ingredients:

1 goose, about 8 lbs.
Juice of a lemon
Salt and pepper
1/2 yellow onion, peeled and chopped
1 head garlic
2 tablespoons flour
2 cups chicken stock (for gravy)
1 teaspoon dried thyme

Rub the goose all over with the cut half of a lemon. Put the halves inside the goose. Season the goose with salt sprinkled liberally over the skin. Cut off the top of a head of garlic and place it inside the goose.

Place the goose breast-side up on a rack in a roasting pan and into the oven. After the goose has cooked for about 20 minutes, add root vegetables such as carrots, parsnips, turnips, potatoes and/or rutabagas, peeled and chopped into large chunks to the roasting pan.

You can also use this time as an opportunity to spoon

From Wikipedia

out some of the goose fat that may be collecting in the bottom of the roasting pan. Put it in the pot with the rendering goose fat.

When you're done, put the goose back into the oven for another 25 minutes.

When a total of 45 minutes of cooking time has elapsed, carve off the whole breasts getting down to the bone. Goose is a red meat and should not be cooked until well-done. Remove the breasts and tent with foil.

Finish cooking the rest of the goose for another 45 minutes until the legs are done. Finish the breasts off by placing them skin-side down in a hot pan with goose fat until the skin is crispy. Do not cook the meat side.

Napa Valley, California. More than 25 years a bindlestiff, this man walked from the mines to the lumber camps to the farms. He is the type that formed the backbone of the Industrial Workers of the World in California before the war.

Photo by Dorothea Lange for the Farm Security Administration

House was chalked by hobos

Lenora Gaerisch Rohde

Born 1930 in Seattle, Washington

Born in 1930, I was a little girl during the Depression in Seattle, Washington. So this is what I remember, or what was told to me:

My mother, Hanna Ronvik, was from Norway, and my father, Werner Gaerisch, was from Germany. We lived in a small house in a little area named Happy Valley between the Magnolia and Ballard neighborhoods north of downtown Seattle — lots of Scandinavians lived there.

Our home was nothing fancy but it was warm and cozy. I was born in this house, the youngest of four children. My sister and brothers were nine, 12 and 14 years older than me, so if they were living today they would have more to say than what I can remember. I never felt that we were poor, but we must have been. We always had food on the table and nice clothes — not expensive, of course. Between my mom shopping at second-hand stores and sewing our clothing, she and my dad gave us a good life. But as a kid, I never knew the extent of what the Depression was doing to our family. To me, this was a normal kid's life — play, eat and all the good things to do.

My dad worked for Safeway as a baker. He sure smelled good when he came home. Bread was baked in a huge warehouse-type bakery. I remember the massive ovens where my dad put in huge baking pans full of bread dough. He had to put his head into the ovens to feed in the pans. I was very impressed when we got to see that.

My mom was a tailor in downtown Seattle before she married. Mom never had another outside job after that. She worked hard doing daily chores, and could mend anything.

At home, we had a few chickens for their eggs. We also had a garden for fresh vegetables, and cherry trees, a pear tree, a plum tree, some raspberries. Food was never an issue. There was a lot of exchanging going on amongst neighbors.

Hobos came to our door to work for a meal. We lived close to the train tracks that were hidden by a small hill. Mom said our house must be "marked," likely with chalk, because there were quite a few hobos who came by. The most important thing that I remember learning is that these men were not there for hand-me-outs. They chopped wood or did any job to pay for their meal. And what a meal they would get! Mom was a good cook and always had left-overs. The men were invited into our home and sat at our breakfast nook. They were very polite and very thankful, just good men that had fallen on hard times. The WPA gave jobs to them after awhile and that helped a lot.

Seattle's "Hooverville" was a large, open area by the railroad tracks that jobless people built. I say, "built," because that's what they did. Scraps of lumber and anything they could find would be their home in this "city." It was actually in a neighborhood called Interbay, located between Queen Anne Hill and the Magnolia neighborhoods. It is within walking distance from my home today.

Here is where the homeless families kept warm, fended for themselves and for each other, depending upon people to feed them and help them. They were part of our community; their kids went to school just as every other kid did.

At school we were given soda crackers and tomato juice every morning. I thought that was what schools did all the time. In Kindergarten, we lined up to get a tablespoon of cod liver oil. Each child had their own spoon. I loved it! Until one morning I almost gagged because it was rancid. Our teacher, whom I adored, had put the bottle of cod liver oil in the window of our cloakroom. She found out not to put it in the sun.

Seattle can be very cold and wet through most of the year, so it would have been hard for some people to stay warm. In front of our house was a dirt road with rocks that had large planks for pedestrians to walk upon. Sometimes the planks were taken, probably for wood to burn. We had a wood/coal range for our house. In fact, I still have it, and it works. As a little girl, my job was to get a bucket of coal to fill the big bin when needed. It was such nice, warm heat for our house, and good to cook with. I used it not too long ago one Thanksgiving when our electricity went out and I had a turkey in my electric stove. I fired up the coal stove and we had a good dinner. Gravy made by candlelight — my guests thought it was great. Me, not so much.

Being so young, I didn't realize there was a Depression. All that I knew was that life was wonderful. I needed more children to play with, but going to school solved that problem. I was allowed to go play with "the kids up the way," but had to be home before dark — and this was maybe six blocks away. I had trees to climb, railroad tracks to run on — I was good at that. I walked to the Hiram M. Chittenden Locks and crossed over them to the Ballard neighborhood. We played around water and sometimes collected bark for the stove. I didn't miss a thing. Outdoors was the best playground ever. Nowadays a parent would have a fit to hear what all of us kids did. Oh, but such fun!

Perhaps the most important lesson that I learned from growing up during the Depression is that you can be happy with what you have — and I've never been jealous of those who have more. If I wanted more, I worked for it until I could afford it. Family and friends are what is important.

Lenora "Lynn" Rohde, Washington

Cod liver oil was public policy

In 1930s America, children reluctantly lined up at home or at school for their daily dose of a spoonful of cod liver oil.

Except Lenora Rohde.

"In Kindergarten, we lined up to get a tablespoon of cod liver oil. Each child had their own spoon. I loved it! Until one morning I almost gagged because it was rancid. Our teacher...had put the bottle of cod liver oil in the window of our cloakroom. She found out not to put it in the sun." ~ Lenora Rohde, Seattle

Rickets and other health issues that arose during the Depression because of a lack of Vitamin D in children's diets were kept at bay when the daily dose of the fermented Atlantic fish's liver oil became public policy for the good of children.

The nasty-tasting stuff contained vitamin D along with vitamin A and omega 3 fatty acids, but it's the vitamin D that was believed to be key in fighting infections and strengthening bones, hair and teeth, and skin.

With the fortification of milk with vitamin D – also in the 1930s -- cod liver oil fell out of vogue. Drinking milk was much easier and tasted lot better.

1930 bus advertisement. Minnesota Historical Society

Wife of WPA (Works Progress Administration) worker living in Arkansas River bottoms. Webbers Falls, Oklahoma.

Russell Lee, June 1939, Library of Congress

He believed strongly in preserving dignity

Yvonne (Green) Taylor

Father born 1921 Tifton, Georgia

My father, Fred Green, was born in Tifton, Georgia in 1921 and grew up in rural Cordele. Including my father, there were four children: his sisters Princess and Velvie, then my father, Fred, and youngest boy, Wright.

My grandparents Bernard and Dovie Green were poor. They had a small farm and raised sugar cane, watermelons, cantaloupes, and a garden with various vegetables, peaches, corn and pecans. They had a few chickens for eggs and for roasting on special occasions. They also had a couple pigs and a milk cow. My grandfather used a hand plow pulled by a mule to till the fields.

They lived in a small, three-room, poorly insulated, wooden farmhouse that sat on blocks and barely protected the family from cold. At night they used a porcelain pot for personal use and an outhouse during the day. The house was sparsely furnished and utilitarian; the boys slept on one side together in a small single bed and the girls slept together on the other side. But they were warm under the feather blankets my grandmother sewed by hand.

Once a week they bathed with water pumped from the Baptist church's well across the street. They all used the same bath water in the kitchen on Saturday night, sitting in a round, tin tub. The water was heated on the wood stove in the kitchen. There was also a bucket of water on the front porch with a tin dipper for drinking and cooking.

My father was about eight-years-old in 1929 when the Depression began. One of his chores was to get up with Wright to milk the cow at sunrise when the roosters crowed. When they returned to the kitchen with a fresh bucket of milk, more often than not they found my grandmother kneading biscuit dough in a tin pan while the girls collected eggs from the chicken house just outside the door.

My grandmother worked hard to take care of her family: she ground corn to make hominy grits, hand-separated cream from milk to make buttermilk — even sitting down to rest on the porch was time for work while she made butter in a churn. She also made lye soap for bathing, cleaning dishes and washing clothes. Clothes were scrubbed on a washboard, and then the girls hung them on the line to dry. That was their favorite part wandering among the clothes on the line with sunshine on their faces and a breeze bringing the clean smell around them.

Although the Greens were poor, they always had food because they raised it themselves. They fed strangers who wandered through the countryside looking for jobs in exchange for food. My grandfather never turned anyone away who was hungry. He understood that even though he had little, if Providence brought someone to his door he had to share what little he had. He believed strongly in preserving dignity and found a task for the guest to do in exchange for a meal.

When they didn't have cash, the family traded for other things they needed. In season, Grandfather loaded melons, sugar cane, peaches or pecans on a wagon every Saturday and went to town to sell or trade for whatever essentials he couldn't make or grow. Sometimes they went without.

They wore the same clothing every day until they literally wore out. Then Grandma used the rags to stuff blankets or patch holes into the porous walls of the house. Winters were mild but still freezing at night. Nothing was wasted.

My father had to quit school in third grade because they couldn't afford shoes for all four children. One story in particular is heart-rending to me: Grandmother took the children to church; they were dressed poorly and had no shoes. My father was nine-years-old when he overheard a church lady say, "How can they bring this child to church without shoes?" My father's heart filled with shame and he never went back. His eyes filled with tears even to his old age every time he told this story. It wasn't until much later in life that he became reacquainted with the Lord.

They all understood that it required the full-scale effort of every family member if they were going to survive this indefinite Depression. Welfare or help from the government wasn't put in place yet, and even if there had been, Grandfather would have died trying to avoid it before he would have accepted that kind of charity. Every member of his family was essential for survival and worked hard from morning until night. Most families had four or more children who were precious resources on the farm.

But there was time for fun. My father played a small guitar that he re-fashioned after finding it in the old barn where the mule was kept. His quick wit and natural musical ability provided merriment for the family.

My mother, Betty Marcellus, and father met after WWII in Pasadena, California when he returned from Iwo Jima. They married after just two weeks and were together until he died in 1994 of a stroke. My mother died in 2009 from heart failure.

My parents were entrepreneurial and fiercely independent, preserving the ethics they learned by surviving the Depression and passing them on to their children. My parents had a small sewing store in their latter years, my brothers owned small businesses, and my husband and I owned a photo studio and home-schooled our two children.

It was the indomitable spirit I saw in my parents that inspired me to believe that my family could solve problems that confronted us. I never thought there was any situation that couldn't be worked through. My mother also grew up on a farm and knew how to fix just about anything. She taught me to can food, make bread, sew and to never give up!

The scriptures say, "Men perish without a vision." I firmly believe that vision was a palpable reality that took shape in my parents after they endured those hardships. It inspired me and my children — that indeed we can survive without the help of the government, and with a faith to sustain us.

Yvonne Taylor, Texas

True grits

"My grandmother worked hard to take care of her family: she ground corn to make hominy grits, [and] hand-separated cream from milk to make buttermilk..."

Yvonne Taylor, Texas

True hominy is dried corn kernels that have been soaked and cooked in an alkaline solution to remove the hulls. During the Depression, lye solution that was used to make soap was also used to soak corn to make "grits." Soaking in lye removed fungus from stored corn and made the kernels easier to grind.

To make hominy grits from scratch:

Sort through dry corn kernels to pick out broken ones and discard chaff. Broken kernels soften and swell faster than whole ones and make it harder to determine the point where the corn turns into hominy.

Soaking

Soak dry corn in lye (alkaline) water until the skin and the little "nib" at the point come off. This might take a day or two. Stir the hominy occasionally. When the skin comes off, the corn will be swelled enough to break the skins. Wash thoroughly — many, many times — to remove all of the lye.

Overnight Soak

- Add the alkaline solution to the pot, stir, then add 2 cups of corn for 4 cups of grits
- Cover and let rest about 12 hours

Quick Soak

- Add alkaline solution to the pot, stir, and then add 2 cups of corn
- Cover, bring to a boil, turn off the heat, and let rest for 2 hours

Prepared grits from Wikipedia

Ready to cook

Simmering

A slow-simmer near 190F for two hours is a critical factor in making homemade hominy. When the hominy is at that temperature, there will be slight movement or bubbles in the water. If the temperature is too low, it takes longer to make hominy. If the temperature is too high, some kernels will cook faster than others.

Oven Simmer

Bring a covered pot to a boil on the stove, then place in a 250F oven. Check the water temperature after 30 minutes — it should be about 190F. If you don't have a thermometer, make sure there's just slight movement or bubbles in the water. Otherwise, turn the oven up or down a little.

Stove-top Simmer

Bring a covered pot to a boil, then turn down to low heat. Check the water temperature after 15 minutes. It should be about 190F. Between 180 and 195 is okay.

Bite Testing for Doneness

To determine if the hominy is done, rinse several kernels very well, then bite into them. Some kernels finish faster than others so you'll have to bite more than one kernel each time. To rinse for tasting, use a stirring spoon to put about six kernels in a small bowl with a little liquid. Add cold water to the bowl, then dump the kernels into your hand and rinse under running water for a few seconds. Bite into them and spit them out if they are under-cooked.

As a rule of thumb, remove the hominy from the alkaline when 10 percent of the kernels are over-cooked and starting to dissolve, 10 percent are still slightly crunchy, and 80 percent are done. You can finish cooking the kernels after removing them from the alkaline solution. The crunchy ones will soften in the cooking liquid long before the others become too soft.

Cook and eat

Cook the corn until tender, cover it with a generous amount of butter, salt to taste and dig in.

1936 farmer. Minnesota Historical Society

Tears left dirt streaks on his face

K. E. (Brummer) Wass
Father born 1913 in Mitchell County, Kansas

The Great Depression was painful to most American families. But for my family, the drought nearly struck a death knell with the dust storm of Black Sunday in April 1935.

My dad, John Brummer, was born late in June 1913 in Kansas. He is the oldest of 12 children born to John I. Brummer and his wife, Katie Simeon Brummer. They lived on a 160-acre farm in Mitchell County, Kansas with my dad's paternal grandparents. They grew wheat and potatoes and raised hogs.

Dad went to school until the eighth grade, but he was needed to work on the farm, so higher education was out. It was apparent from an early age that he was mechanically inclined, and that made him valuable for many farm tasks in addition to helping with pigs and working the golden wheat fields.

On April 13, 1935, my 21-year-old dad went about his normal chores. Dust swirled around him as he led Pat and Mike, two large plow horses, down to a nearby creek. Afterward, he tied them to a cottonwood tree and unbuttoned his trousers to relieve himself onto the ground. His cap slid to the top of his eyes as he watched his urine soak quickly into the parched earth. Everything he wore was too big — it had once been his father's or his grandfather's. Clothes hung on his lithe body like rags. But everyone else was dressed the same.

After the short rest, Dad tied the harness to a plow and created furrows in the farmland; his father told him that those would help keep their topsoil from blowing into Colorado.

When Dad followed behind the slow, steady horses, his mind usually wandered. He didn't understand all that was going on in large cities, but he had heard enough on their Zenith radio to know that men all over the country were out of work and families were going hungry. Dad's family had no money in the stock market when it collapsed because they simply had no money; but they were optimistic — at the very least, they had their land.

Listening to the radio was a nightly ritual. After the family ate potato soup and recited the Rosary, they sat on the floor in front of the wireless. His dad turned it on for exactly one hour to catch up on the latest news. My dad overheard conversations between his dad and grandfather: the roaring '20s was suddenly over, there were food lines, and war was on the horizon. He felt lucky to be stuck on their farm with three generations. At least they had potatoes, wheat for bread and meat from their hogs.

Dad had tried to get Joe at the Oldsmobile shop to let him work a little for extra money to help his family. Dad listened when the older farming men spoke about working in the fields. The consensus was that they were better off because they had their land, animals, and each other. And yet, my grandfather worried that recurring windstorms combined with drought would destroy the land they needed in order to exist.

As the sun dropped below the flat Kansas horizon, my dad headed back up to the house. It was Saturday and he needed a bath in the galvanized tub of shared water so he would be presentable at church the next morning. His parents always loaded up all 10 of the oldest children and made the drive to Osborne every Sunday. But Dad thought about how many things around the farm needed repairs and how little there was left to use for those repairs. He was a natural mechanic and could fabricate most parts needed for their few pieces of machinery. But not even a genius could create a new set of gears for the tractor without any iron to grind.

As the oldest, he was given the job of taking care of the horses, too. After working the field he led them to their tumble-down barn, fed them a strictly-measured portion of hay, and filled the water trough with the last of the water from his canvas water bag. He didn't need to be attentive as he did his chores, because for the past 10 years of his life this was routine: nothing was thrown away, every portion of food for human or animal was carefully preserved, doled out, and eaten without complaint.

If he didn't eat his day's potato, he took it back to the bag in the cellar. He always noticed the ever-shrinking collection of jars and recycled coffee cans on shelves. Canned vegetables and applesauce that were made at the end of summer were gone by the end of winter. They usually had sausage from the last hog they butchered, but hams were typically traded to pay the doctor for medicine that his grandmother needed. Sometimes he wished that they could have ham for breakfast. Or even eggs. Anything but potatoes.

On the eve before the Black Sunday dust storm, Dad's mother asked him to double-lock the cellar door. The wind was kicking up and she didn't want to shovel dirt off the few potatoes and rhubarb stalks that were left. In later years, he told me how he finished his chores and stood on the porch that circled the farmhouse. He looked north and sensed that a windstorm was brewing. They always prayed for rain every night, but God left the earth as parched as a drunkard's mouth the morning after a binge.

Dad said the wind blew all night. When they woke up, the sky was brown from dust. The old barn creaked and clattered which caused Pat and Mike to be restless. My grandfather decided that the trip to town for church would be dangerous. The car was the only mechanical piece that still ran, so it remained in the garage which was the only structure of value on the property.

The family house had missing windows on the north side from the last storm. Because there was no money, they were not replaced. My grandpa used boards from the barn to cover the openings. He hoped to get new windows through a trade of wheat or bacon, but who knew when that would be?

That dusty Sunday, women cut old sheets into masks to cover everyone's faces, including the babies to keep dust out of their lungs. Later, the masks were used to patch clothing.

The wind blew into the next day and finally stopped. The men went out to assess the farm and were mostly silent. They stopped to shake their heads in disbelief at the carnage of what had once been a somewhat successful farm. Help from their neighbors would not be coming because they had either fled the dust from other storms or lost their farms to the bank.

My dad said he was dazed as the true meaning of the Great Depression sunk in. The pigsty was filled with dust, and parts of the barn were gone so the animals were exposed to the filthy air. To top it off they had no crops to trade, and no money to buy anything.

My grandpa couldn't go to town to work for capital to restore the farm — the Plains state banks were hit hard by the crash and certainly could not give them a loan. Dad said that they looked out over the fields where such a short time ago the golden wheat waved softly. Now the crop was ruined. Tears of frustration left streaks in the dirt on his dad's face.

The summer that followed Black Sunday gave the family little relief. However, one stroke of luck came when Joe the Oldsmobile dealer finally came out to see if Dad could work for him because his son was going into the Army. Dad was a skilled mechanic and before long Joe frequently needed him. Dad's earnings were all that kept his family of 16 alive.

After awhile, the desperation of the city dwellers was thrust upon farmers who were still trying to hold on. Starving travelers trying to escape cities were often begging at their farmhouse door or stealing from the family's meager garden.

Perhaps one of the saddest things was the orphan train that stopped frequently in Osborne. Only farmers without children took an orphan — they wanted older ragamuffins as labor for their farms.

Dad hated seeing the train and the terror on faces of the little passengers. It haunted him for days. My grandfather used their existence as a reminder to his own children that things could always be worse. It's because of the children in his own family that he would never leave the 160 acres they got through the Homestead Act of 1862. Dad told us how much his family and other German settlers living around them valued their land. After immigrating from the western agricultural part of Germany, having their own land was paramount. So they hung on.

Three events occurred in December of 1935 that changed the course of Dad's life forever: on September 15 the Nuremberg Laws were passed in Germany which assured the coming war in Europe; the first measurable rain in months fell on his family's parched farm, which renewed his family's determination to stay and persevere; and in that same month my dad met Lois, a blue-eyed beauty who taught at a little school down the road — his heart was completely captured.

Throughout those years of struggle for survival on their Kansas homestead farm, Dad learned that he was a survivor, and that if his faith could get him through the Great Depression and the dust storms, he could get Lois's love and a better life in the future. And he did both.

K.E. Wass, California

Potato Soup

"We ate this soup when I was a child — with fresh, homemade bread and cheese if we had it. I find it amusing that we grew into adults loving potatoes and fried chicken even though they were all we had on several occasions. I can still see the entire family around the plank table, with Grandpa at the head, eating soup out of an odd collection of bowls and spoons." ~ K.E. Wass

15-20 medium-sized potatoes cut into cubes about the size of your thumbnail
One large, finely diced yellow onion
3 cups of cream (add water to fill a 12-quart stock pot)
3 pinches each of salt and pepper
3 tablespoons of butter (if available) or lard

Cook over medium fire until potatoes are soft but not mushy. Stir frequently to avoid boil-over.

If ham is available, add 2-3 cups cut into cubes of the same size. Add ham just as potatoes are softening.

Makes 25-30 1-cup servings, enough for 8-10 adults and children.

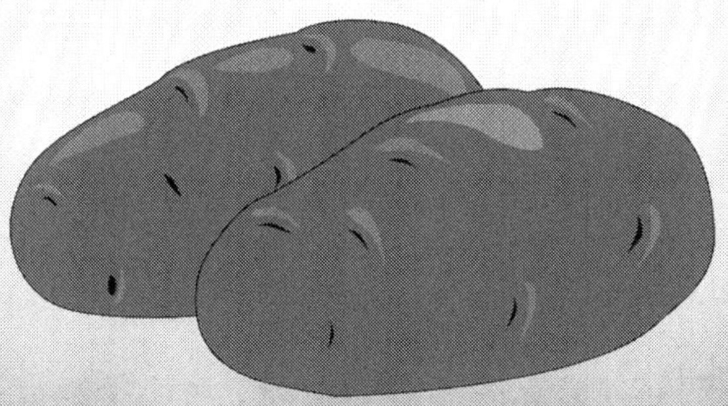

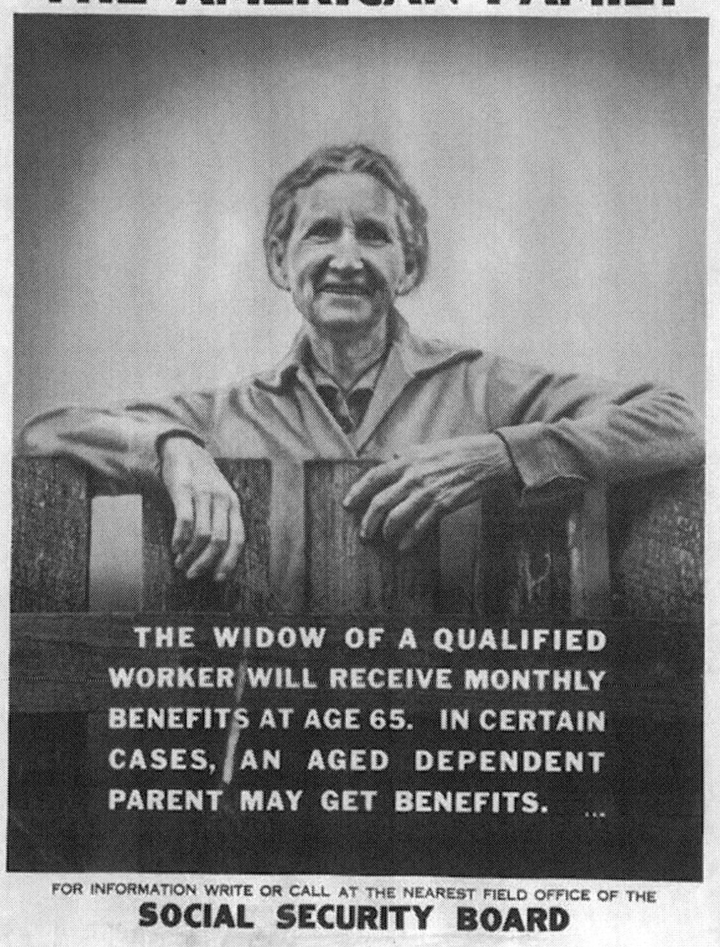

The elderly and families who lost wage-earners to death eventually benefitted from Roosevelt's new Social Security Act.

Franklin Delano Roosevelt Library

The family was already poor

Kathy (Johnson) Young

Mother born 1912 in Beaumont, Texas

When my mother, Anna Dell Light Johnson, was born in 1912 in Beaumont, Texas, she was the eighth of 11 children. Only seven survived.

The family was already poor. My grandparents Charlie and Annie Vasbinder Light had moved from San Antonio to Beaumont the previous year for a promised job in the new oil industry. They struggled to house, feed, and clothe their large family.

Then disaster struck in 1926. My grandfather had a stroke while working at the Magnolia Oil Refinery (now Mobil) and died at the age of 54. My grandmother (Mamaw) took boarders into their three-bedroom house. Now they were even poorer than before.

But it got worse. Disaster struck the family again a few years later in the form of the Great Depression.

When Mom graduated from high school in 1929 there were no jobs. She tried selling cosmetics door-to-door, but nobody was buying.

Mom's brother Leonard worked as a baker in Jasper, supporting himself and his wife, Carrie. One day his boss told him that money was too tight. He was going to have to ask Uncle Leonard to work on his day off — but not for any more pay. So he would be expected to work seven days a week without a raise. Uncle Leonard said, "No," and they shook hands.

Uncle Leonard and Aunt Carrie moved back to Beaumont and in with Mamaw and the remaining younger siblings. Each morning he reported to the refinery gate hoping to be hired for the day. Sometimes he was, but it wasn't until after the Depression that he was hired permanently. He worked there for the rest of his life.

Mamaw worried constantly about making the monthly house payment. Mom's youngest brother Jack owned a donkey at her place, which he sold for $5. "I'll keep the money for you," Mamaw told him. She used it to make the house payment. Jack never got his $5. Every penny Mamaw had went to making the house payment and feeding hungry mouths. It always bothered my mom that Uncle Jack never got his $5 for his donkey.

Mother told me about putting cardboard into her shoes because the holes went all the way through the sole. Nobody could afford new ones; every pair got handed down to a younger sibling no matter how badly the shoes were worn. Except for in the coldest weather, the boys went barefoot. Mom and her sister Lola learned to sew their own clothes, but fabric and thread cost money. No scrap was wasted. Once in a while their married older sister Lillian would buy them fabric and thread.

As siblings married, they usually brought the new spouse

Mamaw (Felicia Ann 'Annie' Vasbinder Light) on the right, and a friend, about 1930

The homestead at 2655 Sycamore, Beaumont, TX, now torn down and the land part of the Mobil Refinery

and moved back in with Mamaw and the rest of the family. Babies arrived in the crowded house too. Privacy wasn't even a concept.

"Where did you all sleep?" I once asked Mom. "I don't know," she said. "Everywhere."

The screened back porch had a bed in it — even when I was a child growing up in the 1950s. A tiny wash-house behind the garage was re-purposed as a bedroom and eventually rented out. All three bedrooms had one or two double beds crammed into them. Someone always slept in the dining room. The oldest sister's husband worked for Gulf Oil and had a job. My oldest uncle Howard worked for an oil company in Central America but finally moved back home, too. But they all contributed cash to the family.

Mamaw had a garden, pecan trees, fig trees, chickens, ducks, and a cow — all in the back yard of a city lot. My mother learned gardening from a boyfriend named Phillip Newman and she helped grow vegetables for the family. The neighborhood was full of immigrants mostly from eastern Europe. My grandmother always helped those who had even less than she did.

At least life was not without its entertaining moments in

a household so full. One morning Mamaw came in from milking. She was boiling mad and "got her tang all toungled up." "That cow switched her face right in my tail!" she snapped. Her children roared with laughter and never let her forget it.

The most important thing in their lives was the understanding that they were family. They went to church together. They helped one another. They helped poorer neighbors. Not everybody got along well, but Mamaw never let family members fight, even if they weren't good friends. They were family; together the whole family survived and eventually thrived.

But habits learned during those lean times died hard. Saving was a way of life that I learned when I grew up in that same house with my divorced mother and Mamaw. We still didn't have much money. Every rubber band was saved. Mamaw had a ball of string to which she added every new bit of string she came across. If we needed string we took a piece off the ball. It might consist of eight short pieces tied together, but it would have to do. Need glue? Mix flour and water.

We also saved bacon grease. I wore my cousin Linda's hand-me-downs, and Mom sewed. Coffee grounds went into the garden. Jars became drinking glasses. Flour sacks became dishtowels. Old clothes were made into quilts. Mamaw darned socks. They sewed their own potholders. They made other items from rags in the rag drawer. Mamaw saved nails and screws and washers. I learned thrift too, and made toys out of apple boxes from the grocery store, cut bows and arrows from tree limbs, shaped toy dishes from clay in the yard. Mamaw and Mom never stopped talking about the Depression years and how they

My oldest aunt, Lillian Light Benthall and son Fred Jr. and Mamaw, about 1930

managed to get through them. They were proud that they never took charity.

I didn't live through the Depression; I was born in 1944. But I learned lessons from those who did; those lessons are far-reaching. I recycle clothing into costumes, and yard waste into compost for my garden, shop at thrift stores, swap books with friends, still use Mamaw's cookware and tools, crochet afghans and caps and shawls from scraps of yarn, save brass for reloading on the firing range and drive my cars until the wheels fall off.

But I buy string and glue at Home Depot when I need it. Enough is enough.

Kathy Johnson Young, North Carolina

Shoes wore out

"Mother told me about putting cardboard into her shoes because the soles went all the way to the sole. Nobody could afford new ones; every pair got handed down to a younger sibling no matter how badly the shoes were worn. Except for in the coldest weather, the boys went barefoot."

~ Kathy Johnson Young, North Carolina

The Depression era slogan, "Make Do or Do Without, Use it Up or Wear it Out" was never so true as when it applied to shoes and clothing. The average cost of a good pair of shoes was $4. Some cost $2 or $3, but were poorer quality and didn't last long. Especially in large families, shoes and boots needed to endure several children and seasons, making their way from oldest to youngest.

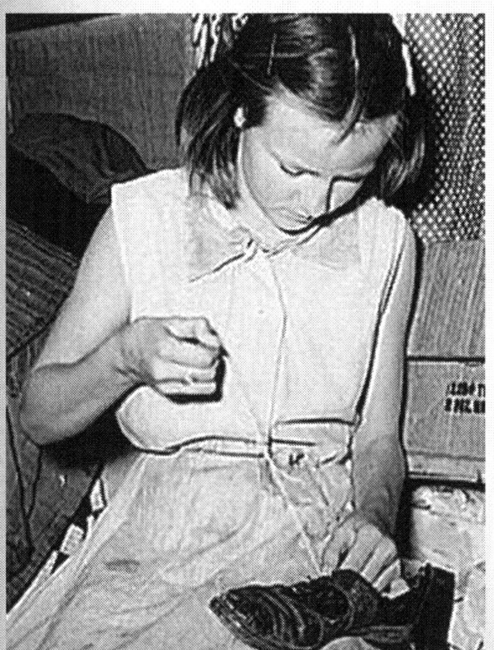

Girl sewing a shoe.
by Russell Lee, Library of Congress

Clara Wanner Lacy grew up in North Dakota. She remembers becoming first in line: *"The worst thing about clothing is that I was hard on shoes. I never walked, I skipped, and my shoes wore out very fast. When the bottoms wore out we used kits that had scrapers, glue and a half-sole. My biggest joy was when I got bigger than my older sister and no longer had to wear hand-me-downs."*

Clara's family was unusual in that her father had a repair kit. Most families relied on newspaper or cardboard to stuff their shoes when the soles wore out. *"In summer we went barefoot until school started. We always got a new pair for school and we wore them all winter. When the shoes wore out, we stuffed newspaper and cardboard in the soles."*

~Russell Weikle, California

Most often, children went barefoot during the warm months. New shoes were purchased before cold weather set in which usually coincided with the start of the school year.

"Mostly we went barefoot but did have shoes. Mother would place our foot on paper on the floor and draw around it, and sent it to Sears." ~Esther Tissing, Texas

When new shoe season came around, it was memorable.

"I vividly remember my first pair of shoes I ever had. I was probably nine-years-old. My mother fitted me in the store and picked them out two sizes too big. They flopped around for awhile, but I grew into them soon, just as mother knew that I would."

~Al Sanborn, Massachusetts

They had meat; they had food

Anthony Frank Zimmerman

Father born 1916 in Pittsville, Wisconsin

My father, Anthony Alfred Zimmermann, was born January 10, 1916 in Pittsville, Wisconsin, the second son of Anton Zimmermann and Anna Stehlik.

Anton was born September 1875 in Bohemia. My grandfather immigrated to America under the sponsorship of his brother-in-law and arrived at the age of 32 on the ship *Ringelshaim*. He left because the King of Bohemia was anti-Catholic and recruited Catholic males to be part of a regiment that he planned to kill off by sending/loaning them to other kings to fight their wars.

Anton was quite serious about a Bohemian girl whom he met in Austria in the late 1800s and had dated for a while. But their circumstances took them in separate directions. In 1907, Anton moved to Milwaukee and then to Pittsville, a smaller town that was mostly a farming community in 1910. A butcher by trade, he built a shop and bought a house.

In July 1913 he ran into his Bohemian sweetheart, Anna Stehlik, in Milwaukee. She was a secretary to an opera star who was playing there. He wasn't letting go of her this time, so they married that same month. Their son Albert followed on Oct. 3, 1914, and my father, Anthony, in 1916. The boys grew up in Pittsville and helped in their father's butcher shop to learn the trade of preparing meat for sale. During the time of the Great Depression they operated the shop in town that was surrounded by dairy farms and close to an Indian reservation.

On one memorable day, my dad and Albert were supposed to prepare a bull for slaughter. They tied a rope onto the nose of the bull, ran the rope through the ring in the floor of the butcher area, and were to strike the bull's head with a sledgehammer so that all of its parts could be used, including the tongue and brains.

The boys had used the sledgehammer for quite awhile without checking it for wear. Albert hit the bull with the sledgehammer and the rotten head broke off — angering the bull, not killing him. My father was stuck with his back to the wall and holding the rope with a dazed, angry bull in front while Albert ran off to get the rifle to shoot the bull. I don't think my father ever forgave his older brother for leaving him to hold the rope rather than being the responsible older brother who took the rope and sent him off to get the rifle.

Something my grandfather disliked about his job, especially during those lean Depression years, was finding out that a cow he had just bought for slaughter was pregnant. This meant that much of the weight of the cow was not sellable. Only about half of the weight is sellable when a cow on the hoof is purchased.

My grandfather was a very strict Roman Catholic. Albert was voted Prom King of the high school in the early '30s, but because he had to dance with the Prom Queen, his father would not let him attend. When my father was a senior two years later, he too was elected Prom King. His father's attitude had not changed about public dancing. This time, however, the men of the town "visited" him. They made a deal he could not refuse — either let Anthony go and dance with the Queen, or not only would they not bring their animals for butcher, but neither would they allow their wives to buy from him — ever. Dad danced and his brother Al fumed. It was better for my grandfather to give in than lose money and business during such hard financial times.

My grandmother wanted my father to be a teacher. At her request he went to a teacher's college during the middle of the Depression. After graduation, he headed to northern Wisconsin and taught for two years. One benefit of teaching was free room and board. However, the trouble was that he lived upstairs in the superintendent's house, so a young, single man had no opportunity for any kind of wild life.

With nothing to do one evening, he looked out his window and noticed a light on in the barn. He went to see what was going on. He caught the superintendent and several members of the local ruling gentry red-handed with a deer strung up and ready to be butchered. It was not hunting season.

Those men were caught red-handed like naughty schoolboys. Everybody knew deer season dates, and this kill was outside of deer season. I'm sure they had hunted the deer for free meat because the times were so hard.

My father saw what they were doing and that they were doing it all wrong. He told them to give him the knife so that he could show them how not to ruin good meat. He had them raise it up correctly; then he gutted, properly skinned and butchered it so that each person's share was maximized. After that, he was "golden" with the school board.

After his teaching stint, my father continued his education in business school and graduated with an Associate of Arts degree in Business Administration. With that, he was able to leave his father's butcher shop for good and became an assistant manager of an A&P grocery store.

Grandmother died of colon cancer in 1937 toward the end of the Great Depression. A doctor had cut out much of her intestine and she had to wear a diaper on her side at the opening. This was a great embarrassment to her. She stopped going to Sunday Mass because of the smell — she had no control of the movement of what bowels she had left. However, she went to daily Mass and sat in the back where she would not offend people.

This was their life in rural Wisconsin during the Depression: of church and community tied to an agricultural area. They had meat; they had food. Often people sold their animals to my grandfather who would trade part of the butchered animal back to the farmer in exchange for the cost of the meat.

My maternal grandmother, Sudie Doster, lived in rural Rochelle, Georgia. As a young woman she inherited a racetrack, but unfortunately it burned down. She married William Cross, also known as Pop Cross, and he started working for Coca-Cola.

My mother, Christian Cross, was born around 1920 in Rochelle. She grew up on a farm, but her grandfather was relatively wealthy by the standards of the area because of his job with Coca-Cola. During the late '30s the family moved to Fort Pierce, Florida where Pop managed the Coca-Cola plant. My mother, who was a young teen then, had a choice of either taking care of her little sister or going to work with her dad. Because he was the manager, he provided fairly well for his family.

Earl R. Dean's original 1915 concept drawing of the contour Coca-Cola bottle - Wikipedia

My mother loved taking orders over the phone from salesmen, or writing them out for them because they didn't like to. The salesmen called in their orders and she wrote them down. To answer the crank-style phone on the wall, she took empty Coca-Cola crates and stacked them on top of each other so she could reach. Not only did she have a great time doing that, it got her out of the house so she didn't have to take care of her baby sister — something her older sisters resented.

Pop bought property out on the edge of town and Sudie raised chickens. She had that chicken coop for a number of years until a hurricane came and blew the coop and all the chickens away.

As my mother grew up, she went to secretary school

where she learned dictation. After Pearl Harbor the Army was hiring people, so she took a civil service secretarial exam which required shorthand. She was hired at Morrison Field which later became Homestead Air Force Base. She worked with the organization that ran the commissary.

During the late '30s, my father was successful as an assistant manager of the A&P store. It was a store that was built with new modern engineering techniques called "flat roof," which worked well for covering areas -- but they usually collapsed under Wisconsin winter snows.

One night there was heavy snowfall and the owner of the A&P store called my father at his rooming house and told him to get his crew together and get the snow off the roof so that it would not collapse. He added that the store had to open on time at 8 am. The owner called from his boat in Miami!

My father got the crew together and shoveled all night on the roof. He took the last shovelful and threw it as far as he could into the neighbor's yard. An Army recruiter had been trying to get my father to join, so Dad and his crew went to the recruiter's office when it opened that day. My dad asked, "Can you send me to a place where you guarantee no snow?"

The recruiter gave him a deal and promised, "No snow" at Morrison Field, Florida. My father got on a train with the other guys right behind him. When they got off the train, a second-ranking general met them there.

Because my father had been to business school and ran a grocery store, he was assigned to the commissary. He had also learned shorthand in business school. At the time, the Army prohibited fraternization with local civilians, especially while on the job. Fraternization could get you court-

USO - FDR's birthday 1943. Franklin D. Roosevelt Presidential Library & Museum

martialed immediately and sent to the infantry in either Europe or the Pacific campaigns. But my parents learned how to read each other's shorthand and wrote love notes back and forth anyway.

Eventually they married, in April 1942. My grandmother Zimmermann died in 1937, my grandfather Zimmermann died in 1952, my grandfather Cross died in 1966 and my grandmother Cross died in 1976.

Anthony Frank Zimmerman, Tennessee

Aboard a trap fishing boat, Provincetown, Massachusetts.

By Edwin Rosskam, summer 1937, Library of Congress

Stole coal with a lobster fishing dory

Mel Nelson

Father born 1905 in Gloucester, Massachusetts

My grandpa Oscar Nelson was born November 15, 1859 in the small fishing village of Fjallbaka, Bohulsan, Sweden. It is located on the west side of a large bay that runs north and south between Sweden and Norway. He was a fisherman all the way up the west coast between Norway and Sweden, but was an apprentice cobbler who completed all his requirements.

Grandpa bailed out of Sweden when he was 33 or 34 in about 1890 and made tracks for a farm job in New Jersey. He was friends with an Erickson family who had immigrated to Gloucester, Massachusetts. The best way to immigrate was to have a job lined up, so the Ericksons arranged for him to work as a "weed picker" on a farm.

After spending a bit of time farming, Grandpa skipped out and headed for Gloucester where he became a full-time cobbler for Mr. Damiano on Main Street, mending and making shoes for his living.

In 1893, Oscar married Amanda Martina Hanson from Marstrand Island, Sweden. The family thinks he must have had her shipped over. Their wedding certificate says it is her first marriage, but she brought over a three-year-old daughter, Viola Danner. Her father is unknown to us — perhaps he was German. She married Audun Audunson who was drowned and lost at sea in February 1933 while lobster fishing with my dad.

Oscar and Amanda settled down and started their family together in Gloucester. Their daughter Dagmar was born in 1900, and my father followed about five years later. Amanda died soon after from childbirth complications. Oscar turned to whiskey. Mr. and Mrs. Damiano were instrumental in raising Nils until he was about 9 or 10.

In 1919, when Nils was about 15-years-old, Oscar moved both of them to Beverly, Massachusetts to earn a living by making specialty shoes for deformed feet. He opened his cobbler business in part of a building on the corner of Cabot Street and Broadway. Oscar bought a house on Elm Street about 150 yards from his workshop.

People paid a lot of money during the Depression for Oscar's custom shoes.

Oscar not only made custom shoes — which kept him in whiskey — he made six violins. There is only one left that I know of, owned by my sister's son.

My dad went to school at South School on Stone Street in an area above the waterfront known as Fish Flake Hill. It is a historic district founded in 1626 by settlers who had come from Salem — before the Witch Trials. The name of the district comes from the "flakes," or cod fish drying tables, of the fish drying yards that which were found there up until the late 1800s. I grew up there too, hanging out every summer and during other weeks of school vacation.

When he was 20 in 1925, Nils began a career in lobster fishing. In those days, dory lobstermen rowed up to five miles per day and dory tub longliners rowed up to eight miles per day. Dorys are small, flat-bottomed rowboats with a high bow and stern. He earned his living this way until December 23, 1963.

Dad married Vera Grant in 1927 in Beverly. I am their firstborn and made my appearance in November 1928. My little sister Jacqueline was born in December 1931.

If you live near the ocean where the tide goes out far enough to uncover the flats, you will never starve in any Depression. We had plenty of fish to eat. Ma pre-chewed it for us kids until we had teeth. One of my favorite dishes that she made was spaghetti with ground up conch meat and olive oil. Conches were a food bonus when they crawled into the lobster traps.

Nils was a good lobster fisherman. Wealthy people ate lobsters during the Depression. Dad also longlined cod, haddock and yellow-tail flounder. We ate the species he caught that didn't sell: cusk, wolffish, and Conger eel. A superb meal was fried cod spawn. We also had occasional haddock or cod that had been scarred from sand shark bites.

In the winter my dad fished on the Dragger *Newton,* a 116-feet long by 23-feet wide boat launched in 1930 that towed fishing gear out of Boston Fish Pier. The captain was his aunt Dagmar's husband, Christian Christiansson.

Well, it caught fire in February 1933 and that is when Viola's husband, Audun "Snowy" Audunson, drowned and was lost at sea along with one other crewman. The engine was running at full throttle on the dragger when it caught fire and took out the steering, which was in full-circle position. A vicious northwest wind smashed it into the fishing dory.

My dad drank more whiskey than his father, Oscar — but only in month-long spurts. Where Oscar was a maintenance drinker and always in control, my dad was a binge drinker. He always looked terrible when he found his way home after "missing" us. He'd be completely out of it for three or four days, or away from home from a week up to a month, then suddenly return as if nothing had happened. My dad was the greatest guy on earth when he was sober, but a complete recluse when he was drunk. His early death at 58 was most likely a result of his binges.

One time Dad went missing for over a month. It was a bitterly cold November and we ran out of coal. I rowed a dory to get underneath the Girdler Coal dock. I was 13-years-old. I pried loose a piece of plank that covered a hole underneath a pile of coal. I moved the dory underneath to fill it evenly. When I was done, I tried to replace the plank and couldn't. I was afraid the dory would sink with all the coal in it, so I had to move away. I rowed over to a ramp next to the Gulf Oil Company wall. Thank goodness it was high tide. I got a wheelbarrow and took all that coal uphill to our home. It took all day Sunday to shovel it through the cellar window and into the bin.

Up until Prohibition ended in 1933, Nils and other lobstermen helped run bootleg whiskey. Every two weeks, Pete McFarland and his brother Harry made a run out of

Provincetown, Massachusetts, summer 1937.

By Edwin Rosskam, Library of Congress

Beverly to a vessel offshore for a load of whiskey. My dad and crew helped unload Pete's boat *Trudy* right up against the seawall that was the edge of Water Street. There was an unoccupied building there where the whiskey was stored that hadn't been trucked away before daylight. The story is that it was old Joe Kennedy's source of income, and the brand of whiskey was Old Fitzgerald. Old Joe Kennedy was John F. Kennedy's father.

When I was 11 in the summer of 1939, I went into the lobster fishing business too. But my dad was twice the lobster fisherman that I was. My first lobster traps were like vegetable shipping crates. I made six of them. I cut out two square areas on opposite sides. I salvaged heads (netting) from old traps and laced them into the crates. I tied two red bricks inside each end and baited them with fish skeletons from the fish market on Water Street or trash fish that my dad had given me. I used old, salvaged line to tie them to the dock pilings. Every morning that summer I pulled them up to check.

One spring, Dad found a flat-bottom skiff drifting in the bay. It was banged up, probably from lobster fishing or longlining. I repaired and re-painted it, then used it to rake mussels off the pilings under coal docks and on the Beverly end of the Beverly-Salem bridge. I got $1 a bushel if they were full-size mussels. Longliners used them to bait hooks.

My sister Jackie was friends with Ann Morgan. Ann had a date for the prom with a certain boy she knew, but he ended up not being able to take her. Jackie told her, "Ask my brother. He's better than nothing." That has stuck to me forever. We were married in 1950 and lived in Beverly. Our two sons, William and Scott, were born in 1951 and 1953.

I stopped lobstering in 1955 when I was 23 in order to build boats. I did that until 1991. In spite of my grandfather's and father's problems with whiskey, I enjoyed a little beer now and then with my friends in the Jubilee Yacht Club cellar.

Mel Nelson, Massachusetts

Teach a man to fish...

"If you live near the ocean where the tide goes out far enough to uncover the flats, you will never starve in any Depression...We had plenty of fish to eat. Ma pre-chewed it for us kids until we had teeth. One of my favorite dishes...was spaghetti with ground-up conch meat and olive oil. Conches were a food bonus when they crawled into the lobster traps."

~ Mel Nelson, Massachusetts

Mel Nelson and his little sister Jacqueline grew up in a fishing village in Massachusetts. When he wasn't out to sea in his lobster-fishing boat, Mel's father, Nils, frequently went on drinking binges. But the family never went hungry because of where they lived.

Conch is a durable shellfish but needs to be tenderized before it's cooked for a tender, easy bite. Mel's mother, Vera, likely pre-chewed it when making the simple spaghetti and olive oil dish the children loved.

Large eastern conch. Photo by ChildofMidnight via Wikipedia

Following is another version:

Swedish Spaghetti

2 lbs. spaghetti noodles
1/3 c. vinegar
1/3 c. sugar
2 tsp. dry mustard
enough conch meat for personal preference
salt and pepper to taste

There is a short window of time to cook conch; undercooked or overcooked conch tends toward a consistency akin to rubber. Conch does best with a high-and-dry cooking method, or when it's cooked over high heat with a little oil for a short period of time. Shallow frying and sauteeing conch work best for a quick seafood fix.

"We ate the species he caught that didn't sell: cusk, wolffish, and Conger eel. A superb meal was fried cod spawn..." ~ Mel Nelson

A Swedish treat also known as fried cod roe, Mel Nelson's cod spawn is a meal made from intact cod egg sacs. Following are instructions:

Fried cod spawn

Choose egg sacs that are intact — small eggs will flow out of any major tear during cooking.

Poach the sacs in salted water that is barely bubbling, with a couple of tablespoons of white vinegar.

Cooking might take 20-30 minutes

Cool cooked ovaries overnight. When ready, slice them ½-inch thick, dust with flour and fry briefly until golden brown. Season with salt and pepper.

Fun facts about the 1930s

Matt Redhawk

1930: Hostess Twinkies, Snickers and Wonder Bread were introduced. Cartoon hottie Betty Boop first appeared in 1930, although she looked more like a poodle. She became human-like in 1932. Mickey Mouse toys made their first appearance as popular Christmas gifts. Best Film Oscar winner: *All Quiet on the Western Front.*

1931: The British freed Gandhi and agreed to discuss his demands regarding the British monopoly on salt, which was his boldest act of civil disobedience against British rule in India. Airstream trailers were introduced to the public, invented by Wally Meryle Byam. Nearly two-thirds of these camping vehicles ever produced are still in use. First Christmas appearance: Battleship. Best Film Oscar winner: *Cimarron.*

1932: In response to the Depression, Hoover reduces his salary by 20 percent and asks the Vice President and cabinet to do the same. *Time* magazine's Man of the Year was Franklin D. Roosevelt who repeated the honor in 1934 and 1941. Twenty-month-old Charles Lindbergh, Jr. was kidnapped on March 1 and found dead on May 21. Bruno Hauptmann was found guilty of the crime and executed in 1936. First Christmas appearance: Tripoly game. Best Film Oscar winner: *Grand Hotel*

1933: Roosevelt is elected president of the United States -- the first of four terms -- and takes office in March. Jack Benny becomes a radio sensation as a perpetual 39-year-old miser who owns an old Maxwell automobile and keeps his money in a basement vault. Quote of the year: "The only thing we have to fear is fear itself"- Franklin Delano Roosevelt in his first inaugural address. One of his first acts as President was to repeal Prohibition, which was the first and only constitutional amendment that actually withheld a right from American citizens.

1934: John Dillinger is killed by federal agents after seeing *Manhattan Melody* at the Biograph Theatre in Chicago. Other master criminal deaths: "Baby Face" Nelson in a police shoot-out in Chicago, Clyde Barrow and Bonnie Parker during a police ambush in Louisiana, and "Pretty Boy Floyd" was killed by 14 FBI bullets in Ohio. A sad realization came to six-year-old Shirley Temple when a department store Santa asked her for her autograph. *It Happened One Night* won the big five Oscars (grand slam) - Best Picture, Best Director, Best Actor, Best Actress and Best Writing. First Christmas appearance: Sorry!, Radio Flyer

1935: The rhumba becomes the latest dance craze. October 31, 1935 - Orson Welles' famous *War of The Worlds* broadcast airs for the first time, causing a mass panic throughout the United States. First Christmas: Monopoly, Fire Fly Sled. Best Film Oscar Winner: *Mutiny on the Bounty*

1936: A *Fortune* poll indicates that two out of every three women use some form of birth control. Baseball Hall of Fame founded in Cooperstown, New York -- Ty Cobb got more votes than Babe Ruth in the inaugural Hall of Fame roster. Ty was a great player, but apparently not well-liked by his peers; only four members of the baseball community attended his funeral. Pastime: Reading Margaret Mitchell's *Gone With The Wind*. Best Film Oscar Winner: *The Great Ziegfeld*

1937: John D. Rockefeller dies at age 98, leaving an estate worth nearly $1 billion. Scandals: movie star Marie Prevost died of malnutrition. Hindenburg burned and crashed in Lakehurst, New Jersey on May 6, killing 36 people. May 28, San Francisco's Golden Gate Bridge opened. Disney's *Snow White* became the biggest film of all time. Hewlett-Packard was founded; Disney's first big job was *Fantasia*. Amelia Earhart and her plane were lost flying over the Pacific Ocean. Best film Oscar Winner: *The Life of Emile Zola*

1938: The Jefferson nickel goes into circulation. American auto-maker Henry Ford received Germany's highest honor for a non-German, The Order of the German Eagle along with a personal note from Adolf Hitler. Best

Film Oscar winner: *You Can't Take It With You*

1939: College fads include swallowing goldfish, knock-knock jokes, roller-skating and Chinese Checkers. NBC broadcast its first black-and-white television images, but only about 1,000 homes had television sets in the New York area. John Steinbeck's *Grapes of Wrath* is published. First Christmas: Batman Comics, View-Master. Best Film Oscar winner: *Gone With the Wind*

27151420R00231

Made in the USA
Middletown, DE
12 December 2015